THE NEW TESTAMENT

A CONTEMPORARY INTRODUCTION

THE NEW TESTAMENT

A CONTEMPORARY INTRODUCTION

Colleen M. Conway

WILEY Blackwell

Registered Offices
John Wiley & Sons, Inc., 111 River Street, Hoboken, NJ 07030, USA
John Wiley & Sons Ltd, The Atrium, Southern Gate, Chichester, West Sussex, PO19 8SQ, UK

Editorial Office
9600 Garsington Road, Oxford, OX4 2DQ, UK

For details of our global editorial offices, customer services, and more information about Wiley products visit us at www.wiley.com.

Wiley also publishes its books in a variety of electronic formats and by print-on-demand. Some content that appears in standard print versions of this book may not be available in other formats.

Library of Congress Cataloging-in-Publication Data
Names: Conway, Colleen M., author.
Title: The New Testament : a contemporary introduction / Colleen M. Conway.
Description: Hoboken, NJ : Wiley-Blackwell, 2022. | Includes
    bibliographical references and index.
Identifiers: LCCN 2022028173 (print) | LCCN 2022028174 (ebook) | ISBN
    9781119685920 (paperback) | ISBN 9781119685951 (adobe pdf) | ISBN
    9781119685968 (epub)
Subjects: LCSH: Bible. New Testament–Criticism, interpretation, etc. |
    Bible. New Testament–History. | Bible. New Testament–History of
    contemporary events.
Classification: LCC BS2361.3 .C66 2022 (print) | LCC BS2361.3 (ebook) |
    DDC 225.6–dc23/eng/20220804
LC record available at https://lccn.loc.gov/2022028173
LC ebook record available at https://lccn.loc.gov/2022028174

Cover Design: Wiley
Cover Image: Julio Romero de Torres, *Christ and the Samaritan Woman*, 1920 (public domain)

Set in 9.5/12pt STIXTwoText by Straive, Pondicherry, India
Printed and bound by CPI Group (UK) Ltd, Croydon, CR0 4YY

C106576_170822

CONTENTS

LIST OF FIGURES   xi

LIST OF MAPS   xiii

LIST OF BOXES   xv

PREFACE   xvii

ACKNOWLEDGMENTS   xix

TIMELINE   xxi

PROLOGUE: ORIENTATION TO THE ACADEMIC
STUDY OF THE NEW TESTAMENT   1

Chapter Overview   1
A Contemporary Introduction to the New Testament   1
Different Designations and Different Bibles   4
The Contents of the New Testament   6
Abbreviations, Translations, and Annotations   7
New Terminology for Old Texts   13
Prologue Review   15
Resources for Further Study   15
Appendix: Translation and Paraphrase Comparison of John 1:18   15

1   THE NEW TESTAMENT WRITINGS IN MULTIPLE CONTEXTS   17

Chapter Overview   17
A History of Trauma under Imperial Rule   17
The New Testament Writings in their Ancient Literary Context   21
The New Testament Writings in their Ancient Social Context   22
Focus Text: Acts 16:11–40   25
Conclusion: The New Testament in a Complex World   27
Chapter One Review   28
Resources for Further Study   28

2 THE JESUS MOVEMENT IN THE CONTEXT OF THE ROMAN EMPIRE   29

Chapter Overview   29
Rome Comes to Jerusalem   29
Searching for the Historical Jesus: Problems and Proposals   33
The Earliest Jesus Traditions   39
Chapter Two Review   43
Resources for Further Study   43

3 INTRODUCING PAUL AND HIS LETTERS   45

Chapter Overview   45
Introduction to the Study of the Pauline Letters   46
Paul's Earliest Surviving Letter: 1 Thessalonians   51
Paul's Letter to the Philippians   54
Paul's Letter to Philemon   57
Chapter Three Review   59
Resources for Further Study   60

4 READING PAUL WITHIN JUDAISM: GALATIANS AND ROMANS   61

Chapter Overview   61
Paul's Gentile Problem in Galatia   62
Paul on his "Earlier Life" (Gal 1:13)   64
Why and Why Not Circumcision in Galatia?   65
Paul's Letter to the Romans: The Righteousness of God in Relation to Jews and Gentiles   69
The Problem of Israel and the Place of the Gentiles (Romans 9–11)   75
Chapter Four Review   77
Resources for Further Study   77

5 CONFLICTS WITH THE CORINTHIAN CHRIST GROUP   79

Chapter Overview   79
The Urban Setting of Corinth   80
Status Problems in Corinth   83
Conflicts over the Body and Sexuality in Corinth   85

Conflicts over Meat Consumption in Corinth   87

Disputing Ritual Practices in Corinth   88

Afflictions and Accusations in 2 Corinthians   90

Disputes Regarding the Collection for Jerusalem (2 Corinthians 8–9)   92

Paul's Self-Defense against Gendered Status Attacks   93

Focus Text: 2 Cor 11:16–12:13   94

Chapter Five Review   95

Resources for Further Study   95

6 Claiming Pauline Authority: Later Trajectories of Pauline Traditions   97

Chapter Overview   97

Ancient Pseudonymity and the New Testament Writers   98

Three Deutero-Pauline Letters: 2 Thessalonians, Colossians, and Ephesians   99

Conforming to Roman Imperial Values: The New Testament Household Codes   104

More Deutero-Pauline Letters: 1 and 2 Timothy and Titus   105

The Paul of Legend: The Acts of Paul and Thecla   108

From Local Letters to Scriptural Authority   109

Chapter Six Review   111

Resources for Further Study   111

7 The Gospel of Mark: Suffering and Trauma under Imperial Rule   113

Chapter Overview   113

The Jewish War (66–70 CE)   114

Clues to the Dating and Context of the Gospel of Mark   115

The Story of Jesus in the Gospel of Mark   118

The Rising Popularity of Jesus and Rising Conflict with the Authorities   118

Teaching and Misunderstanding "on the Way"   122

Mark's Suffering Messiah   126

An Enigmatic Ending   129

Focus Text: Mark 12:1–12   130

Chapter Seven Review   132

Resources for Further Study   132

**8   THE GOSPEL OF MATTHEW: DEFINING COMMUNITY
IN THE WAKE OF DESTRUCTION   133**

Chapter Overview   133
The Synoptic Problem   134
The Structure of the Gospel of Matthew   136
The Matthean Jesus and Jewish Tradition   138
The Matthean Jesus, Righteousness, and Torah Obedience   140
The Matthean Jesus, Wisdom, and Torah   142
Matthew's Apocalyptic Vision and the
Kingdom of Heaven   143
The Matthean Polemic against the Pharisees   146
Focus Text: Matt 25:31–46   150
Chapter Eight Review   152
Resources for Further Study   153

**9   THE GOSPEL OF LUKE: LEGITIMIZING THE JESUS MOVEMENT
IN THE MIDST OF EMPIRE   155**

Chapter Overview   155
Reading the Clues in the Lukan Prologue   156
The Lukan Jesus in Continuity with Israel's Past   158
God's Plan of Salvation for Israel and the Gentiles   160
The Lukan Jesus and Imperial Imitation   160
The Role of the Holy Spirit in the Lukan Narrative   164
The Travel Narrative and Lukan Parables   165
Focus Text: Jesus's Sermon in Nazareth (Luke 4:14–30)   168
Chapter Nine Review   170
Resources for Further Study   170

**10   THE SPREAD OF "THE WAY" IN THE ROMAN EMPIRE:
THE ACTS OF THE APOSTLES   171**

Chapter Overview   171
Salvation to Israel and to the Gentiles in Acts   171
The Role of the Spirit in Acts   174
The Acts of Jesus and the Acts of the Apostles   175
Looking Beyond the Leading Men of Luke–Acts   177
Paul and the Spread of "the Way" in the Roman Empire   179
Focus Text: Acts 8:26–40   180

Conclusion: Luke–Acts' Ambivalent Response to Empire   183
Chapter Ten Review   183
Resources for Further Study   184

11 The Gospel of John and the Johannine Letters: Turning Inward as a Strategy for Life in the Empire   185

Chapter Overview   185
Who Is the Johannine Jesus?   186
The Johannine Prologue: Jesus as Pre-existent Logos Made Flesh   186
The Johannine Jesus as God's Divine Agent in the World   189
The "I Am" Sayings in the Gospel of John   191
Knowing and Believing in the Johannine Jesus   192
Opposition from the World   194
The Problem of "the Jews" in the Gospel of John   196
Focus Text: John 17   200
The Johannine Letters   201
Chapter Eleven Review   203
Resources for Further Study   203

12 Following Christ in the Empire: Diverse Approaches in the New Testament   205

Chapter Overview   205
The Revelation to John: Visions of "Conquering" Roman Power   206
Focus Text: Revelation 17–18   213
Hebrews: Platonic Perspectives on Christ   214
1 Peter: Living as Aliens and Accommodating to the Empire   218
Conclusion: Three Different Relationships to the Roman Empire   221
Chapter Twelve Review   222
Resources for Further Study   222

Epilogue: The Final Formation of the New Testament Canon   223

Glossary   227

Appendix: A Brief Overview of Some Interpretive Approaches to the Bible   233

Index   237

LIST OF FIGURES

0.1   The end of the Gospel of Luke and beginning of the Gospel of John in Codex Vaticanus, fourth century.   9

2.1   Excavation of the remains of an outer stairway and arches of the Second Temple in Jerusalem.   31

2.2   Proposed reconstruction of the outer stairway and arches of Jerusalem.   31

2.3   Model of first-century CE Jerusalem.   32

2.4   The Forum of Augustus in Rome.   32

2.5   Painting of Moses from a third-century CE synagogue (Dura Europos).   36

2.6   Parchment illustration of a scene from the Infancy Gospel of Thomas where Jesus brings clay birds to life.   42

3.1   Statue of Augustus showing him wearing the veil of the *pontifex maximus* ("greatest priest").   49

3.2   Remains of the *Via Egnatia*, Rome's primary artery to the east.   49

4.1   Third-century CE wall painting depicting a baptism from the Catacomb of St. Callistus in Rome.   69

5.1   Ruins of the Temple of Apollo in Corinth in front of the Acrocorinth.   81

5.2   Doorways of shops in ancient Corinth.   81

6.1   Wall painting of Paul and Thecla discovered near Ephesus (sixth century CE).   110

7.1   Silver shekel minted about 67 CE during the Jewish revolt.   114

7.2 The pillaging of the Jerusalem Temple depicted on the Arch of Titus.   115

7.3 "Judaea Capta" coin minted in Rome to commemorate victory over the Jewish rebels.   116

8.1 A diagram of the synoptic relationships.   135

8.2 Roman coin indicating the ruling power of Augustus as he subdues the earth under his foot.   146

9.1 A coin minted by Caesar Augustus around 18–19 BCE.   161

9.2 Base of an honorific column in Rome showing the deification of a second-century CE emperor and his wife.   163

10.1 Rembrandt van Rijn – The Baptism of the Eunuch (1626).   181

11.1 Papyrus fragment, Rylands Library P52, containing lines from John 18.   190

11.2 Medieval Christian image of the church preferred over the synagogue.   198

12.1 Fourth-century CE catacomb painting illustrating how early Christians viewed their own experience of the Roman empire through the lens of the biblical text.   212

12.2 Revelation's figure of the "whore of Babylon" as depicted by the artist and poet William Blake.   213

LIST OF MAPS

0.1 The Roman Empire in the 1st century CE.   xxii

1.1 The reach of three of the major empires that dominated Israel and/or Judah: the Assyrian, Babylonian, and Persian empires.   19

1.2 The Hellenistic kingdoms and the Hasmonean state around 90 BCE.   20

3.1 Map of cities addressed in the Pauline letters.   48

7.1 Palestine in the first century CE.   123

12.1 Cities of Revelation.   207

13.1 Spread of Christianity across the Mediterranean world by 300 CE.   225

List of Boxes

Special Topic Boxes

Contents of the Hebrew Bible/Tanakh/Old Testament	5
The Origins of Chapters and Verses	8
More on Textual Criticism	10
More on the Historical Jesus Search	35
Eschatology versus Apocalypticism	37
The Infancy Gospel of Thomas: The Boy Jesus and His Superpowers	41
The Structure and Composition of Paul's Letters	50
More on Paul and Jewish Apocalypticism	52
The Question of Circumcision for Gentiles	63
Changing Perspectives on Paul	67
Paul's Rhetorical Use of Scripture	72
On Paul and "Unnatural" Sex	74
The Composition of the Corinthian Correspondence	82
Women, Paul, and the Jesus Movement	90
Markan Priority	117
An Exorcism of Rome?	120
More on the Messianic Secret	125
Intercalation, or the Markan "Sandwich"	127
A Glimpse of Life under Roman Occupation	128
More about the Q Document	135
Gender and Matthew's Genealogy (Matt 1:1–17)	139
The *Ekklesia* in the Gospel of Matthew	144
Who Were the Pharisees?	147
The Priene Calendar Inscription	162
The Paul of Acts versus the Paul of the Letters	179
Was There a Johannine Community?	198
Tacitus's Account of Nero's Persecution of Christians in Rome	208

Basics Boxes

Basics on 1 Thessalonians	50
Basics on Philippians	55
Basics on Paul's Letter to the Galatians	62
Basics on Romans	70
Basics on 1 Corinthians	84

Basics on 2 Corinthians 91
Basics on 2 Thessalonians 100
Basics on Colossians 103
Basics on Ephesians 103
Basics on 1 Timothy 106
Basics on 2 Timothy 107
Basics on Titus 107
Basics on the Gospel of Mark 116
Basics on the Gospel of Matthew 137
Basics on the Gospel of Luke 157
Basics on the Acts of the Apostles 173
Basics on the Gospel of John 188
Basics on the Revelation to John 208
Basics on the Letter to the Hebrews 216
Basics on 1 Peter 219

Contemporary Voices Boxes

Contemporary Voices: Ongoing Critiques and the Future of Historical Jesus Research 38
Contemporary Voices: A Dalit Feminist Engagement of Gal 3:28 66
Contemporary Voices: Queering Paul's Letters 86
Contemporary Voices: The Syrophoenician Woman and the Politics of "Sass" 122
Contemporary Voices: Decolonizing the Story of the Canaanite Woman (Matt 15:21–8) 149
Contemporary Voices: Latin American and Intercultural Interpretation of Luke 167
Contemporary Voices: Disability Studies and John 5:2–15 191
Contemporary Voices: Asian Americans, Perpetual Foreigners, and 1 Peter 220

PREFACE

This book builds on my work in *A Contemporary Introduction to the Bible: Sacred Texts and Imperial Contexts* (Wiley Blackwell, 2021) co-authored with David Carr. As is the case with that book, my goal here is to offer a concise introduction that is well suited to a one-semester course. For those teaching a yearlong introduction to the Bible, this book would be well paired with David Carr's *The Hebrew Bible: A Contemporary Introduction to the Christian Old Testament and the Jewish Tanakh* (Wiley Blackwell, 2021).

A major goal of the book is to introduce students to the broad range of interpretive methods for the study of the New Testament. While the book is historically focused throughout, students will also be able to sample the interpretive results of multiple contemporary approaches. As I explain in the Prologue, I have intentionally woven insights from postcolonial theory, gender theories, and other theoretical perspectives into the body of the text. My goal was to integrate diverse scholarly perspectives into the student's introduction to the academic study of the New Testament. Some readers may find this integration startling at points. Hopefully, it will become less so as biblical scholars continue to recognize historical critical scholarship as one among many important ways to critically analyze the New Testament. I am all too aware of approaches that are not included in this book. Nonetheless, my hope is that even this necessarily limited introduction will encourage students to continue to explore the wide world of critical biblical studies.

The timeline provided in this textbook is adapted from *A Contemporary Introduction to the Bible*. The translations of biblical texts are my own unless noted otherwise.

Finally, I have been helped by many in the course of writing this book. Seton Hall University granted me a year of sabbatical leave, providing the time I needed for writing. Many thanks, as always, to my spouse, David Carr. This book would not have been written without his steadfast partnership, not to mention his ever-ready expert consultation on all matters biblical. Maia Kotrosits and Sarah Emanuel have been supportive of my "introduction" efforts for many years. Indeed, Maia assisted with the glossary definitions at an early stage, and her work lives on in this book. Adele Reinhartz generously read portions of the John chapter, for which I am grateful. I also had the benefit of comments from several anonymous reviewers of my initial draft. The textbook is better for their excellent feedback and suggestions. My work-study assistant, Emily Nix, proofread several chapters during a very busy semester. Clelia Petracca, Monica Rogers, Sinduja Abirami and Rajalakshmi Nadarajan of Wiley Blackwell were very helpful in bringing the book to production. Clelia was patient and supportive as I rejected multiple possible cover images. I could not be more pleased with what we decided on together. The painting of Christ and Samaritan Woman by Julio Romero de Torres does what I hope the book will do – bring to the foreground the often marginalized figures in the New Testament.

I am also especially grateful to Giles Flitney for his keen copyediting eye. Also, in a truly delightful development toward the end of my work, my son Ian Grant offered his professional editorial services to this endeavor. This meant that I benefitted from his superlative copyediting skills and Ian learned more about what his mom had been up to during the pandemic. The book is better because of Ian's exceptional editorial insight, and his humor kept me entertained along the way. I wish I could have followed his suggestion to coin the term "Johnsplaining" for the Johannine discourses.

Finally, our dear friends Hester Oberman and Sander Zwart opened their desert home to David and me for six weeks of Tucson sunshine and many delicious meals, all of which bolstered my energy when it flagged. I wrote several of the early chapters of this book during our stay. Hester and Sander are excellent conversation partners on topics from the Bible to gender reassignment to mountain biking. I dedicate this book to them.

ACKNOWLEDGMENTS

The author and publisher gratefully acknowledge the permission granted to reproduce the copyrighted material in this book:

Figure 0.1   Art Collection / Alamy Images

Figure 2.1   Todd Bolen / BiblePlaces.com

Figure 2.2   Vodnik / Wikimedia Commons / CC BY SA 2.5

Figure 2.3   Berthold Werner / Wikimedia Commons / Public Domain

Figure 2.4   Mary Evans Library / Adobe Stock

Figure 2.5   Marsyas / Wikimedia Commons / Public Domain

Figure 2.6   Unknown author / Wikimedia Commons / Public Domain

Figure 3.1   Adam Eastland / Alamy Images

Figure 3.2   Todd Bolen / BiblePlaces.com

Figure 4.1   Heritage Image Partnership Ltd / Alamy Images

Figure 5.1   Greg Balfour Evans / Alamy Images

Figure 6.1   Unknown author / Wikimedia Commons / Public Domain

Figure 7.1   Courtesy of the American Numismatic Society.

Figure 7.2   Unknown author / Wikimedia Commons / Public Domain

Figure 7.3   www.BibleLandPictures.com / Alamy Images

Figure 8.2   Stephen Jenkin / THE CLASSICAL ANTHOLOGY

Figure 9.1   Carlomorino / Wikimedia Commons / CC BY SA 3.0

Figure 9.2   Photo Scala

Figure 10.1   Museum Catharijneconvent / Wikimedia Commons / Public Domain

Figure 11.1   The University of Manchester Library / Wikimedia Commons / Public Domain

Figure 11.2   State Museums in Berlin / Wikimedia Commons / Public Domain

Figure 12.1   DEA / V PIROZZI / De Agostini Editore / AGE Fotostock

Figure 12.2   British Museum / Wikimedia Commons / Public Domain

At points throughout the translations have been used from the New Revised Standard Version of the Bible copyright 1989, by the Division of Christian Education of the National Council of the Churches of Christ in the United States of America. Used by permission. All rights reserved.

The publisher apologizes for any errors or omissions in the above list and would be grateful if notified of any corrections that should be incorporated in future reprints or editions of this book.

TIMELINE

BCE	Beginning of Israelite monarchy
	Saul's "chieftainship"
	David (1010–970)
1000	Solomon (970–930)
	Northern Tribes form their own Kingdom
900	
800	
	Assyrian domination of Judah begins (734)
	Assyrian destruction of Israel (722)
700	
	Domination of Judah by Babylonia
600	First wave of exiles (597)
	Destruction of Jerusalem and second wave of exiles (586)
	Third wave of exiles (582)
	Persian conquering of Babylonian empire (539)
	First wave of returnees (538)
	Another wave, beginning of Temple restoration (532)
	Another wave, completion of Temple rebuilding (520–515)
500	
400	
	Alexander's conquering of Persian empire (332)
300	
200	Maccabean revolt against Antiochus Epiphanes IV (167–164)
	Hasmonean dynasty's independent rule (142–63)
100	Roman takeover of Palestine (63)
	Rule of Herod in Palestine (40)
	Beginning of Roman empire with reign of Caesar Augustus (Octavian) (27)
	Birth of Jesus (4?)
CE	**Paul's letters (50s)**
	Jewish War (first Jewish revolt against Rome) (66–70)
	Destruction of the Second Temple (70)
	Gospel of Mark (70)
	Gospels of Matthew and Luke (80–85)
	Revelation of John (90–95?)
	Gospel of John (90–100)
	Acts of the Apostles (90–100?)
100	**Pastoral Epistles (c. 100)**

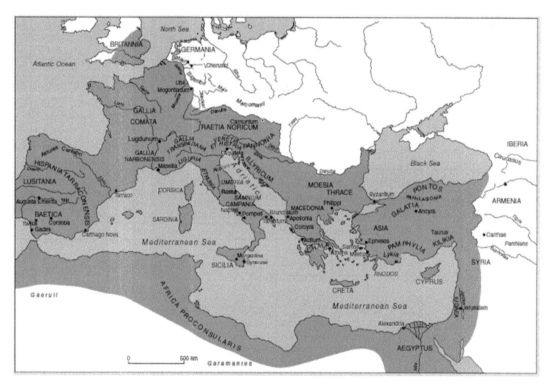

MAP 0.1

The Roman Empire in the 1st century CE

Chapter Outline

Chapter Overview	1
A Contemporary Introduction to the New Testament	1
Different Designations and Different Bibles	4
The Contents of the New Testament	6
Abbreviations, Translations, and Annotations	7
New Terminology for Old Texts	13
Prologue Review	15
Resources for Further Study	15
Appendix: Translation and Paraphrase Comparison of John 1:18	15

Chapter Overview

This prologue introduces you to what is distinctive about the academic study of the Bible. I discuss how several academic approaches have been applied to the New Testament, including historical, postcolonial, gender, and intersectional analyses. Also, you will learn about the content of the New Testament and the differences between English translations of the Greek text. Finally, the Prologue begins to familiarize you with the Bible that you will be using for your study across the upcoming chapters.

A Contemporary Introduction to the New Testament

The title of a book offers a promise of what is to come. In this case, the promise is that readers will be introduced to the New Testament and that this introduction will be contemporary. If you are already familiar with the collection of ancient writings called the New Testament, it may seem like they need no introduction. But just as there are

The New Testament: A Contemporary Introduction, First Edition. Colleen M. Conway.
© 2023 John Wiley & Sons Ltd. Published 2023 by John Wiley & Sons Ltd.

different ways of knowing another person, there are different ways of knowing the New Testament. One way to know the Bible is through one's sociocultural experience. For example, perhaps you or someone you know is familiar with the New Testament through church services, Sunday school classes, youth groups, and Bible study groups. In such settings, what one learns about the New Testament often concerns how it informs life in one's community and how it relates to one's personal morality and religious practice.

Another way of knowing the New Testament comes simply from living in a culture with a centuries-long history of centering the Bible as an authoritative text. Even if you have never been part of a Christian community, perhaps you have watched a film with a plot that includes a "Christ figure," heard someone use the expression "Good Samaritan," or encountered paintings of New Testament scenes in a museum. You can probably think of many other examples where living in Western culture involves encounters with biblical traditions.

Yet another way of knowing the New Testament comes from learning about it in an academic setting from scholars who have made a career out of the analytic study of the Bible. This academic discipline is known as "biblical studies." Though both focus on the Bible, biblical studies and Bible study are different. Biblical studies is an academic discipline that typically takes place in colleges, universities, and seminaries. In contrast, Bible study typically occurs in private, small group settings in homes and churches, with a devotional focus rather than an academic one.

The academic study of the Bible can also take many shapes. What biblical scholars refer to as the "historical critical approach" to the New Testament first emerged in Europe, especially Germany, during the Renaissance and Enlightenment periods. In this sense, historical criticism of the Bible began as an enterprise of white, European, Protestant Christian, educated men working in academic institutions. Seeking a supposedly rational and scientifically objective approach, these scholars began to ask questions about the human origins of the Bible. They analyzed the New Testament in its original Greek language and theorized about matters such as dating, authorship, setting, and the potential oral and literary sources of each New Testament book.

The historical critical approach has dominated the field for more than two hundred years, with mixed results. On the one hand, we have learned a great deal about the historical setting of the New Testament writings. On the other hand, we now know that because the historical approach began as a primarily white, European, and male enterprise, it had certain limitations and blind spots at its core. These limitations have become increasingly evident as academic biblical studies has expanded to include other approaches and (all too slowly) a more diverse group of scholars. One goal of this contemporary introduction to the New Testament is to be mindful of the limitations of the historical critical approach while also introducing its often highly illuminating results. As I will detail further below, another goal of the textbook is to illustrate what additional insights become possible through the use of other academic approaches to the study of the New Testament.

The historical critical approach requires us to think about a variety of factors that contributed to the formation of each of the New Testament texts. These factors include the historical and political contexts of the authors and their audiences. We also need to consider various influences on New Testament authors, such as the cultural ideas and practices that were common in the authors' time and place. Finally, we must consider how the authors were influenced by the various literary genres that were popular at the time, such as history writing, biographies, moral treatises, letters, romance novels, and dramas.

Although taking all these elements into account may seem complicated, it is completely consistent with how one would study other types of literature in an academic setting. For example, if you were to take a class on Shakespeare, you might learn a great deal about late-sixteenth-century England to help you understand the playwright's literary works. The same will be true of our study of the writings in the New Testament. While we will certainly analyze the content of the gospels and the letters of Paul, we will also explore how different aspects of the first-century CE Mediterranean world helped to shape these ancient texts.

Like any other academic subject, interpretations of the New Testament writings in their ancient context (the historical critical approach) continue to be revised as scholars recognize mistakes made in past scholarship and propose new readings based on new knowledge. I do not assume – and nor should you – that the contemporary scholarship reflected in this textbook offers the final word for understanding the New Testament. Many aspects of the ancient world remain a puzzle, and interpreters of every generation have blind spots. Nevertheless, historical scholarship has made important advances in the twenty-first century, and this book offers an introduction to this recent work.

As mentioned above, along with the discussion of historical questions in the textbook, I will also introduce you to insights that come from other academic perspectives. Often grouped under the label "contemporary approaches" to the New Testament, these studies draw on theories that are widely used across the humanities for social and cultural analysis. For example, postcolonial theory considers the effects of colonization on groups of people. In the case of the New Testament writers, this includes considering how the effects of living under Roman imperial rule might have influenced how they experienced and wrote about the Jesus movement. Feminist theory, gender theory, and critical masculinity studies all examine how ideas and assumptions about gender contribute to the meaning, interpretation, and application of New Testament texts. Intersectional approaches consider how issues of race, class, gender, and sexual orientation may affect the writing and interpretation of the New Testament. Still other approaches to the New Testament consider different social locations and ethnic identities in the interpretive process. This textbook is designed to introduce you to some of the insights we gain from reading the New Testament through these diverse perspectives. In many cases, this scholarship is woven into the main body of the textbook. In others, boxes marked "Contemporary Voices" feature the work of New Testament scholars who offer important ideas to consider in our study of the New Testament writings.

Different Designations and Different Bibles

The English title "New Testament" comes from the Latin translation (*novum testamentum*) of the Greek designation "New Covenant" (*kaine diatheke*). Originally, this "new covenant" was understood in theological terms. Christ-followers believed that God had made a new covenant that was the fulfillment of the old covenant of God with Israel. Sometime in the second century CE, the term "new covenant" began to serve also as a designation for the collection of writings that were becoming authoritative for Christ-followers. An unfortunate legacy of the use of "old" and "new" to designate the two parts of the Christian Bible is that the terms contributed to the idea of Christian **supersessionism**. This is the assumption that God's covenant with the world through Christ superseded any prior covenant that God made with Israel. For people who subscribe to this idea, the **Old Testament** is often treated as the old and *supplanted* Testament. It is seen as the outdated book of the "law," as opposed to the New Testament, which is understood to be the truly scriptural word about Jesus, love, and grace. More recent forms of supersessionism depict the New Testament as superior to the Old Testament in its treatment of female figures, violence, and other issues important to contemporary readers. Old or new, supersessionist interpretations generally reflect a lack of close reading of both the Old and the New Testament. Worse, reading the New Testament as superior to the Old Testament has contributed to a long, violent history of Christian anti-Semitism.

In this textbook, I will use the term "**Hebrew Bible**/Old Testament" to refer to the collection of writings that are sacred scripture to both Jewish and Christian communities. The term is not ideal. Jewish people do not call their scriptures the "Hebrew Bible." They use the designation TaNaK (or Tanakh), from the Hebrew names of the three main parts of the Jewish Bible: **Torah** (the first five books of the Bible – Genesis, Exodus, Leviticus, Numbers, and Deuteronomy), *Neviim* ("prophets"), and *Ketuvim* ("writings"). Moreover, not all of the writings in this collection were written in Hebrew. Portions of the books of Ezra and Daniel, for example, were written in a common spoken language called Aramaic. Finally, there are differences in what books are considered part of this collection, depending on one's faith tradition. The box "Contents of the Hebrew Bible/Tanakh/Old Testament" shows the differences between the Jewish Tanakh; the Protestant Old Testament, which contains the same books as the Tanakh but in a different order; the Roman Catholic Old Testament, which includes some additional books; and Eastern Orthodox collections, which again contain slightly different groups of additional books. For Roman Catholics, the additional books that are not in the Jewish Tanakh are "**deuterocanonical**." The term "**canon**" is used to refer to a collection of sacred texts, and "deutero" means second. Thus, these books belong to a "second canon." For Protestants, books that are not in the Jewish Tanakh are not considered true scripture – that is, they are not "canonical" but rather "**apocrypha**," meaning "books hidden away." Of course, they are not literally hidden away; in fact, they were quite important to many New Testament writers, as I will discuss in Chapter 1.

Contents of the Hebrew Bible/Tanakh/Old Testament

Jewish Tanakh	Protestant OT	Roman Catholic OT (*italics* = not in Tanakh)	Eastern Orthodox OT (*italics* = not in Tanakh)
Torah	**(Pentateuch)**	**(Pentateuch)**	**(Pentateuch)**
Genesis, Exodus, Leviticus, Numbers, Deuteronomy	Genesis, Exodus, Leviticus, Numbers, Deuteronomy	Genesis, Exodus, Leviticus, Numbers, Deuteronomy	Genesis, Exodus, Leviticus, Numbers, Deuteronomy
Prophets (Neviim)	**(Historical Books)**	**(Historical Books)**	**(Historical Books)**
Former prophets Joshua, Judges	Joshua, Judges, Ruth	Joshua, Judges, Ruth	Joshua, Judges, Ruth
1–2 Samuel	1–2 Samuel	1–2 Samuel	1–2 Samuel
1–2 Kings	1–2 Kings	1–2 Kings	1–2 Kings
	1–2 Chronicles	1–2 Chronicles	1–2 Chronicles
Latter prophets	Ezra-Nehemiah	Ezra-Nehemiah	Ezra-Nehemiah
			1 *Esdras* (2 *Esdras* in Russian Orthodox)
Major prophets		*Tobit*	*Tobit*
Isaiah		*Judith*	*Judith*
Jeremiah	Esther	Esther (*with additions*)	Esther (*with additions*)
Ezekiel		1–2 *Maccabees*	1–3 *Maccabees*
Minor prophets/ book of the twelve	**(Poetical Books)**	**(Poetical Books)**	**(Poetical Books)**
	Job	Job	Job
Hosea, Joel, Amos,	Psalms	Psalms	Psalms (with Psalm 151)
Obadiah, Jonah,	Proverbs	Proverbs	Proverbs
Micah, Nahum,	Ecclesiastes	Ecclesiastes	Ecclesiastes
Habakkuk,	Song of Solomon	Song of Solomon	Song of Solomon
Zephaniah, Haggai,		*Wisdom of Solomon*	*Wisdom of Solomon*
Zechariah, Malachi		*Sirach*	*Sirach*
Writings (Ketuvim)	**(Prophets)**	**(Prophets)**	**(Prophets)**
Psalms	Isaiah	Isaiah	Isaiah
Proverbs	Jeremiah	Jeremiah	Jeremiah
Job	Lamentations	Lamentations	Lamentations
		Baruch	*Baruch*
Five festal scrolls		*Letter of Jeremiah*	*Letter of Jeremiah*
Song of Songs	Ezekiel	Ezekiel	Ezekiel
Ruth	Daniel	Daniel (*with additions*)	Daniel (*with additions*)
Lamentations	Hosea, Joel, Amos,	Hosea, Joel, Amos,	Hosea, Joel, Amos,
Ecclesiastes	Obadiah, Jonah,	Obadiah, Jonah,	Obadiah, Jonah,
Esther	Micah, Nahum,	Micah, Nahum,	Micah, Nahum,
	Habakkuk,	Habakkuk,	Habakkuk,
Daniel	Zephaniah, Haggai,	Zephaniah, Haggai,	Zephaniah, Haggai,
Ezra–Nehemiah	Zechariah, Malachi,	Zechariah, Malachi,	Zechariah, Malachi,
1–2 Chronicles			4 *Maccabees* (appendix)

In spite of these problems, for our purposes, the designation Hebrew Bible/Old Testament has the advantage of reminding of us that (1) there is not one but multiple versions of this collection of writings, (2) in their various forms, these collections are sacred to multiple faith communities, and (3) while the term "old" has a history of pejorative uses, it is by now a longstanding designation for the first part of the Bible among Christians. Given this last point, some Christians emphasize a more ancient understanding of "Old" in "Old Testament" as implying something good, rather than the more contemporary idea of "old" being something that is outdated. Certainly, the authors of the New Testament writings saw it that way. Indeed, the interpretation of the New Testament depends on an understanding of how these authors turned to and used these authoritative scriptures to understand the person and meaning of Jesus.

The Contents of the New Testament

The New Testament is a collection of 27 "books" written in the period from around 50 CE to the early second century CE. Unlike the different collections of the Hebrew Bible/Old Testament, this list (see box "The New Testament Canon") is common among Christian denominations, even though it took several hundred years to stabilize. I discuss this process of "canonization," meaning the designation of certain writings as part of a collection of sacred texts, in the Epilogue.

The New Testament Canon

The Gospels

Matthew	Luke
Mark	John

Acts of the Apostles

Pauline Letters
(also known as Pauline Epistles)

Romans	1 Thessalonians
1 Corinthians	2 Thessalonians
2 Corinthians	1 Timothy
Galatians	2 Timothy
Ephesians	Titus
Philippians	Philemon
Colossians	

General Letters (or General Epistles)

Hebrews	1 John
James	2 John
1 Peter	3 John
2 Peter	Jude

Revelation

The four gospels narrate stories about the words and deeds of Jesus of Nazareth, his conflict with authorities in Jerusalem, his eventual execution by Rome, and his resurrection. The Acts of the Apostles is an account of the growing Jesus movement after the death of Jesus. It was written by the same author as the Gospel of Luke and picks up where the gospel ends, although the two books are separated in the New Testament by the Gospel of John. The earliest New Testament writings are the letters written by the apostle Paul. Though he was not a follower of Jesus during Jesus's life, Paul became a leading figure in the spread of the Jesus movement about two decades after Jesus's death. The New Testament also includes a number of later writings that are attributed to Paul (for example, 1 and 2 Timothy and Titus). Still other writings are attributed to leading figures in the Jesus movement, such as Peter and James. Finally, the New Testament concludes with the Revelation to John, an apocalyptic text directed toward Christ-followers living in the cities of Asia Minor.

Abbreviations, Translations, and Annotations

Complete the following exercises to familiarize yourself with the idea of Bible translations and the basic features of your study Bible.

READING

1. Using the parallels provided in the appendix to this prologue, compare the translations (and the Living Bible paraphrase) of John 1:18. What differences do you notice?
2. Look at two pages of a biblical book in your Bible. Make a list of all types of elements on those pages aside from the actual text of the Bible. Consider where these elements come from and how they contribute to your understanding of the biblical text.

EXERCISE

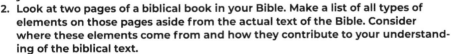

Here, I introduce a few basic aspects of English translations of the Bible that will assist you going forward. The first matter concerns how to understand citations of the Bible. When books and articles cite biblical passages by chapter and verse, they usually follow this order: the abbreviation of the biblical book, followed by the chapter number, followed by the verse. An example is Rom 1:13 (chapter 1, verse 13). If more than one verse is cited, dashes and commas can be used: Rom 1:13, 16 or Rom 1:13, 16–17. Using abbreviations of biblical books is standard practice when citing biblical texts. Here are some standard abbreviations for biblical books shared by the Jewish and Christian Bibles (given in the order followed by most Christian Bibles).

Gen = Genesis	Esther = Esther	Hos = Hosea
Exod = Exodus	Job = Job	Joel = Joel
Lev = Leviticus	Ps or Pss = Psalms	Amos = Amos
Num = Numbers	Prov = Proverbs	Ob = Obadiah
Deut = Deuteronomy	Eccl = Ecclesiastes	Jon = Jonah
Josh = Joshua	Song = Song of Songs	Micah = Micah
Judg = Judges	(also known as Canticles, and Song	Nah = Nahum
Ruth = Ruth	of Solomon)	Hab = Habakkuk
Sam = Samuel	Isa = Isaiah	Zeph = Zephaniah
Kgs = Kings	Jer = Jeremiah	Hag = Haggai
Chr = Chronicles	Lam = Lamentations	Zech = Zechariah
Ezra = Ezra	Ezek = Ezekiel	
Neh = Nehemiah	Dan = Daniel	

Here are the abbreviations for books in the New Testament:

Matt = Matthew	Eph = Ephesians	Heb = Hebrews
Mark = Mark	Phil = Philippians	Jas = James
Luke = Luke	Col = Colossians	1–2 Pet = 1–2 Peter
John = John	1–2 Thess = 1–2	1–2–3 John = 1–2–3 John
Acts = Acts	Thessalonians	Jude = Jude
Rom = Romans	1–2 Tim = 1–2 Timothy	Rev = Revelation
1–2 Cor = 1–2 Corinthians	Titus = Titus	
Gal = Galatians	Phlm = Philemon	

The Origins of Chapters and Verses

The earliest manuscripts of the Bible lack any chapter or verse numbering (see Figure 0.1). The first Bible with numbered verses was produced in 1555 by a Parisian bookseller, Robert Estienne (also known as Stephanus). He is reported to have divided a copy of his New Testament into the present 7,959 verses while riding on horseback from Paris to Lyon. He also numbered the chapters and verses of both the Old and New Testaments. Today, these verses are used in scholarly editions of the Hebrew Bible and Greek New Testament as well as in translations of the Bible.

FIGURE 0.1

The end of the Gospel of Luke and beginning of the Gospel of John in Codex Vaticanus, fourth century. Note the absence of both verse numbers and spacing between words.

A second issue concerns the process of translation. Because most students cannot read ancient Hebrew or Greek, they rely on translations of the Bible. A well-informed reader should keep in mind what the production of such translations involves. In terms of the New Testament, every translation requires many decisions by the translator of the Greek text. In some cases, translators do not know the precise meaning of ancient Greek words. In others, it is difficult to convey the meaning of ancient Greek into English or other contemporary languages. Also complicating matters is that we have no original manuscript of any biblical book. Instead, we have thousands of different copies of biblical books, or fragments of books, all handwritten by ancient scribes. Not surprisingly, these copies contain thousands of minor changes that were introduced by the scribes (both accidentally and intentionally) as they copied their copies. Because the materials used for copying manuscripts were expensive, scribes used the limited space on a sheet of papyrus as efficiently as possible. Ancient New Testament manuscripts were written either with all capital letters or all lowercase letters. Moreover, scribes did not use punctuation marks or spaces between words. This can make reading ancient manuscripts challenging. Try it for yourself:

IMAGINEHAVINGTOREADWITHOUTTHEHELPOFSPACESORPUNCTUATIONESPE-
CIALLYIFTHEMATERIALINCLUDESLONGLISTSOFNAMESOROTHERUNFAMILIAR-
MATERIALTHISCOULDPROVECHALLENGING

In fact, sometimes the results of *scriptio continua* (the Latin term used for this type of scribal practice) are ambiguous. A well-known English language example of such ambiguity is the phrase GODISNOWHERE. Is this an assertion or refutation of divine presence? Or how about the sentence THEYSAWABUNDANCEONTHEDINNERTABLE. Did they see a lot of food on the table or was the table shaking? You get the idea.

Given such textual problems, some scholars specialize in a discipline called **textual criticism**, which focuses on determining what wording is most likely closest to the original manuscript. Over the past several centuries, much progress has been made in uncovering ancient manuscripts and learning to identify copying errors and other changes in such manuscripts. In addition, there has been continual progress in knowledge about biblical languages.

These advances in knowledge about the text and language of the Bible mean that the academic study of the Bible requires the use of up-to-date translations of the biblical text. The King James Version (also known as the KJV or "Authorized Version"), though beautiful and cherished by many, is not an up-to-date translation. It was done four hundred years ago, when scholars knew far less about biblical languages than they do now. Moreover, the King James Version, and especially its New Testament portion, is based on unusually corrupt manuscripts that have more errors and expansions than higher-quality manuscripts used today. Therefore, the KJV should not be used for readings in a twenty-first-century academic course on the Bible.

More on Textual Criticism

Textual criticism of the Bible attempts to reconstruct the wording of the original version of a biblical writing. Because all such original versions are long lost to us, attempts to determine the original wording require detective work. The ancient manuscripts that have survived (all copies of copies of the original) are referred to as witnesses. They bear witness to earlier versions of biblical texts even if their "testimonies" do not all agree. Scribes regularly introduced changes into new manuscripts as they hand-copied from earlier ones. Some changes were introduced when a scribe accidentally confused letters or copied a given line twice. Others were more intentional, where a scribe added a clarification of a place name or inserted a theological correction or expansion. An example of scribal expansion occurs at the end of the Gospel of Mark, where two different scribal endings have been added after Mark 16:8. An example of theological editing occurs at John 1:18. If you are using a Bible designed for academic study, you will find a footnote at this verse indicating the different wording found in ancient manuscript witnesses concerning the verses's references to "God" or "son."

A translator or translation committee often needs to decide word by word whether to follow a reading in one manuscript tradition or another. To do this, most scholars use "critical editions" prepared by text critics that gather and compare the readings found in ancient biblical manuscripts with each other. For the study of the New Testament, the critical edition is called the Nestle-Aland after two prominent translators, Eberhard Nestle and Kurt Aland.

Translations also vary in theological perspective. The New Jerusalem Bible (NJB) and New American Bible (NAB) were produced by Catholic scholars. The New Revised Standard Version (NRSV), newly updated in 2022, aims to be an ecumenical and interfaith translation, that is, suitable in Roman Catholic, Protestant, Christian Orthodox, and Jewish contexts. Still, the translation stems from a line of Protestant revisions of the KJV. The New International Version (NIV; now available in updated form as Today's New International Version) is a Protestant evangelical alternative to the NRSV.

Translations also vary in style. They may aim to stay as close to the biblical languages as possible or, alternatively, to maximize readability. **Formal correspondence** translations aim to stay as close as possible to word-for-word translations of the Hebrew, Aramaic, or Greek text. As a result, these translations are good tools for study but may also be more difficult to understand. Translations that tend toward formal correspondence include the NRSV, NIV, and the New American Standard Bible (NASB). Other translations tend toward **dynamic equivalence**, which aims for equivalent meaning rather than a word-for-word translation. This results in translations that are more readable but can also contain more interpretation on the part of translators. Examples of translations that tend toward dynamic equivalence include the NJB, NAB, and several other translations produced by Protestant groups, such as the Good News Translation (GNT; also known as the "Good News Bible" and TEV – Today's English Version) and the Contemporary English Version (CEV). These translations should be distinguished from resources such as the Living Bible or Amplified Bible. The latter are not direct translations of the Hebrew and Greek texts but paraphrases or expansions of other translations. For example, the Living Bible is a paraphrase of the nineteenth-century American Standard Version. Since such paraphrasing adds yet another level of interpretation between the reader and the ancient text, it is not helpful for academic work on the Bible.

One more way that contemporary Bible translations vary is in the extent to which they aim to use gender-neutral language, such as "humanity" instead of "mankind." Though older writing conventions endorsed the use of "man" for "human" or "he" for "he or she," many now argue that the general use of such male-focused language reinforces a male-centered society. Some translations revise male-specific language in the Bible in two ways. In some cases, past English translators used male-specific words to translate Hebrew or Greek expressions that were gender-neutral. The recent revision of the NIV translation, Today's New International Version (TNIV), aims to correct such mistranslations to what it terms "gender-accurate" English expressions. Compare the following two translations:

> "Come, follow me," Jesus said, "and I will send you out to <u>fish for people</u>." (TNIV)
> He said to them, "Come after me, and I will make you <u>fishers of men</u>." (NAB)

The first translation more accurately reflects the meaning of the saying because we know that the Jesus movement included women as well as men!

Some other translations go further in their effort to be gender-inclusive. For example, the NRSV and the NJB revise other references to human beings toward gender-neutral English terms, even in cases where the original biblical languages use masculine nouns. So, for example, in places where the apostle Paul writes to "brothers," the NRSV translates the Greek word for brothers, *adelphoi*, as "brothers and sisters." The translators opt for this more inclusive translation both because Paul also addressed women with his letters and because many contemporary churches want gender-inclusive language to be part of their worship and ministry. In this textbook, I generally follow the policy of using gender-inclusive language by avoiding male pronouns to refer to God and using gender-neutral references to human beings. Nevertheless, I also take account of the fact that the Bible was formed in a culture that privileged masculinity and conceived its God in largely masculine terms.

Finally, readers should recognize that all these translations are published in different editions, each with its own perspective and added resources. For example, the *New Oxford Annotated Bible with Apocrypha* and the *HarperCollins Study Bible* are not different translations but different publishers' packaging of the NRSV translation. Each one has a different introductory essay, introductions to the biblical books, and brief commentaries on the biblical text written by biblical scholars commissioned by the publisher. Indeed, whenever you use a given translation, it usually includes many other elements that were added by the publisher of the particular edition that you are using: headings for different sections of the biblical text, marginal references to other biblical passages, maps, and other additions. These can be helpful resources. Nevertheless, users of such editions should be aware of how these additional elements – none of which are actually part of the biblical writings per se – can subtly influence how one reads a given biblical passage.

In the end, there is no single contemporary translation that scholars agree is decisively better than all others. Arguments can be made for a variety of the contemporary translations that are listed in the Appendix to this prologue. You can get a good sense of the translation issues that arise in a particular passage by comparing multiple up-to-date translations. You may want to consult online resources for such comparisons, such as Bible Study Tools (www.biblestudytools.com\compare-translations) or the Bible Gateway (www.biblegateway.com). However, note that such online resources often contain a number of out-of-date translations and neglect others. If you use them, be sure to compare up-to-date resources.

Finally, I urge you to consider one more crucial point about your study Bible. This textbook is designed to be used *alongside* your translation of the New Testament, whatever version you are using. While it can be tempting to focus only on the textbook and not on the primary text we are studying, you will learn much more if you take the time to read and study the New Testament writings themselves. As a reminder to do this, I have included "Reading Exercises" throughout the textbook. Taking time to read the assigned biblical texts and reflect on the questions will prepare you to better understand the discussions that follow.

New Terminology for Old Texts

Most chapters of this textbook conclude with a focused look at a passage in the New Testament that illustrates the ideas that I have discussed in the chapter. In this case, I offer the following verse as the focus of the last section of this prologue. The verse highlights another difficulty with translating an ancient text into our twenty-first-century setting.

> So it was that for an entire year they met with the church and taught a great many people, and it was in Antioch that the disciples were first called "Christians." (Acts 11:26b NRSV)

This verse, taken from the book of Acts, uses two words that may seem unremarkable to find in a New Testament writing: "church" and "Christians." At the same time, you might have noticed that I have not used either of these terms in my discussion so far. Instead, I have used the terms "Christ-followers" and "Jesus movement" rather than "Christians" and "Christianity" to refer to the early followers of Jesus and to the emerging church.

I use this terminology for several reasons. First, the term "Christian" appears only three times in the New Testament: twice in Acts (11:28 and 26:28) and once in 1 Peter (4:16). Meanwhile, the term "Christianity" never appears at all in the New Testament because Christianity did not yet exist as an organized religion distinct from Judaism. Even in Acts, where the word "Christian" does occur, the author does not adopt the term. Instead, the character Paul says he is a follower of "the Way" (Acts 24:14). Another problem with using the designations "Christian" and "Christianity" for the academic study of the New Testament is that these words evoke a set of associations that would be completely anachronistic to the first century CE. Twenty-first-century Christianity is the product of two thousand years of history and evolving traditions. Moreover, there is not just one type of Christianity today but rather a wide variety of Christian beliefs and practices.

We encounter similar translation problems with the word "church" in the New Testament. Most people who hear the word "church" may well think of a building where Christians gather or of a specific religious institution (as in "church" versus "synagogue" or "temple"). Yet, the Greek word behind the English translation "church" is *ekklesia*, which did not refer to a building or a specific type of religious institution. In ancient Greece, *ekklesia* referred to a public assembly, typically a political one. In the first century CE, the word could be used as a designation for both civic assemblies and non-civic associations in Jewish and Greco-Roman contexts. Indeed, *ekklesia* could be used to refer to Jewish synagogue communities. In this textbook, I typically use the word "assembly," or sometimes "Christ group," rather than "church" to translate *ekklesia*. These translations avoid evoking anachronistic images of steepled church buildings, or suggesting that already in the time of the New Testament writings, a distinct group of Christians attended churches while Jews attended synagogues.

All that said, it is likely that terms like "Christ-followers" or "Jesus movement" will seem odd and unfamiliar to you. Likewise, it may feel uncomfortable not to read about Paul's "churches." My translation choices are not meant to take away from the value of the New Testament writings as scripture for Christian churches today. Rather, they are designed to help you remember that we are studying writings that reflect the earliest stages of a movement that took around one hundred years (some would argue even longer) to gain recognition as a distinct group within the Roman empire. In other words, throughout this textbook, we will keep at the forefront of our study that the New Testament writings represent just the very beginning of a centuries-long process of (1) the development and establishment of rituals and doctrines that would come to define normative Christianity and (2) the eventual separation of Christianity from Judaism.

Here is one last important point about the terminology used in the coming chapters. In what follows, you will encounter references to the "historical Jesus," the "Markan Jesus," the "Matthean Jesus," the "Lukan Jesus," and the "Johannine Jesus." These are common ways of referring to the different representations of "Jesus" that biblical scholars discuss. They are used to reinforce two points. The first is that the person who lived and died in the first century, referred to as the "historical Jesus," is not identical with the different presentations of Jesus that are evident in the gospels. This leads to the second point. Each of the four canonical gospels offers a picture of Jesus that is in keeping with the author's understanding of the significance of this figure for Christ-followers. Each gospel develops themes linked to these particular understandings of Jesus. So, a term like the "Markan Jesus" is used to refer to the literary portrayal of Jesus in the Gospel of Mark, compared to, say, the "Johannine" Jesus who is depicted in the Gospel of John. Some students assume that this is one and the same Jesus, with only some minor differences in the details of how he is portrayed. But attending to these different literary details is the beginning point for the academic study of the gospels. Indeed, one of the goals of our study of the gospels will be to show how these differences matter for appreciating the unique visions of each of the gospel writers. Another goal will be to perceive how the gospel writers defined the significance of Jesus in light of their particular historical, social, and political contexts. Finally, we will often use the term "audience" rather than "readers" to refer to the ancient groups for whom these writings were intended. This is because most people in the first-century CE Mediterranean world could not read or write. Even if they could, they likely would not own manuscripts to read on their own. Instead, the early writings of the Jesus movement were intended for use in assemblies of Christ-followers where they were read out loud. In imagining how most ancient people experienced the gospel narratives or the letters of Paul, we should envision an audience of listeners rather than a reader alone in a private study. With these ideas in mind, we turn now to the study of the New Testament.

PROLOGUE REVIEW

1 Know the meaning and significance of the following terms discussed in this prologue:
- apocrypha
- canon
- deuterocanonical
- dynamic equivalence
- *ekklesia*
- formal correspondence
- Hebrew Bible
- Old Testament
- supersessionism
- textual criticism

2 What do labels such as "Markan Jesus" or "Lukan Jesus" designate, and why do scholars use them for the academic study of the New Testament?

3 What are some ways that English translations of the Bible differ? Identify what Bible translation you are using for your study of the New Testament.

RESOURCES FOR FURTHER STUDY

Moxnes, Halvor. *A Short History of the New Testament.* London: I.B. Tauris, 2014. This book includes a useful chapter on the emergence of the academic study of the Bible in modern Europe.

Porter, Stanley, and Andrew W. Pitts. *Fundamentals of New Testament Textual Criticism.* Grand Rapids, MI: Eerdmans, 2015.

APPENDIX: TRANSLATION AND PARAPHRASE COMPARISON OF JOHN 1:18

New Revised Standard Version	New American Standard Bible	New International Version	Today's English Version (Good News Bible)	King James Version	Living Bible	New Jerusalem Bible
No one has ever seen God. It is God the only Son, who is close to the Father's heart, who has made him known.	No one has seen God at any time; the only begotten God who is in the bosom of the Father, He has explained *Him*.	No one has ever seen God, but the one and only Son, who is himself God and is in closest relationship with the Father, has made him known.	No one has ever seen God. The only Son, who is the same as God and is at the Father's side, he has made him known.	No man hath seen God at any time; the only begotten Son, which is in the bosom of the Father, he hath declared him.	No one has ever actually seen God, but, of course, his only Son has, for he is the companion of the Father and has told us all about him.	No one has ever seen God; it is the only Son, who is nearest to the Father's heart, who has made him known.

The New Testament Writings in Multiple Contexts

1

Chapter Outline

Chapter Overview	17
A History of Trauma under Imperial Rule	17
The New Testament Writings in their Ancient Literary Context	21
The New Testament Writings in their Social Context	22
Focus Text: Acts 16:11–40	25
Conclusion: The New Testament in a Complex World	27
Chapter One Review	28
Resources for Further Study	28

Chapter Overview

As you read in the Prologue, there are many different aspects of the ancient world that we could study to help us understand what we read in the New Testament. This chapter provides overviews of three such aspects: the historical context, ancient literary context, and social context of the New Testament writings. I begin with a historical overview of key events in the history of ancient Israel. Knowing the events that helped shape the writings of the Hebrew Bible/Old Testament will be important for understanding many aspects of the New Testament. I then turn to a discussion of the ancient literary context of the New Testament, focusing especially on a collection of Jewish writings that influenced New Testament authors. Finally, I offer an overview of the social context of everyday life in the hierarchical Roman world.

A History of Trauma under Imperial Rule

In this section, I offer a brief overview of the history of ancient Israel, which provides important context for understanding the events in the first century CE that shaped the New Testament writings. Note first, that the history of Israel is not the same as the biblical story, or the **canonical** story, as it is also called. The word **canon** refers to a collection of authoritative scriptures. The Christian canonical story begins with the creation

The New Testament: A Contemporary Introduction, First Edition. Colleen M. Conway.
© 2023 John Wiley & Sons Ltd. Published 2023 by John Wiley & Sons Ltd.

of the world in the book of Genesis and ends with a proclamation of a new heaven and earth in the book of Revelation. Christian theologians sometimes refer to the canonical story as a "**salvation history**." This "history" moves from creation to sin to redemption and the anticipation of the final consummation of God's reign. The canonical story is not history in the academic sense and not the history I discuss in what follows. Instead, studying the historical context of the Bible means learning about the historical circumstances that shaped the people and culture that produced the biblical writings.

All of the New Testament texts were written during a time of Roman imperial domination. For the Jewish people of this period, including the Jewish authors of the New Testament, the experience of Roman imperialism was simply the most recent episode in a long history of foreign domination. The detailed examination of that history is a topic for a textbook on the Hebrew Bible/Old Testament. Nevertheless, for our study of the New Testament, we need to situate first-century CE Roman imperialism within a larger story that includes the people of Israel's experiences of earlier imperial oppression. In the discussion below, I briefly mention the ways that this history produced writings that would later influence the New Testament. In later chapters, I explore in more detail the ways that Christ-followers relied on ancient traditions to understand their experience of Jesus.

For this purpose, I begin with the formation of an Israelite monarchy in the tenth century BCE. The book of 1 Samuel suggests that Israel's first king, Saul, emerged as a sort of warlord or /proto-king. He rallied different tribes in the land to resist invasions from nearby city-states (1 Samuel 10–11). Following Saul, David conquered the Jebusite city of Jerusalem and made it the capital of the kingdom (2 Samuel 5). David's son Solomon assumed the throne after David. He built a temple to Yahweh and a palace for himself (1 Kings 6–7). Solomon was the last to reign over both the northern and southern tribes. When he died, the northern tribes, dissatisfied with the treatment they experienced under Solomon, split from the south to form their own kingdom called Israel (1 Kings 12). Meanwhile, the Davidic monarchy (the line of kings descended from David) continued to reign over the southern kingdom of Judah until the sixth century BCE. A group of biblical psalms known as the "royal psalms" provide evidence of the importance of the Davidic monarchy, portraying the king as one chosen and empowered by God (see, for example, Psalm 2). Many centuries later, Christ-followers reinterpreted such royal psalms in relation to Jesus.

Meanwhile, to the northeast, the Assyrian empire was growing in strength and expanding its reach. In the eighth century BCE, Assyria conquered the northern kingdom, driving the inhabitants of Israel from their land and exiling them across the Assyrian empire. Judah survived only barely and was terrorized by Assyria and forced to pay tribute to the Assyrian king. Two centuries later, in the sixth century BCE, Judah suffered a devastating defeat by another regional superpower, the Babylonian empire. The conquering Babylonian army destroyed the city of Jerusalem, including the Temple, in 586 BCE. Most of the elite, including the king, were forcibly deported to Babylon. This period, known as the **Babylonian exile**, was so pivotal to the people of Judah that biblical history is typically periodized as "pre-exile," "exile," and "post-exile." Note that the genealogy of Jesus that opens the Gospel of Matthew is divided into the periods before and after the deportation to Babylon (Matt 1:11–12). Moreover, some of the biblical prophesies that spoke to the experience of exile were reinterpreted by Christ-followers as prophecies about Jesus. For example, the depiction of Israel as a suffering servant of God became an especially important image for connecting the fate of Jesus to the Jewish scriptures (see Isa 42:1–4; 49:1–6; 50:4–7; 52:13–53:12).

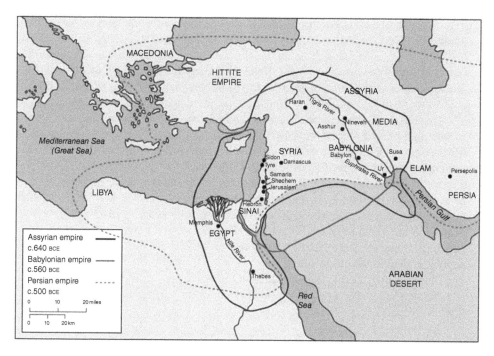

MAP 1.1
The reach of three of the major empires that dominated Israel and/or Judah: the Assyrian, Babylonian, and Persian empires. Redrawn from www.bible.ca, Abingdon Press, 1994.

Several decades after the Babylonian deportation, the Persian ruler, Cyrus, conquered the Babylonian empire (see Map 1.1). So began a period of Persian rule over Judah that lasted over two hundred years. Cyrus and his successors allowed the Judean exiles to return to Judah in several stages to rebuild the Jerusalem Temple and their community; it is no wonder that Cyrus is referred to as God's **"messiah"** in Isaiah 45:1 (Hebrew, "annointed one"). The prophet saw him as God's chosen liberator of the deportees. Still, although they were permitted to return, the Judeans remained under foreign rule. The designation **Second Temple period** refers to the period beginning in 515 BCE, when Persian authorization made it possible to rebuild the Jerusalem Temple. The period ends in the late first century CE when this temple is destroyed by Rome.

Returning to our historical overview, the Persian empire came to an end with the conquering Greek army of Alexander the Great. Alexander and the Hellenistic rulers who came after him spread Greek culture throughout the eastern Mediterranean region. (The terms **"Hellenistic"** and **"Hellenization"** come from the Greek word *hellen*, the term that ancient Greeks used to refer to themselves.) This period of Hellenization had far-reaching consequences, one of which was the spread of a Greek dialect known as **Koine** ("common") across the region. The spread of the Greek language had a direct impact on the Bible. First, beginning in the third century BCE, the Hebrew scriptures were translated into Koine Greek. This Greek translation is known as the **Septuagint**, from the Latin word for 70 (often abbreviated as **LXX**). The name of the translation comes from a legend about the production of the Greek translation. According to the story, 72 scribes were appointed by the high priest in Jerusalem to go to Alexandria in Egypt to translate the Hebrew scriptures into Greek for inclusion in the famous Alexandrian library. The legend states that the translation was produced in exactly 72 days. While few scholars think this story is authentic, the translation attests to the needs of a Greek-speaking Jewish community in the Hellenistic period. The even longer-term effects of Alexander's conquest are evident in the New Testament. All of the New Testament authors wrote in Koine Greek, quoting from the Septuagint in their writings.

The introduction of Greek culture produced a new kind of imperial pressure for the Judeans living in and around Jerusalem. Because there were social, economic, and political advantages to adopting Greek culture and customs, some of the Judeans living in Jerusalem were open to the process of Hellenization. Others saw the adoption of Greek culture as a threat to the Jewish people. These differences led to internal disputes that came to a crisis when the Hellenistic Seleucid king, Antiochus IV, decided to settle the matter by forbidding Jewish practices such as circumcision and dietary regulations. His actions resulted in an armed resistance by some of the Judeans (see 1 and 2 Maccabees for two different accounts of these events). The successful "Maccabean revolt," so named after the family that led the rebellion, began a period of independent rule for the Jewish people. The Hasmonean dynasty (the descendants of the Maccabees) ruled in Jerusalem for some one hundred years, even expanding to claim some of the surrounding land (Map 1.2).

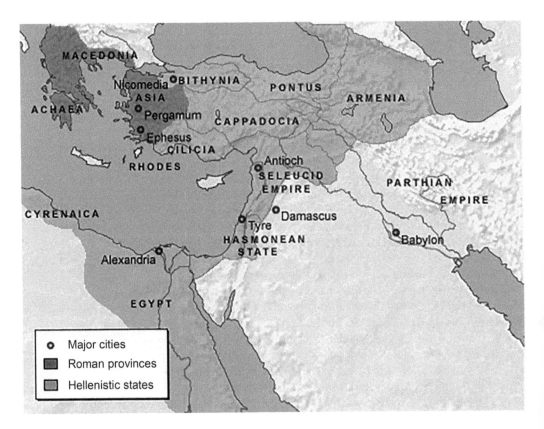

MAP 1.2
The Hellenistic kingdoms and the Hasmonean state around 90 BCE.

This relatively brief period of independence for the Jewish people came to an end with the occupation by Rome in 63 BCE. However, as these events require more detailed attention in terms of their relevance to the New Testament writings, I leave them for discussion in the next chapter.

The New Testament Writings in their Ancient Literary Context

Ancient literary influences also informed the writings of the New Testament. Writing styles and genres of communication change over time, and such change can present problems for modern people attempting to understand ancient texts. Although we can read the translated words of an ancient text, we may be unaware of how those words contribute to a particular genre, how they function rhetorically in an argument, or how they convey certain moods or tones, like humor or sarcasm. Indeed, we may miss the author's meaning entirely. One contemporary example of changing literary forms and modes of communication illustrates the point: less than two decades before this textbook was written, the idea of communicating with something called a "tweet" did not exist. Since its invention in 2006, Twitter has not only become a central means of sharing information but has also encouraged the creation of new types of literature. "Twitterature" is formed by blending older poetic genres like haiku with the 140-character format of Twitter. Meanwhile, the ubiquitous hashtag has found its way into everyday speech, useful for expressing sarcasm or humor. Perhaps by the time you are reading this, the use of Twitter and hashtags is already fading in light of new media forms. Centuries from now, people might be #clueless about understanding writings from our time if they are unfamiliar with the literary practices associated with a #early2000s company called "Twitter."

So, too, we may misunderstand aspects of biblical writings if we are not familiar with first-century CE literary genres and ancient rhetorical conventions. For this reason, attention to ancient literary contexts will be part of our discussion of New Testament texts. For example, later in this book, you will learn about a rhetorical style called the diatribe that Paul used in his letter to the Romans. Similarly, I will discuss conventions of Greco-Roman biographies to help with interpreting the birth stories of Jesus. These are just two examples of how attending to ancient literary contexts and genres will help you learn more about the New Testament.

Another important part of the literary context of the New Testament concerns how the authors drew on Jewish scriptural traditions for their own writing. What Christians now call the Old Testament was simply called "the scriptures" or the "law and prophets" for Jesus and his followers (see, for example, Matt 7:12; Acts 13:15; Rom 3:21). I have already pointed to some of these scriptural influences, and we will see more in the coming chapters. Here, I want to focus on another important but less well-known collection of writings that also informed the authors of the New Testament: the Jewish literature written in Greek and Aramaic in the third to first centuries BCE. Scholars often refer to these writings as Second Temple literature because they were written in the Second Temple period. Some of these Jewish writings did not become part of the biblical canon. As I discussed in the Prologue, some are now considered deuterocanonical in the Roman Catholic church and some make up the apocrypha in Protestant denominations. Here, I will mention just a few examples of influential Second Temple texts as a way of anticipating later discussions.

The first example is a Jewish writing known as 1 Enoch, which is not included as part of any sacred canon despite its influence. The work is a good illustration of some common elements of Jewish literature from the Second Temple period. First, the writing is attributed to an ancient biblical figure, Enoch, rather than the actual ancient scribe who wrote it. This literary practice was a way of giving authority to an esteemed biblical figure and indicating that the text should be read as a continuation of the scriptural tradition. Although Enoch is mentioned only briefly in the Hebrew Bible (Gen 5:21–4), the figure captured the attention of later Jewish writers. Indeed, 1 Enoch is actually a collection of several writings from the Second Temple period that were attributed to Enoch. A second element in 1 Enoch that is common to Second Temple literature is the way it draws on, interprets, and sometimes expands biblical traditions. In this way, it shows how Jewish writers engaged with scripture to address their own contemporary contexts. The popularity of 1 Enoch is evident in the many copies of the book that were found among the scrolls discovered at a place called Qumran, an archeological site on the western shore of the Dead Sea. The authoritative status of 1 Enoch is further attested by the fact that the New Testament book of Jude contains a direct quotation from it (Jude 14–15).

The second example is not one text but a group of Jewish writings that scholars refer to as Wisdom literature. These writings praised a semi-divine figure of Wisdom ("*sophia*" in Greek, often represented as a feminine figure). One such wisdom book written during the Second Temple period is called the Wisdom of Solomon (an additional example of a pseudonymous text). Another example is a book called the Wisdom of Ben Sira (also known as Sirach or Ecclesiasticus). This is one of only a few Jewish writings in which the author identifies himself. Both of these books transmit a collection of wisdom sayings that demonstrate the elevation of the wisdom tradition in the Second Temple period. In later chapters, I will show how the personified figure of Wisdom from this literature influenced New Testament traditions about Jesus.

The most important thing to know about Jewish writings from the Second Temple period is that they contain many ideas that are centrally important to the New Testament authors but are not found in the Hebrew Bible. For instance, only in Jewish literature from the third century BCE do we find references to God's final judgment, resurrection from the dead, the afterlife, and a coming messiah – all concepts that are central to the first- to second-century CE New Testament writers.

Some of these ideas, like speculation about an afterlife, were likely influenced by interaction with Persian and Greek cultures, yet another example of the influence of imperial conquest and cultural mingling on the development of the Bible. Finally, we should note that for the authors of the New Testament, there was likely little distinction between writings that we now designate as "biblical" versus other non-biblical Second Temple writings. These authors drew on a broad range of Jewish traditions that were important to them in understanding the significance of the figure of Jesus.

The New Testament Writings in their Ancient Social Context

In this last section of the chapter, I turn to the social and economic reality of everyday life under Roman rule. Sometimes readers of the New Testament assume that it is a collection of religious writings concerned primarily with individual heavenly salvation – that is, a benefit one receives after death. However, ancient audiences likely understood the Jesus movement's promises of restoration and salvation as relevant to their *present* lives. What follows is a brief description of the social world of the Roman empire that I will build on in later chapters.

Roman society was hierarchical. It privileged men over women, freeborn people over enslaved people, wealthy people over poor people, and Roman citizens over non-citizens. For its most elite members, family ancestry was a major factor. The "patricians," as they were called, claimed ancestral connections to the founders of Rome. Most people were commoners, or "plebians," though citizenship and wealth were still factors in their status within this group, as was a person's status as freeborn or a freedperson. Those who were formerly slaves might eventually become quite wealthy but were never afforded the same status as freeborn people. Toward the bottom of the social hierarchy were people who owned no property and worked menial jobs for pay. At the lowest end were slaves, who were legally considered property rather than people.

Such social gradations meant that one's quality of life depended on a complex combination of intersecting factors. A person might rank above someone else in one area (freeborn rather than freedperson) and below them in another area (a woman rather than a man). Accordingly, the New Testament authors show a keen awareness of social status. Note, for example, the apostle Paul's observation to the Corinthians, "Not many of you are of high birth" (1 Cor 1:26). In the Gospel of Mark, a wealthy Torah-obedient man becomes an object lesson about how difficult it is for a rich person to enter the kingdom of God (10:17–22). Revelation offers a biting critique of Roman extravagance with a detailed list of luxurious cargo sold to Rome that concludes with "slaves – and human lives" (Rev 18:11–13). Such passages, and many others, demonstrate the relevance of economic and social status to the New Testament writers. These examples also show the importance of including an intersectional approach in New Testament interpretation. Recall that such an approach examines how multiple social categories intersect to affect one's place in social power structures.

While the idea of a social hierarchy based on family, wealth, and possessions is not a new concept for twenty-first-century readers, other aspects of the socioeconomic system of Rome may be less familiar. For example, an important element of the Roman social hierarchy was a long-standing system of patron–client relationships that operated at both the public and private levels. At the public level, a wealthy patron might sponsor a guild or religious association, or even a small city. He or she might give funds for a public building or provide public entertainment. A private patron could support an individual, whether a freedperson who had been a slave for the patron or a freeborn person of lower status. Under this arrangement, the lower-status client would be obligated to perform services for the patron in exchange for that patron's provision of funds or legal protection. The apostle Paul provides an example of such a patron–client relationship in his letter to the Romans. In the closing chapter of the letter, Paul commends a woman named Phoebe for being "a benefactor of many including myself" (Rom 16:2). This is all we know about Phoebe. Nevertheless, this intriguing reference points to the existence of patron–client relationships among Christ-followers, in this case between Paul and a woman with enough means to provide him with support. In another example, the author of the Gospel of Luke and the Acts of the Apostles prefaces both writings with a direct address to "most excellent Theophilus." This is just the way a client would refer to a patron who had sponsored his work.

Another aspect of Roman society – indeed, one that was deeply interwoven in the fabric of the ancient world – was the institution of slavery. The system of slavery was an assumed part of life in the Greco-Roman world. Past scholarship sometimes underestimated the significance of this fact because ancient slavery differed from more recent iterations of slave labor in the Americas. To be sure, there are differences between ancient slavery and the modern slave trade of the sixteenth to nineteenth centuries. In the Roman empire, slaves were often war prisoners or the children of war prisoners. Also, slaves in the Roman period were not all agricultural or household workers. The labor required to make Rome's imperial expansion a profitable enterprise was enormous, requiring many types of labor from thousands, and at times, millions of slaves. Nevertheless, the dependence on slave labor to turn a profit was similar in both ancient and modern contexts. In both cases, slaves had no legal rights or recourse whatsoever. Slaveowners could do what they wished with their slaves.

References to slaves and slave owners occur frequently throughout the biblical writings. The presence of enslaved characters is not always apparent to English-language audiences because English translations often soften the Greek words *doulos* (slave) or *paidiske* (slave-girl) with the English word "servant." Perhaps this translation choice is a way to avoid the discomfort of confronting the reality of the ancient slave culture and how deeply embedded the institution of slavery was for the New Testament writers. Here, I list just a few examples among many that could be cited to illustrate the point. Apart from references to enslaved characters (for example, the enslaved girl who identifies Peter as a disciple of Jesus, Luke 22:56), enslaved figures populate the teachings of Jesus. Especially Jesus's short narratives, known as parables, often refer to slaves as a way to teach audiences about the kingdom of God, as in "the Kingdom of heaven is like a king who wanted to settle accounts with his slaves" (Matt 18:23). Several parables describe the violent treatment of enslaved men (for example, Mark 12:1–12 and Luke 19:12–27). An enslaved girl in the house of a Christ-follower named Mary is used in an attempt to add humor to the narrative in Acts, which was a common use of enslaved figures in Greek literature (see Acts 12:12–15). Paul's letters are peppered with references to slaves. For example, in one letter Paul mentions a report that he received from "Chloe's people" (in Greek, "those of Chloe," 1 Cor 1:11). This is likely a reference to slaves owned by a Christ-follower named Chloe. Paul also writes a brief letter to a man named Philemon that seems to be advising Philemon about a slave named Onesimus. Again, these are just some of the many places where slaves play a role in the various writings that make up the New Testament.

So far, I have discussed a number of identity markers that were central to one's place in Roman society, but I have not yet discussed the idea of religious identity. This may seem odd. Contemporary readers of the New Testament might reasonably assume that religion would be the most important category to discuss. Yet here again, we are confronted with different ways of thinking in the ancient world. The idea of religion did not exist in any form similar to how we now think of this social practice. People were not members of an institutionalized religion that was distinct from other religions, let alone distinct from other aspects of their lives. Instead, the beliefs and practices of ancient people were linked to locally specific deities and particular ethnic identities. The implications of this ancient way of conceiving of divine–human relationships will become evident across this textbook. To note just one example as a preview of coming discussions, Paul's letters address a major debate among Jewish Christ-followers regarding the place of gentiles (non-Jews) in the Jesus movement. As we will see, the question concerns whether gentiles could be part of the movement *as gentiles*, since they were not part of ethnic kinship structure associated with the God of Israel.

Acts 16:11–40

FOCUS
TEXT

I conclude this chapter on the multiple contexts of the New Testament with a close look at a passage from the Acts of the Apostles. We will learn more about the book of Acts later in this textbook. Here, I focus on Acts 16:11–40 to demonstrate what it means to attend to the multiple contexts of the New Testament.

The passage relates two episodes that take place in the city of Philippi. Both episodes describe Paul's encounters with other people in the city. As you read through the passage, pay attention to how gender, ethnicity, citizenship status, patron–client relationships, and slave status factor into the narrative.

Considering the ancient literary context of the work, note that Acts 16 *tells a story* about Paul and Silas – that is, it is written in narrative form. Curiously, the narrative shifts from the use of first person "we set sail. . ." to third person; the "we" disappears at verse 19 only to resume at Acts 20:5. This intermittent use of the first person is a puzzle for interpreters of Acts that I discuss further in Chapter 10. For now, note that we are reading stories *about* Paul shaped by the author of Acts. The story begins with Paul and Silas arriving in Philippi (16:11–15). The narrator describes the place as a leading city in the Roman province of Macedonia (see Map 1.2). Philippi was also a Roman colony, which means that it was occupied and governed by Romans. Thus, the story is set in a Greek urban center under Roman control.

Paul and Silas's first action occurs on the sabbath, when they go looking for a "place to pray." It is unclear what this phrase designates. One would expect Paul and Silas to be heading toward the local synagogue given the mention of the Sabbath. However, the author does not choose this word, despite doing so elsewhere (Acts 13:14–15; 14:1; 17:1; 18:4, 19). All we know is that Paul and Silas find women gathered in a ritual space for prayer. This sets the stage for their encounter with a woman named Lydia.

The character Lydia offers a good example of the intersecting identities that we discussed earlier in the chapter. Like Paul, she is not local to Philippi but is from Thyatira, another Greco-Roman city located in modern-day Turkey. Inscriptions from Thyatira provide evidence for this city's thriving trade in textiles and dye. Lydia's name may also provide clues about her identity. The region in which Thyatira was located was called Lydia. It may be that the name Lydia describes the woman's origin, and it could indicate her former slave status since slave names were often linked to place names. The story explicitly affirms that Lydia is a businesswoman: she sells purple cloth in Philippi. The narrator also describes Lydia as a "worshipper of God," an expression that could mean that she is a gentile who is interested in Jewish rites. Alternatively, the term may simply signal Lydia's piety, with "god" being used in a general sense. The description of a group of women gathered in a ritual setting more closely matches descriptions of gentile women's cultic activity in non-Jewish settings. For instance, the worship of the Egyptian goddess Isis was prominent in Philippi and popular among ancient women generally.

In either case, the story goes on to depict Lydia's interest in Paul's teaching. Upon hearing it, she and her household are baptized. The mention of Lydia's household and the fact that she immediately invites Paul and Silas to stay there give the impression that she has some financial resources. Indeed, by the end of the focus text, Lydia's home has become a meeting place for Paul, Silas, and other "brothers" in Philippi (16:40). Thus, in this brief episode, we meet a woman with multiple intersecting identities. Lydia is a gentile, a businesswoman, and a devout cultic practitioner (or perhaps a synagogue attendee). She is relatively wealthy, possibly a freedwoman, is newly baptized, and becomes a host and thereby enters a patron relationship with the Christ group.

We can contrast this encounter between Paul and Lydia with the second, longer episode that is narrated in Acts 16:16–39. Again, Paul and Silas meet a woman as they are going to "the place of prayer." This time, they cross paths with a young, enslaved girl who makes money for her owners with her powers of divination. In contrast to Lydia, we learn nothing about this young woman except that she is profitable. The plot thickens when Paul becomes annoyed after hearing the young girl proclaim for many days that he and Silas are "slaves of the Most High God who preach to you a way of salvation" (16:17). In a seemingly impulsive response, Paul casts out her spirit of divination.

When the owners see their source of income slip away after the young woman loses her spirit of divination, they seek retribution through the city officials. Nevertheless, the charges that the owners bring against Paul and Silas do not focus on their economic loss. Rather, the men claim that Paul and Silas are Jews who are promoting customs that are not legal for the men to accept or practice "being Romans," as they emphasize (16:21). From out of nowhere, "the crowd" joins in the attack against Paul and Silas, apparently eager to condemn two Jewish men. In response to the unrest in the city, the officials have Paul and Silas stripped and beaten in public and then imprisoned. In this way, the story depicts the use of Roman identity within a Roman power structure to exact revenge against suspicious non-Romans.

But the story does not end there. Only *after* succumbing to this humiliating treatment, only *after* an earthquake occurs and Paul's jailer is baptized, and only *after* the magistrates order that he and Silas be secretly released, does Paul reveal that he is a Roman citizen! Paul could have mentioned this crucial detail much earlier in the story, but the narrative delay allows for the dramatic divine intervention as well as the conversion of the jailer and his household. The response from the magistrates is also quite dramatic. Without asking for proof of Paul's claim, the magistrates fearfully and quickly apologize and grant Paul's request for an escort out of the prison. What do they fear? The narrator does not make this explicit, so we should assume that the audience would understand that subjecting Roman citizens to bodily harm without a trial could endanger the magistrates' own positions; after all, they are among many expendable officials who work at the behest of the emperor. The entire episode in Philippi ends where it began, with Paul and his co-workers staying at the house of Lydia.

A close reading of Acts 16:11–40 illustrates how intersecting identities affected one's social standing and relations in the ancient first-century CE world, as they also do in our present world. Together, these two episodes also present some uncomfortable challenges to the assumptions that a twenty-first-century reader might bring to a New Testament text. Perhaps the most disturbing is the contrast between the powerless, nameless female slave and the businesswoman, Lydia. The slave, economically exploited by her owners, is little more than a plot device. Even though she correctly divines the identity of Paul and Silas, they pay her no mind until her constant prophesying annoys Paul to the point of action. The story does not show Paul casting the spirit out of the young woman because of concern for her (nor is she consulted about the matter). He simply reacts out of irritation. Once the young woman's plot purpose is fulfilled, she disappears from the story. Indeed, Paul shows more concern for his unnamed jailer, whom he eventually baptizes (16:28–34). As we have seen, Paul also baptizes the woman of higher status, Lydia, who makes her home available to Paul and his co-workers. As Paul moves on in his journey, the narrative leaves us to imagine the Christ group in Philippi continuing to meet in Lydia's house. In this way, her role in the story comports with evidence from Paul's letters that relatively wealthy women functioned as patrons to the growing Jesus movement. In contrast, we have no idea what becomes of the enslaved woman who is no longer profitable to her owners.

Finally, the story also portrays the benefits of Roman citizenship in occupied cities in contrast to non-citizens' vulnerability to violence. In addition, it shows the susceptibility of those viewed as outsiders – in this case, those identified as Jews. The owners of the enslaved woman know how to trigger the local crowd and the civic authorities to incite violence against Paul. Meanwhile, Paul knows how to leverage his citizenship to embarrass the officials and gain his freedom.

Conclusion: The New Testament in a Complex World

This chapter has introduced you to multiple ancient contexts that influenced the New Testament writings. I have moved rapidly through a review of the New Testament's historical context, I have asked you to consider the literary influences on the New Testament writers, and I have discussed the social environment of the first century CE. This is quite a lot to take in at once! Keep in mind that the goal of this chapter has been to illustrate the complexity of the world we enter when we study any ancient text, including the New Testament. We will have occasion to revisit many of the ideas I have introduced here as we study the writings themselves in the chapters to come.

Finally, the focus text offers an example of how this textbook will explore the leading male figures of the New Testament writings while also calling attention to the characters on the margins. The first part is all too easy because the legacy of white Eurocentric scholarship has always been to center figures like Paul while mostly ignoring figures like Lydia and the nameless enslaved young woman. My goal for this contemporary introduction to the New Testament is to situate this collection of ancient writings in the midst of a complex world in which all sorts of people lived and longed for a safe and full life. My hope is that doing so will offer a more fully informed way of bringing the texts into conversation with our own complex world.

CHAPTER ONE REVIEW

1 Know the meaning and significance of the following terms discussed in this chapter:
   - canon/canonical
   - Babylonian exile
   - Koine
   - LXX
   - messiah
   - salvation history
   - Second Temple period
2 List the different empires that ruled over Israel and/or Judah. What is one example of how the trauma of imperial domination is reflected in the New Testament?
3 Give some examples of how Alexander's conquest played a role in how the New Testament was written.
4 What are some of the different contexts that influenced the writers of the New Testament?
5 (Focus text: Acts 16:11–40) What aspects of Acts 16:11–40 are illuminated by attention to ancient intersecting identities? How might your own intersecting identities affect your understanding of the New Testament?

RESOURCES FOR FURTHER STUDY

Ascough, Richard. *Lydia: Paul's Cosmopolitan Hostess*. Collegeville, MN: Liturgical Press, 2009.

Carr, David M. *The Hebrew Bible: A Contemporary Introduction to the Christian Old Testament and Jewish Tanakh* (2nd edition). Chichester: Wiley Blackwell, 2021.

Henze, Matthias. *Mind the Gap: How the Jewish Writings between the Old and New Testament Help Us Understand Jesus*. Minneapolis: Fortress Press, 2017.

The Jesus Movement in the Context of the Roman Empire

2

Chapter Outline

Chapter Overview	29
Rome Comes to Jerusalem	29
Searching for the Historical Jesus: Problems and Proposals	33
The Earliest Jesus Traditions	39
Chapter Two Review	43
Resources for Further Study	43

Chapter Overview

In the last chapter, I offered an overview of the history of the people of Israel up to the time of the independent rule of the Hasmoneans. Chapter 2 begins with the Roman occupation of the regions of Judea and Galilee. I then invite you to envision some of the long-term effects of this occupation through an imagined tour of Jerusalem as it looked during the time of Jesus in the first century CE. The second part of the chapter turns to the figure of Jesus as one among many people who lived under Roman rule. In this section, I discuss the scholarly problem of the historical Jesus and what it means for reading the New Testament. Finally, I consider what we know about the **oral traditions** about Jesus because the transmission of these traditions constitutes the earliest stage of the formation of the New Testament.

Rome Comes to Jerusalem

By the second century BCE, the Roman Republic had taken control of much of the area that is present-day Europe and was pressing eastward. Meanwhile, despite the successful Maccabean revolt against Antiochus IV, Judea did not transition smoothly into independent rule. Instead, the power vacuum left after the revolts was filled with ongoing disputes about who should hold the high priesthood. It was during this time that distinct groups within Judaism began to take shape, such as the Pharisees, the Sadducees, and the Essenes. More will be said about these different groups in later

The New Testament: A Contemporary Introduction, First Edition. Colleen M. Conway.
© 2023 John Wiley & Sons Ltd. Published 2023 by John Wiley & Sons Ltd.

chapters. The important point here is that these tensions hastened Rome's entry into Jerusalem in the person of the Roman general Pompey.

In 63 BCE, Judea was embroiled in a civil war between two Hasmonean brothers, Hyrcanus and Aristobulus. At various points in this struggle for power, both brothers sought assistance from Pompey, the Roman general who was then stationed in Syria. Pompey responded by moving his army into Jerusalem to take control of the region. Unlike the much earlier invasion of Babylon, there was no massive destruction of Jerusalem or its Temple when the Roman empire seized control of Judea. Nor was there a major deportation of the residents. Instead, Pompey inflicted minimal damage on Jerusalem, ordered the Jewish priests to properly purify the Temple after his military advance, and reinstated one of the brothers, Hyrcanus, as high priest.

These actions were in keeping with the way that Rome expanded and maintained its empire. The Roman army could not depend on military rule across Rome's conquered lands – the army was simply not big enough. Instead, the typical Roman practice was to choose local leaders to rule on their behalf. These **client kings**, or procurators, as they were sometimes titled, were typically the elite men of the local communities who stood to benefit from demonstrating their loyalty to Rome. One such local elite man was Herod the Great, who, after carefully working his way into Roman favor, was designated as king of Judea by the Roman Senate in 37 BCE.

Herod, whose reign lasted more than forty years, is a prime illustration of the cultural complexity that existed in Roman **Palestine** during this time. As part of his interest in gaining the confidence of Rome, he began an extensive building program in Jerusalem and throughout Roman Palestine. Because of an ongoing interest in Greek culture, newly formed Roman cities across the Roman empire closely resembled the Hellenistic urban centers established by Alexander the Great. Accordingly, the Jewish King Herod built cities in Judea complete with Greek-styled theaters, agoras, and gymnasiums. Herod's Roman patrons were likely impressed with the colossal size and grandeur of his building projects. Similarly, the people of Jerusalem could hardly object to the massive renovation and expansion of the Jerusalem Temple that Herod funded or the construction of roads and aqueducts that improved the infrastructure of the region. Nevertheless, Herod himself was from Idumea, a region south of Judea whose inhabitants had been forced to convert to Judaism when the Hasmoneans expanded their kingdom. Given this, local Judeans remained skeptical of Herod's Jewish identity.

Imagine, then, that you are a first-century CE traveler to Jerusalem. Perhaps you are going at the time of the Passover festival to commemorate God's deliverance of the Hebrews from slavery in Egypt. In the first century CE, while the Jerusalem Temple still stood, the festival required a pilgrimage to the city to offer a Passover sacrifice in the Temple. Approaching the city, you would see the massive foundation of the Temple with its surrounding walls and fortified corners, known as the Temple Mount (see Figures 2.1 and 2.2). As you made your way up the wide stone staircase to the Temple, you would pass under impressive archways. You might take a stroll on Solomon's Porch (Figure 2.3), the beautifully colonnaded walkway on the east side of the Temple. The size of the Temple plaza itself would have rivaled any of the finest open civic esplanades in the Roman empire (see Figure 2.4). Adjacent to the Temple Mount you would see the refurbished Antonia fortress, named after Herod's patron,

FIGURE 2.1
Excavation of the remains of an outer stairway and arches of the Second Temple in Jerusalem, built on the site of Solomon's Temple c. 520 BCE and expanded under Herod in 1 BCE.

FIGURE 2.2
Proposed reconstruction of the outer stairway and arches of Jerusalem.

FIGURE 2.3
Model of first-century CE Jerusalem. The Antonia fortress is on the right of the Temple Mount. The colonnade known as Solomon's Porch (or Portico) is visible behind the Temple.

FIGURE 2.4
The Forum of Augustus in Rome. Compare the colonnaded porticos to those on the Jerusalem Temple Mount.

the Roman general Marc Antony. Gazing out over Jerusalem from the height of the Temple Mount, you would see the Greek-styled amphitheater for the performance of Greek and Roman plays, the hippodrome for chariot races, and the elaborate palace of King Herod with its three enormous, fortified towers.

The point of this imaginary journey is to make vividly clear the cultural and political landscape during Herod's rule over Judea and Jesus's life in Galilee: the countryside was inhabited predominantly by Jews, with urban cities like Jerusalem infused with Greek culture, all of which was ruled by the Romans. Such was the situation across the period that the New Testament writers put stylus to papyrus sheet. As we turn to examine the study of the historical Jesus and the earliest traditions about him, we will keep in mind this complex cultural and political mix.

Searching for the Historical Jesus: Problems and Proposals

Beginning with the study of Jesus may seem like an obvious choice for an introduction to the New Testament. In fact, the decision is complicated. The problem is that the Jesus we read about in the New Testament is not the same, or at least not exactly the same, as the figure biblical scholars call the **historical Jesus.** The need for this distinction is evident in the gospels themselves. As mentioned in the Prologue, the gospels differ in their presentations of Jesus. This brief example of the last words of Jesus illustrates the point:

- In Mark 15:34, Jesus cries out in a loud voice: "My God, my God, why have you abandoned me."
- In Matthew 27:46, Jesus cries out in a loud voice: "My God, my God, why have you abandoned me," which is followed by a second loud cry (see 27:50).
- In Luke 23:46, Jesus cries out in a loud voice: "Father, into your hands, I entrust my spirit."
- In John 19:30, Jesus says: "It is finished."

As you can see, the last words of the Markan and Matthean Jesus differ from the last words of the Lukan Jesus, which differ also from the Johannine Jesus. The final words of the historical Jesus could not have been all of these differing statements. A close reading across the New Testament gospels reveals many more ways that their portrayals of Jesus differ.

When we consider questions of dating and authorship, the gap between the New Testament and the historical Jesus becomes apparent in another way. The earliest of the canonical gospels, the Gospel of Mark, was likely written around 70 CE, more than forty years after Jesus's death. The other three gospels were written at an even greater distance from the living Jesus. Such a time gap adds to the difficulty of considering the gospel narratives as reliable historical records. In addition, all four of the canonical gospels were written anonymously. It was not until the second century CE, when the four gospels were circulated as a collection, that scribes added titles to the top of the manuscripts. These superscriptions use the same Greek work, *kata*, to assert that each gospel is "according to" a particular authorial figure: Matthew, Mark, Luke, and John, respectively. This is also the time when traditions about these four figures begin to appear, with claims that they were either original apostles of Jesus (Matthew and John) or close associates of other well-known apostles (Mark of Peter and Luke of Paul). Despite these attributions, most scholars do not think any of these people were the original gospel writers. The gospels are not written in a style that suggests their authors were present at the narrated events. Nor is it likely that the disciples of Jesus were able to write, especially not in Greek, the language in which the gospels were written.

Given this evidence and much more that I must leave aside for now, we are left with the reality that the Bible's gospels were written by anonymous Christ-followers decades after the events that they relate. In the rest of this book, I will refer to the gospels using the traditional names associated with each one, even though the gospel writers are completely unknown. These authors, whoever they were, believed Jesus to be the long-awaited Jewish messiah and Son of God, and their writings are an effort to demonstrate the meaning and truth of this faith claim. Thus, while the gospels offer insight into the ancient Christ-followers' faith in and memory of Jesus, they do not offer easy access to the historical Jesus.

Still, once scholars acknowledged the distinction between the historical Jesus and the Jesus of the gospels, they were eager to discover the "real" Jesus in the midst of church traditions about him. The late seventeenth century saw the beginning of the "quest for the historical Jesus" (so named after a 1906 book by Albert Schweitzer, *The Quest of the Historical Jesus*). By now, it is more accurate to say "quests," because there have been several versions of the project. The first, which produced many biographical "Lives of Jesus," abruptly ended with the publication of Schweitzer's book mentioned above. After carefully reviewing the seventeenth- and eighteenth-century attempts to write a life of Jesus, Schweitzer convincingly concluded the following:

> each successive epoch of theology found its own thoughts in Jesus; that was, indeed, the only way in which it could make Him live. But it was not only each epoch that found its reflection in Jesus; each individual created Him in accordance with his own character. There is no historical task which so reveals a man's true self as the writing of a Life of Jesus.

Anyone attempting to construct a historically accurate figure of Jesus should be aware of Schweitzer's insight: people in search of a historical Jesus are likely to "find" a Jesus that suits their needs. It is all too tempting to imagine a Jesus that matches one's beliefs and preferences rather than the historical evidence. On this point, too, Schweitzer had something to say. He argued that if scholars succeed in finding the actual historical Jesus, "[he] will be to our time a stranger and an enigma." By this, Schweitzer meant that we must take seriously the temporal, social, and cultural gap between our world and the world of Jesus. If the historical Jesus we imagine seems at home in the twenty-first century, we probably do not have an accurate historical construction. Instead, our picture of Jesus may reflect our own dreams and ideals. Note also that the New Testament writings offer no physical description of Jesus. We can only surmise how a first-century CE Mediterranean Jewish man might have appeared (Figure 2.5).

More on the Historical Jesus Search

READING

Read and study how each of the four canonical gospels describes the baptism of Jesus (Mark 1:9–11; Matt 3:13–17; Luke 3:21–2; John 1:29–34).

EXERCISE

What details are the same? What differences do you notice? Note also the context for each of these scenes. What comes before and after the baptism in each gospel?

During the second iteration of the quest, in the mid-twentieth century, scholars developed criteria to assess the historical reliability of a given gospel tradition about Jesus. The third quest, in the late twentieth century, focused especially on the Jewish identity of Jesus. In this phase, historical Jesus scholars began to question the usefulness of some of the earlier criteria, especially those that tried to establish how Jesus's teaching and practice differed from first-century CE Judaism. More recently, scholars have broadly challenged the usefulness of the supposedly scientific set of criteria for assessing the historicity of New Testament traditions about Jesus.

Still, some of these principles remain useful. For example, the "criterion of embarrassment" posits that early followers of Jesus would not invent a tradition that conflicted with beliefs about him. For example, Christ-followers would not likely invent a tradition about Jesus being baptized by John for two reasons. First, such a baptism would suggest that Jesus was a follower of John; and it is hard to understand why such a tradition would develop among Christ-followers. Second, John's baptism was associated with repentance for the forgiveness of sins (Mark 1:4), but later traditions about Jesus claimed that he was without sin (2 Cor 5:21; Heb 4:15; 1 Peter 2:22). These sorts of tensions suggest that Jesus *was* baptized by John. This historical fact was remembered, and the gospel writers worked in various ways to explain or downplay this "embarrassing" detail in Jesus's actual life. Thus, Mark's gospel opens with the baptism scene but includes a prediction from John that one will come who is more powerful than he is (Mark 1:7). The Gospel of Matthew deals with the same problem by featuring a conversation in which John objects to the idea of baptizing Jesus, suggesting that Jesus should be the one baptizing him (Matt 3:13–15). In the Gospel of Luke, the baptism of Jesus is reported after it occurs, without an explicit mention of John performing the baptism (Luke 3:21). Meanwhile, the Gospel of John does not report Jesus's baptism at all. Rather, John first declares that Jesus ranks above him and then testifies about seeing the Spirit descend on Jesus (John 1:29–34).

FIGURE 2.5

There are no descriptions of the physical appearance of Jesus in the New Testament. Given his Mediterranean ethnicity, we can be sure he was not the blue-eyed, fair-skinned man seen in countless European paintings. Joan Taylor argues that this wall painting of Moses from a third-century CE synagogue (Dura Europos) may be the closest we can come to picturing the historical Jesus because it shows how a Jewish sage was imagined in the Greco-Roman world. See her discussion at https://www. bbc.com/news/magazine-35120965.

As part of his work, Schweitzer offered his own theory about the historical Jesus. He argued that a "thoroughgoing eschatology" motivated Jesus. **Eschatology** means "study of the last things." Schweitzer highlighted the eschatological themes in Jesus's teaching, demonstrating that, like many other first-century CE Jews, the historical Jesus expected the imminent arrival of the reign of God. According to Schweitzer, Jesus's final pilgrimage to Jerusalem was intended to help usher in this divine kingdom. In more recent years, scholars such as E.P. Sanders, Bart Ehrman, and Paula Fredriksen have followed Schweitzer in showing how the teaching and actions of the historical Jesus align with the role of an eschatological or, more precisely, an **apocalyptic** prophet. By using the term "apocalyptic," these scholars suggest that Jesus, along with some other Jewish people of his time, expected an imminent intervention by God in human affairs. **Apocalypticism** includes the belief that this divine intervention will inaugurate a glorious new age for those who have remained faithful and just. Meanwhile, God will punish the evil powers that have been in control of the world.

Eschatology versus Apocalypticism

While these two terms are sometimes used interchangeably, there is a difference in their meaning in the context of biblical scholarship. "Eschatology" comes from the Greek word eschaton, meaning "last." It is the study of "last things" or end times. "Apocalypticism," however, refers to a specific worldview that expects God's cosmic intervention to set right the injustice of the world. The term "apocalypse" literally means "uncovering."

An apocalypse is also an ancient literary genre. A literary apocalypse purports to reveal special knowledge about heavenly realms as well as God's impending intervention in the earthly realm. Examples of this literary genre began to appear in the third century BCE with Jewish texts like Enoch and the biblical book of Daniel. Apocalyptic thinking continued to grow in popularity and is reflected in many of the writings discovered near the Dead Sea at Qumran. More examples of literary apocalypses were written in the first century CE, such as the Apocalypse of Abraham and the Apocalypse of Moses.

As we will see in the chapters that follow, apocalypticism runs through many of the New Testament writings, beginning with the letters of Paul. Jesus himself likely started as a follower of John the Baptist, a charismatic figure who proclaimed an apocalyptic message, exhorting Jews living in Galilee and Judea to prepare for the coming judgment of God. According to the Gospel of Mark, Jesus's own preaching focused on the coming of the reign of God, and many of his parables were about the coming kingdom. This supports the idea that Jesus was one of many apocalyptic Jewish thinkers living in the first century CE.

In addition to recognizing the apocalyptic worldview of Jesus, any historical construction of Jesus must consider the fact that he was crucified by the Romans. The Romans would not have crucified Jesus unless his words or activities had been perceived as a threat to the Roman civic order. While the gospel narratives do portray Jesus in conflict with Jewish leaders in Jerusalem, it was not the typical practice of Roman rulers to execute someone over intellectual or religious disagreements. We may never know the precise nature of the historical Jesus's disputes with local Jewish leaders, but we know for certain that his activities gained the attention of the Roman authorities in Jerusalem.

One clue as to why this occurred may lie in the report, common to all of the gospels, that Jesus was crucified under the charge that he called himself "king of the Jews." The title appears in various accounts of Jesus's trial before Pilate (Mark 15:2; John 18:33) and in accounts of an inscription that was hung on the cross with Jesus (Matt 27:37; Luke 23:38; John 19:19–21). It does not appear that Jesus's own followers used the title "king of the Jews," and John's gospel may deliberately avoid it (see John 1:49 where Jesus is called "the king of Israel"). In any case, if this was the charge that was brought to the Roman authorities, it may have been the reason for his death at the hands of the Romans. Roman authorities would have viewed such a claim as treason against the emperor and thus cause for execution.

Apart from this charge, the Gospel of Mark suggests that Jesus's disruptive protest in the Temple – overturning tables and driving out buyers and sellers – was a decisive factor leading to his arrest and crucifixion (Mark 11:18; see also Luke 19:47). If Jesus did engage in this act of protest, he would not have been alone in his critique of Temple leadership and practices. There is additional evidence from the first century CE of ongoing disputes about the Temple. For instance, some of the Dead Sea Scrolls suggest that a Jewish group retreated to the Judean desert in protest over the Temple leadership. Given this general time of unrest, it is thus quite conceivable that the historical Jesus also engaged in a critique of the Temple leadership and practices. Perhaps he predicted the Temple's destruction (see Mark 14:58) and symbolically enacted this destruction by causing a disturbance in the Temple precincts. This type of symbolic enactment was common in the prophetic tradition. Moreover, a civil disruption like this would have triggered a strong reaction from the Roman authorities.

Contemporary Voices: Ongoing Critiques and the Future of Historical Jesus Research

Scholarly work on the historical Jesus continues, as do critiques of the project. Elizabeth Schüssler Fiorenza, for example, has long argued that the production of historical Jesus studies for popular audiences effectively maintains the status quo in the male-dominated field of biblical studies. She has also claimed that the proliferation of historical Jesus books is driven by market demands – in other words, the quest has been commodified. Schüssler Fiorenza's long-term project has been to argue that the historical Jesus and his followers were an emancipatory group that included women and men. (For a representative sample of her large body of work, see Resources for Further Study.)

More recently, James Crossley has offered a way forward for the "next quest" (see James Crossley, "The Next Quest for the Historical Jesus," *Journal for the Study of the Historical Jesus*, 19 (2021): 261–264). Crossley asserts that a renewed focus on the historical Jesus must include close attention to the social history of scholarship. This means considering how past scholarly reconstructions of the historical Jesus relate to "the development of the nation state, European colonialism, fascism, capitalism in its various guises . . . and American culture wars." Crossley's overall point is that the study of Jesus as a historical figure lags behind progress that has been made in other areas of the humanities. Thus, he argues that in the next quest, "any claims to religious authority must be treated as academics would treat any other claims in any other historical, religious, or cultural context." Moreover, categories such as class, race and ethnicity, and gender and sexuality must be part of this new effort.

In the end, we can only speculate about the historical realities that lie behind the narratives of Jesus as we find them in the gospels and other New Testament writings. The discussion in the coming chapters will focus more on the different depictions of Jesus that come to us from the New Testament. This is the Jesus known by early Christ-followers living in the midst of the Roman empire. It is this Jesus that lived on in the **social memory** of the early followers and was transmitted first in oral stories and then in written form for later generations. I turn next to a discussion of the nature of social memory and the early stages of oral traditions about Jesus.

The Earliest Jesus Traditions

Read 1 Corinthians 15:3–8 and compare it to the empty tomb and resurrection stories in the four canonical gospels (Mark 16:1–8; Matt 28:1–10, 16–20; Luke 24:1–43; John 20:1–29).

READING

How do the gospel accounts compare to each other and to the tradition that Paul reports he received in 1 Cor 15:3–8? Make a list of similarities and differences.

EXERCISE

Early Christ-followers formed a group identity around shared social memories of Jesus. We need to be flexible in our sense of what the term "memories" designates in this context because human memory is a fluid phenomenon. Community memories of Jesus could certainly have included accounts from immediate followers of Jesus about what he did or said. However, social memories of Jesus would also have included stories about him that indicated his significance to the community, even though the events that the stories relate did not actually happen. A contemporary example of this idea may clarify this point. Most schoolchildren in the United States are taught that the six-year-old George Washington cut his father's cherry tree with a new hatchet. When he was confronted by his father, young George supposedly admitted to the act, telling his father, "I cannot tell a lie." We now know that none of this happened – an American minister and Washington biographer made up the story. Nevertheless, the "memory" has been transmitted in the United States for centuries (including through the ritual baking of cherry pies on President's Day). The story is transmitted as a form of national nostalgia that reinforces a "truth" about the first president of the United States, namely that he was a person of integrity. In a similar way, the social memories of Jesus transmitted to future generations by early Christ-followers conveyed their central truth claims about Jesus.

You can see this process of oral transmission reflected in the apostle Paul's description of the tradition that he "received" about the resurrection of Jesus, an account that he then "delivered" to the Corinthians (1 Cor 15:3). Paul's use of the words "received" and "delivered" indicates the oral communication of tradition. Here, it is important to remember that none of the canonical gospels had been written yet when Paul was writing his letters. Moreover, Paul's resurrection tradition does not match any of the later gospel accounts of the empty tomb and resurrection stories. Indeed, the gospels themselves vary in their accounts of who went to the tomb and what they saw there, not to mention their differing resurrection stories.

When students learn about the oral stage of certain gospel traditions, they sometimes assume that the written gospels differ because an original, historically accurate account was distorted as it passed from person to person. In this scenario, one might imagine a process something like the children's game of "telephone," where a player whispers a phrase to another player who whispers it to another and so on, with the original message shifting as it passes between players. But imagining a *single* game of telephone is not helpful for explaining the existence of the gospels' different stories of the empty tomb and Jesus's resurrection appearances. Rather, from the very beginning, a variety of traditions about Jesus's death, burial, and resurrection circulated orally among the earliest followers of Jesus. If you imagine *many* games of telephone being played at the same time, each beginning with its own phrase, you will be closer to the process of the oral transmission of early Jesus traditions like those of the empty tomb. We cannot determine exactly how, when, and under what conditions these stories about Jesus began to take shape. To be sure, there are core elements common to all of the traditions – that Jesus died, was buried, and was raised from the tomb. But the difference in details shows how parts of the empty tomb story varied among tellers, or perhaps were introduced by the gospel writers.

One example of what we can learn from a close reading of these different empty tomb stories concerns the depiction of women in the tradition. No women are mentioned in Paul's account. (Note that in the Greek text, 1 Cor 15:6 states that "he appeared to more than five hundred *brothers*. . ..") Meanwhile, various combinations of women at the empty tomb are described in the four gospel accounts. For example, the author of the Gospel of Luke takes special care to claim that the male apostles did not believe the women's account of the empty tomb (Luke 24:10–11). This variation of details about the women at the tomb offers one piece of evidence that the role of women was a contested topic in the earliest stages of the Jesus movement. The argument about women's participation is not explicitly spelled out. Instead, it is reflected in different "memories" regarding the testimony and authority of women in the Jesus movement. From a historian's perspective, this contested topic suggests that women played a prominent role in the early movement.

Paul's account in 1 Corinthians 15 provides evidence for the early circulation of resurrection traditions about Jesus. This seems to be the main tradition that Paul "received" when he became part of the Jesus movement, since his letters say very little about the teaching and ministry of Jesus. Nevertheless, the early stages of oral traditions about Jesus must have also included stories about his teaching and healing ministry. Indeed, the depictions of Jesus in the gospels suggest that he had a memorable style of oral communication. The gospel writers portray Jesus teaching in **parables** – that is, by means of short narratives – or comparative language. They also depict Jesus in verbal contests in which he bests his opponents with short, clever **pronouncements**. Note, for example, the Markan Jesus's reply to his opponents when they complain that he is working on the Sabbath: "the Sabbath was made for the sake of humankind, not humankind for the Sabbath" (Mark 2:27).

The difficulty of appreciating the oral quality of the historical Jesus's teaching is that his teaching has been preserved only in written form. Written versions of oral traditions mask the flexibility, fluidity, and repetitiveness that characterize the oral transmission of traditions. For example, reading the account of Jesus's "Sermon on the Mount" (Matthew 5–7), one would understandably get the impression that there was one occasion on which Jesus stood on a mountain and preached the sermon as it stands in the gospel. As we will see in Chapter 12, it is far more likely that Matthew's sermon is a literary creation that reflects the sort of teaching that Jesus did on several occasions in several different places. Similarly, we should imagine Jesus repeating parables and pronouncements on a variety of occasions during his ministry. When he did so, the details likely varied, even as the basic outline of his teachings might have remained the same. The transmission of such sayings of Jesus comprises an early stage of the oral traditions that lie behind the written text of the gospels.

Not long after the death of Jesus, his followers not only transmitted his teachings but also began to tell stories *about* Jesus. These, too, would have been repeated on different occasions in different places. As stories about Jesus began to spread, there would have been demand for additional stories about him. New believers may have wanted to hear more about the circumstances of his birth or what he was like as a boy. Although such details may not have been available to the storytellers, there were plenty of cultural models on which they could develop their own versions of Jesus's early days. Stories of "great men" typically included tales of divine omens regarding their birth and their precociousness as children. For example, in his *Life of Augustus*, the Roman historian Suetonius offers an account of multiple omens surrounding the birth of Octavian, the future Caesar Augustus. According to Suetonius, the omens, which include dreams, lightning strikes, pillars of fire, and more, make it possible "to anticipate and perceive [the] future greatness and uninterrupted good fortune" of Augustus (Suetonius, *Augustus* 94). Similarly, the Gospel of Matthew features astrologers ("magi") following an omen, a star that appeared in the sky at the birth of Jesus (Matt 2:2, 9). Meanwhile, in the Gospel of Luke, divine messengers portend the births of both John the Baptist and Jesus (Luke 1:12, 30–1), and a divine messenger announces the birth of Jesus (Luke 2:10–14). In these ways, the gospel writers imitate common cultural patterns of ascribing greatness to the man about whom they are writing.

As the emerging community of believers met new challenges, it also adapted or created traditions about Jesus to address changing circumstances, for example the inclusion of the gentiles in the Jesus movement. While we might be surprised at the idea of Jesus's followers "making up" stories about him, this is because we do not live in an oral culture. Rather than focusing on whether these oral traditions about Jesus are "true" (where "truth" is unhelpfully equated with historical veracity), we should think in terms of what fundamental convictions about Jesus these storytellers wanted to convey by means of these stories.

The Infancy Gospel of Thomas: The Boy Jesus and His Superpowers

Among the canonical gospels, only the Gospel of Luke mentions Jesus as a young boy, and even this gospel includes only one such episode (Luke 2:41–51). One entertaining non-canonical gospel, known as the Infancy Gospel of Thomas, addresses that gap. The gospel was likely written sometime in the second century CE and fills in details about the precocious boy Jesus creating mischief with his divine superpowers. For instance, a five-year-old Jesus makes birds out of clay, brings them to life, and has them fly away (Figure 2.6). On another occasion, when another boy accidentally bumps into him, Jesus strikes the boy dead. Such behavior earns a scolding and ear-pulling from his father, Joseph. The episodes in this gospel take Jesus from ages 5 to 12. After relating a number of impulsive and arrogant displays of power by Jesus, the narrative depicts him as becoming obedient to his parents and growing in wisdom (echoing Luke 2:51). Overall, this imaginative account of the boy Jesus reads like an ancient coming-of-age superhero story. The Infancy Gospel of Thomas shows how Jesus traditions continued to develop even after the canonical gospels were written. At the same time, it illustrates the sort of invention and development of tradition that are also found in the canonical gospels.

FIGURE 2.6
This parchment illustration from around 1340 CE shows a scene from the Infancy Gospel of Thomas where Jesus brings clay birds to life.

Because this chapter concerns the oral nature of Jesus's ministry and the oral transmission of early Jesus traditions, I will not conclude with a focus text. Instead, I leave you to imagine the village settings of Galilee and the urban setting of Jerusalem where people listened to a Jewish rabbi talking about how God's coming reign would restore justice to an unjust world. Consider how, as the years passed, Christ-followers continued to pass on traditions about Jesus, perhaps while sharing meals or when coming together for rituals. In such settings, these groups also imagined anew the sort of things Jesus might have done and said, especially to address issues in their own time. These new stories of Jesus were also "remembered" and became a formative part of the Jesus movement.

CHAPTER TWO REVIEW

1 Know the meaning and significance of the following terms discussed in this chapter:
   - apocalyptic / apocalypticism
   - client kings
   - eschatology
   - historical Jesus
   - oral traditions
   - Palestine
   - parables
   - pronouncements
   - social memory

2 Describe the earliest stages of traditions about Jesus.

3 Why is it difficult to know much for certain about the historical Jesus? Why do some scholars think it is likely that Jesus had an apocalyptic worldview?

4 Students are often troubled to learn that some of the gospel stories of Jesus may not have happened just as they are reported. The question that seems to follow is, "Are the stories true?" Can you think of a story that communicates something that you think to be true even if the events related in the story did not really happen? What does this suggest about using historicity as the ultimate measure of truth?

RESOURCES FOR FURTHER STUDY

Carey, Greg. *Apocalyptic Literature in the New Testament*. Nashville, TN: Abingdon Press, 2016.

Carter, Warren. *The Roman Empire and the New Testament: An Essential Guide*. Nashville, TN: Abingdon Press, 2006.

Carter, Warren. *Seven Events that Shaped the New Testament World*. Grand Rapids, MI: Baker Academic, 2013.

Kelber, Werner. *The Oral and the Written Gospel: The Hermeneutics of Speaking and Writing in the Synoptic Tradition, Mark, Paul, and Q* (2nd edition). Bloomington: Indiana University Press, 1997.

Kelber, Werner H., and Samuel Byrskog, eds. *Jesus in Memory: Traditions in Oral and Scribal Perspectives*. Waco, TX: Baylor University Press, 2009.

Resources on the Historical Jesus:

Bond, Helen K. *The Historical Jesus: A Guide for the Perplexed*. London and New York: T&T Clark, 2012.

Charlesworth, James H. *The Historical Jesus: An Essential Guide*. Nashville, TN: Abingdon Press, 2008.

Ehrman, Bart D. *Jesus before the Gospels: How the Earliest Christians Remembered, Changed, and Invented Their Stories of the Savior*. New York: HarperOne, 2016.

Moxnes, Halvor, Ward Blanton, and James G. Crossley, eds. *Jesus beyond Nationalism: Constructing the Historical Jesus in a Period of Cultural Complexity*. London and Oakville, CT: Equinox, 2009.

Schweitzer, Albert. *The Quest of the Historical Jesus*. Minneapolis, MN: Augsburg Fortress, 2001. A republished English translation from the 1901 original.

Schüssler Fiorenza, Elizabeth. *Jesus and the Politics of Interpretation*. London and New York: Continuum, 2000.

Schüssler Fiorenza, Elizabeth. *Jesus: Miriam's Child, Sophia's Prophet: Critical Issues in Feminist Christology*. London: Bloomsbury T&T Clark, 2015. A reissue of the original 1994 with a new preface. The book addresses the study of the historical Jesus while laying out a feminist approach to interpreting the Christ figure in Christian scriptures.

Simpson, Benjamin I. *Recent Research on the Historical Jesus*. Sheffield, UK: Sheffield Phoenix Press, 2014.

Introducing Paul and His Letters

3

Chapter Outline

Chapter Overview	**45**
Introduction to the Study of the Pauline Letters	**46**
Paul's Earliest Surviving Letter: 1 Thessalonians	**51**
Paul's Letter to the Philippians	**54**
Focus Text: Paul's Letter to Philemon	**57**
Chapter Three Review	**59**
Resources for Further Study	**60**

Chapter Overview

In this chapter, I turn from the discussion of Jesus traditions to a focus on the figure of Paul and the Pauline letter collection. This turn is in keeping with this textbook's mostly chronological approach to the New Testament writings. Paul wrote all of his letters a decade or more before any other New Testament text. Thus, historically, the letters came first, even if they are not positioned before the gospels in the New Testament canon. To begin the study of Paul, I introduce several concepts that are key to the academic study of his letters: (1) **undisputed** versus **disputed letters** in the Pauline letter collection, (2) the potential gap between what Paul writes and the reality among the Christ groups that he addresses, and (3) the nature of the urban settings of Paul's missionary efforts. With these concepts in mind, I focus on three of Paul's letters. First, 1 Thessalonians shows how Paul's work was directed toward non-Jews as part of his own Jewish apocalyptic worldview. Second, the letter to the Philippians provides an example of reading Paul's letters in light of the particular local setting of his audience. Finally, Paul's letter to Philemon illustrates Paul's rhetorical skills as well as how his letters functioned in later cultural debates.

The New Testament: A Contemporary Introduction, First Edition. Colleen M. Conway.
© 2023 John Wiley & Sons Ltd. Published 2023 by John Wiley & Sons Ltd.

Introduction to the Study of the Pauline Letters

Imagine that you discover a collection of letters written by someone who lived two thousand years ago. Most of the letters are addressed to groups of people living in urban centers of the Roman empire. The tone of the letters ranges from joyous and celebratory to angry and defensive. Your task is to learn as much as you can about the sender and the recipients of these letters. What circumstances led to the writing of the letters? What were the letters meant to communicate? What was the nature of the relationship between the sender and recipients? Such questions are central to the academic study of Paul's letter collection.

While there is much we could learn about each of Paul's letters, in this introductory textbook, I direct our study across the next three chapters to focus on key aspects of Paul and the Pauline letter collection. In this first chapter, we will read 1 Thessalonians, Philippians, and Philemon to learn more about Paul's letter-writing practice and his mission to urban Christ groups. Chapter 4 focuses on Paul's letters to the Galatians and Romans to understand his mission and message to the gentiles in the context of first-century CE Hellenistic Judaism. In Chapter 5, we will read 1 and 2 Corinthians with a focus on the real-life implications for gentiles who accepted Paul's message, including tensions between the members of the Corinthian Christ group and Paul. Along the way, we also consider the occasion for each letter, Paul's style of argumentation, and the use of Paul's letters in contemporary contexts. Before turning to focus on Paul's individual letters, I first provide some guidelines for the general study of the Pauline letter collection.

One fundamental idea that informs the academic study of Paul's letters is that he did not write all of them. Scholars agree that Paul wrote seven of the 13 letters traditionally attributed to him. These seven, listed in the table below, are called the **undisputed letters** because there is no debate regarding their authorship. These seven letters share a common writing style and vocabulary. They were likely written in the span of a single decade: the 50s CE. The authorship of the remaining six letters is **disputed**. Many scholars have raised serious questions about whether Paul wrote these six letters because they differ in writing style and reflect a later stage in the development of the Jesus movement. We will return to the discussion of these disputed letters in Chapter 6. Note that the order of the letters in the New Testament has nothing to do with their chronology. They are simply ordered by length, from the longest (Romans) to the shortest (Philemon).

Undisputed Letters	Disputed Letters
Romans	Ephesians
1 Corinthians	Colossians
2 Corinthians	2 Thessalonians
Galatians	1 Timothy
Philippians	2 Timothy
1 Thessalonians	Titus
Philemon	

The book of Acts raises another question concerning authorship and authenticity related to Paul. While the author of Acts provides a fascinating and colorful picture of the character of Paul, it is important to realize that this is a literary characterization rather than a historical record. In the book of Acts, Paul is a character in a narrative written several decades after the historical Paul was alive. As part of his longer work, the author of Acts tells a story about Paul that suits the author's own purposes. We will study the Paul of Acts in Chapter 11. In the present chapter and in the next two, I focus on the undisputed letters to be sure that we are studying Paul's own writings.

The second basic idea to keep in mind as we read Paul's letters concerns the relationship between what he writes and what was happening in the Christ groups that he was addressing. Every one of Paul's letters addresses a specific set of circumstances regarding a specific group of people living in a particular place. Scholars often refer to these circumstances as the **occasion** of the letter. As we will see, Paul adapts his language and teaching to address these different occasions.

Although it is important to discern the occasion of Paul's letters, we should be careful in our attempts to do so. We may be tempted to read Paul's letters as a mirror that simply reflects the social situation in the groups to whom he writes. However, the circumstances may be more complex than Paul's letters reflect. For example, Paul often uses kinship language, such as referring to his audience as "brothers." He regularly writes of unity and being "one in Christ." However, reading between the lines, his letters attest to disagreements, divisions, and diversity in early Christ groups. In short, we might think of the rosier parts of Paul's letters as aspirational, describing the relationships that he hopes to create. Meanwhile, the more heated parts of Paul's letters likely reveal the actual situations that he encountered in his work. Even here, however, we must be cautious about simply accepting Paul's version of events at face value, let alone his description of himself and his opponents. After all, Paul is interested in establishing and maintaining his authority among the Christ groups to whom he writes.

The third basic point to know before we turn to Paul's letters is that most of his letters are addressed to people who lived in cities located in modern-day Greece (Philippi, Thessalonica, and Corinth). One letter is to people living in a region of Asia Minor (Galatia, in modern-day Turkey) and one is addressed to people living in the seat of the empire, the city of Rome. In other words, Paul's mission was focused on urban populations (see Map 3.1). We will explore these urban settings in more detail in our discussion of Paul's letters, but it will be useful to have a general sense of these cities at the outset.

In general, the cities to which Paul writes were much smaller than most cities in the United States. For example, ancient Thessalonica is estimated to have had a population of 35,000. Philippi was much smaller, with about 15,000 people. In contrast, even a small city in the United States typically has over 100,000 inhabitants. A Greco-Roman city of this period would contain a Greek-styled amphitheater, multiple temples devoted to various deities in which city dwellers offered sacrifices, an outdoor assembly place (called an agora), a gymnasium for athletic competition, and a colonnade leading to important buildings such as the forum for civic affairs.

These urban centers would convey the power of Rome in many forms. Public festivals, processions, and ritual sacrifices provided opportunities to demonstrate allegiance

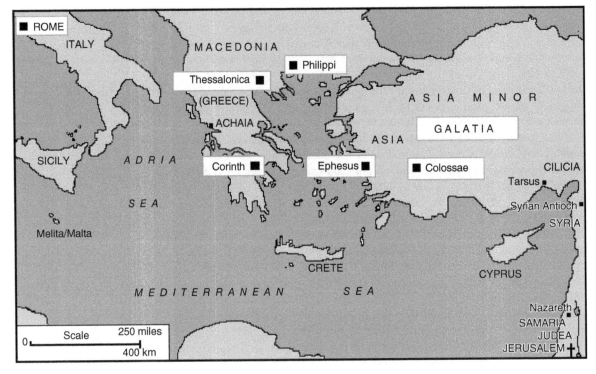

MAP 3.1
Map of cities addressed in the Pauline letters. Note that Galatia is a region rather than a city.

to the Roman emperor. Coins used for daily commerce kept the emperor's image in wide circulation. Public recitations of poetry and hymns proclaimed Rome's divinely given authority and eternal reign. Inscriptions on public pillars celebrated Roman military achievements and honored imperial officials. In short, visual and auditory reminders of imperial power were everywhere, and especially prominent in the ever-present statues of the emperor. Some of these statues would feature the military strength of the emperor. Other statues and marble reliefs conveyed the emperor's priestly role in which he functioned as a mediator between the people and the gods, thus ensuring divine favor toward the empire (see Figure 3.1).

The cities and colonies of the empire were linked by an impressive system of Roman roads built to move the Roman army and to transport material goods between cities. These same roads enabled the spread of the Jesus movement and allowed Christ-followers like Paul and those he refers to as "co-workers" (Greek, *synergos*) to travel between urban centers. Paul would certainly have traveled on the major Roman thoroughfare called the *Via Egnatia* between Philippi and Thessalonica (see Figure 3.2). I turn now to a closer look at Paul's letters to the Christ groups in those two cities.

FIGURE 3.1

Statue of Augustus showing him wearing the veil of the *pontifex maximus* ("greatest priest").
The *pontifex maximus* was the highest priestly position in the Roman state religion.

FIGURE 3.2

Remains of the *Via Egnatia*, Rome's primary artery to the east. Paul would have traveled along this
road first to Philippi and then on to Thessalonica.

The Structure and Composition of Paul's Letters

You are likely familiar with how to properly begin and end different types of written communication, whether a formal letter of application, an email to your professor, or a brief text to your friend. Similarly, Paul followed the first-century CE cultural conventions of written communication, with some modifications. Greco-Roman letters typically adopted the following structure:

- opening salutation (identification of letter writer and the addressee(s))
- health wish, thanksgiving, or blessing
- body of letter (adopting standard rhetorical conventions depending on the purpose of the letter)
- greetings to particular people associated with the addressee(s)
- closing

Paul follows this same basic form with some unique features. He often expands the thanksgiving section in which he praises the community for their acceptance of his message (see, for example, 1 Thess 1:2–10; Phil 1:3–11). Similarly, instead of standard words of closing, Paul ends his letters with a blessing (for example, 1 Thess 5:28; Phil 4:23). In the body of his letters, Paul frequently uses rhetorical patterns that he would have learned as a youth, including deliberative rhetoric (persuading an audience to take a particular course), judicial rhetoric (defending actions), or epideictic rhetoric (praise and blame of others).

In the opening salutation, Paul typically identifies other co-workers who had a role in the composition of the letter. In the case of 1 Thessalonians, he names Silvanus and Timothy (1 Thess 1:1). For the letter to the Philippians, he again includes Timothy in the salutation (Phil 1:1). Following common ancient practice, the actual writing of Paul's letters was done by a scribe. Note, for example, in Rom 16:22, where the scribe who wrote the letter identifies himself as Tertius. In other places, Paul notes where he has written a few words in his own hand (1 Cor 16:2; Gal 6:11). Given the length of many of Paul's letters, we should imagine an extended process of composition rather than a single session of dictation. Moreover, some of Paul's letters as we have them now seem to combine fragments of more than one letter. (See the discussion of 2 Corinthians in Chapter 5).

Basics on 1 Thessalonians

Outline: reassuring and instructing the Thessalonians

I	Salutation		1:1
II	Thanksgiving		1:2–10
III	Body of the letter		2:11–5:22
	A. Paul describes and defends his work among the Thessalonians		2:11–3:14
	B. Instructions and exhortations about an anticipated "Day of the Lord"		4:1–5:22
III	Closing greetings and blessing		5:23–8

Date and composition   None of Paul's letters are dated. Scholars can only offer approximate dates based on some clues from Paul's letters together with the (much later) story of his travels in the book of Acts. One important external clue for establishing a general range of dates (50s CE) comes from a Roman inscription that names the Roman official Gallio, who served as governor of Achaia around 52 BCE. The Acts narrative connects Paul's time in Corinth to the period when Gallio was in office (see Acts 18:1, 18:12–17). Therefore, if Paul wrote to the Thessalonians from Corinth, the letter can be dated to 50 or 51 CE. In terms of composition, scholars agree that Paul wrote the letter with assistance from Timothy and Silas (see 1 Thess 1:1). The occurrence of a second thanksgiving at 2:13–16 is unusual, as is the condemnation of the Jews that occurs in the second thanksgiving section (2:15–16). Both factors raise the question of whether 2:13–16 is a later scribal addition to the letter. While all surviving manuscripts include these verses, that in itself does not decide the question because the verses could have been added at an early stage of transmission.

Paul's Earliest Surviving Letter: 1 Thessalonians

The academic study of Paul's letters involves looking for clues about the occasion for the letter. Read 1 Thessalonians and search for such clues.

READING

Look also for places that tell us something about how Paul views the world and the nature of his message to the Thessalonians. Can you find places in the letter that address specific concerns of the Christ group in Thessalonica? What are these concerns? How does Paul respond?

EXERCISE

1 Thessalonians provides a useful beginning point for studying the Pauline letters. Because it appears to be the earliest surviving letter of Paul, it offers insight into Paul's early teaching. In Paul's time, Thessalonica was the capital city of Macedonia. It stood at a major crossroads of the empire and thus had a cosmopolitan population. We should imagine Paul traveling across the *Via Egnatia* from Philippi to Thessalonica to bring his message to those who would listen to him (see 1 Thess 2:2). After Paul moved on from the city toward his next destination, he sent Timothy back to check on the Christ group in Thessalonica (1 Thess 3:1–3). Upon Timothy's return, Paul composed a letter with the help of Silvanus and Timothy (1 Thess 1:1). This letter is what we know as 1 Thessalonians.

What can we learn about Paul's worldview, his message, and the concerns of this particular Christ group from the letter? Early in the letter, in the thanksgiving section, Paul writes of a mutual "knowing" about each other. On his side, Paul claims, "we know that you all are chosen, because our gospel came to you not in word only, but also in power and in a spirit of holiness, and with much certainty." With respect to the Thessalonians, Paul asserts, "you know how we were among you" (1 Thess 1:4–5). Paul's emphasis on "knowing" one another is the first step in a series of reassurances that he will offer the Thessalonians.

Part of Paul's reassurance comes in the form of praise of their fundamental life change: how, as Paul puts it, the group "turned toward God from idols, to serve a living and true god and to wait for [God's] son from heaven, whom he raised from the dead, Jesus, who saves us from the wrath that is coming" (1 Thess 1:9). With this brief statement, Paul indicates two main elements of his message and mission. First, the description of his addressees as turning toward "a true god" from idols shows that Paul's message was directed toward non-Jews. Paul writes as a Jewish man attempting to change what he views as the misplaced and dangerous allegiance to Greek and Roman gods, or "idols." As we will see, Paul's missionary focus on gentiles, or the "uncircumcised" as he sometimes refers to them, is reiterated many times in his other letters. Second, Paul's statement shows his expectation of a coming "wrath." Later in the letter, Paul reminds the Thessalonians that they are not to act like the gentiles who do not know God, "for the Lord is an avenger in all these things as we have told you before and testified to you" (1 Thess 4:5–6). Such remarks offer clues about Paul's message when he arrived in the city, suggesting that it was shaped by a Jewish apocalyptic worldview that he shared with many other Second Temple Jews. Paul's "gospel of God," as he refers to it in 1 Thess 2:9, involved preaching to non-Jews about the impending judgment by God that would await them if they did not turn to serve a "living and true god" – that is, the God of Israel.

As we will see in more detail in the coming chapters, Paul's work among gentiles is directly connected to his anticipation of God's coming judgment. He, like other Jewish thinkers of the time, viewed gentiles as "ungodly" or "sinners" (see, for example, Gal 2:15; Rom 5:6). In the Second Temple period, many Jews chose to separate themselves from non-Jews, at least in certain contexts, to maintain a state of purity before God. Why, then, did Paul concern himself with gentiles being "delivered" from God's wrath? The answer lies in Paul's Jewish apocalyptic expectations. Some strands of Jewish apocalypticism included the view that God's ultimate triumph would include bringing in the "nations" (that is, the gentiles) under God's reign. This was not a new idea within Judaism. The Book of Isaiah ends with a vision of all nations who had not yet heard of Yahweh now declaring his glory and worshipping him (Isaiah 66:19, 23). 1 Enoch, the popular Second Temple text discussed in Chapter 1, also features the inclusion of the gentiles. Paul's thought fits within this stream of Jewish tradition. He viewed his mission to bring the gospel to the "uncircumcised" non-Jews as contributing to God's plan of salvation. Moreover, Paul's successes with gentile audiences likely reinforced his belief that the day of judgment was imminent.

More on Paul and Jewish Apocalypticism

In the last chapter, I defined an apocalyptic worldview as a belief in an impending divine intervention in which God will reward just and faithful people while punishing the unjust powers in the world. This apocalyptic perspective is evident in Paul's letters when he writes about "the present evil age" (Gal 1:4) and when he describes the present time as one of suffering that will soon be relieved (Rom 8:18).

However, Paul's experience of the risen Christ led him and other Christ-followers to reshape Jewish apocalypticism in a distinct way. For Paul, God's defeat of evil forces was no longer a future event. Rather, Paul thought that God had *already* intervened decisively in the world through the death and resurrection of Jesus. Yet, this event could only be the first step in God's cosmic intervention given the continued suffering of Paul and other Christ-followers. For example, Paul writes to the Corinthians of Christ's resurrection as the "first fruits" of God's saving work in the world (1 Cor 15:20–3). Paul claims that Christ-followers must wait for the return of Christ, which would signal the full completion of God's saving act. This is what Paul means when he describes the Thessalonians as waiting for God's son from heaven (1 Thess 1:10). The return of Christ (Greek, **parousia** = presence) would bring God's final judgment. For this reason, Paul regularly urges right conduct in his letters so that, as he puts it to the Thessalonians, they may be "blameless at the coming (*parousia*) of our Lord Jesus" (1 Thess 5:23).

We should pause over the implications of such a "turning to a living and true god" for the Christ group in Thessalonica. These Christ-followers, and others like them, shifted their cultic allegiance from Greek and Roman gods to Yahweh, the god of Israel. In the Greco-Roman cities where Paul worked, this change likely meant they no longer participated in regular rituals and festivals with their friends and neighbors. Withdrawing from some aspects of their social network may have resulted in disruption in other parts of their lives. For example, Christ-followers may have been excluded from the economic connections on which their livelihoods depended. Note that Paul describes the situation in Thessalonica with the Greek word *thlipsis*, meaning "trouble" or "affliction" (often translated as "persecution," 1 Thess 2:3). If the social tensions they faced were difficult enough, the Thessalonians may have begun to doubt both Paul and his message. Indeed, Paul expresses this very worry (1 Thess 3:1–5). Thus, he takes care to reassure the group of his trustworthiness by reminding them of how he conducted himself among them (1 Thess 2:3–12).

Paul also addresses a specific concern of the Thessalonian Christ group. His initial teaching among them seems not to have focused on details of the resurrection of believers or the nature of an afterlife. As a result, the Thessalonians became worried about those who had died before the proclaimed coming of Christ. They may have assumed that these departed ones would miss out on the glorious salvation promised by Paul. Paul's response to their worries offers additional insight into the apocalyptic scenario he imagined would happen upon Christ's return. He first reminds them about their belief in Jesus's death and resurrection, offering it as an example of what God will do with others who die (1 Thess 4:14). He then explains the following:

> For this we say to you by the word of the Lord, that we who are living, who remain until the Lord's coming (*parousia*), will definitely not go before those who have died. Because the Lord himself, with a shout of command, with an archangel's voice and the sound of God's trumpet, will come down from heaven, and the dead in Christ will rise first. Then we who are living, who remain behind, will be snatched away with them into the clouds to meet the Lord in the air. And so, we will be with the Lord always. (1 Thess 4:15–17)

With Paul's reference to "we who are (still) living," he suggests the coming of the Lord will happen in his lifetime. He imagines a quite spectacular meeting in the air, replete with trumpets blaring and booming cries of command. Such imagery evokes the type of pageantry that would accompany festal processions for the emperor or other high-ranking officials that were typical in urban settings like Thessalonica. In fact, the word *parousia* was used in reference to heralding the arrival of the emperor.

Finally, note that Paul takes special care to remind the Thessalonians that he and his co-workers did not ask for financial support but instead worked "night and day" to support themselves (1 Thess 2:9). Paul's concern to avoid putting financial pressure on the Thessalonians may indicate the group's low social status (1 Thess 2:1–12). This idea is reinforced by Paul's comments in another letter, where he writes of the poverty of the Macedonians (2 Cor 8:1–2). The issue of the social and economic status of the Christ groups to whom Paul wrote is relevant to the interpretation of all of Paul's letters. As we see next, this is certainly the case with his letter to the Philippians, another Christ group in Macedonia.

Paul's Letter to the Philippians

The focus for the discussion of 1 Thessalonians was on what we could learn about Paul and his worldview. Our study of Philippians will illustrate the importance of attending closely to the local situation of the people to whom Paul writes. While we know that Paul's message was directed to gentiles, the daily experience of his letter recipients varied depending on where they lived and their social status. In what follows, we examine how knowledge about the history and inhabitants of ancient Philippi can help us understand what Paul wrote to the Philippians.

The city of Philippi had a history of colonization. Long before Paul's time, it was invaded by Greek tribes who were attracted by its nearby gold mines. Soon after, in 356 BCE, the city was conquered by Philip of Macedon, from whom the city got its name. By 42 BCE, the Romans had colonized the city, initially by settling retired Roman soldiers there. This colonization likely involved the violent confiscation of land by the newly settled veterans and the displacement of local inhabitants. Moreover, what began in 42 BCE continued under the imperial rule of Octavian as he settled more veterans and other Romans in the city.

This history of foreign colonization meant that Philippi was a city of varied and mixed ethnicities by Paul's time. Its inhabitants included descendants of the various colonizers of the past mixed with the Roman colonizers of the present, both living amidst descendants of yet earlier indigenous groups. As we read Paul's letter, we should keep in mind the ethnic diversity of Philippi's inhabitants, as well as their correspondingly diverse mix of social, economic, and political concerns. This diversity means that Paul's group of Christ-followers could have included both descendants of Roman veterans and people whose families had lived on the land long before the Romans took control.

READING

Read Paul's letter to the Philippians.

EXERCISE

Once again, look for clues as to why Paul writes to this group. What is Paul asking of them? For what reasons does Paul "rejoice"?

Paul's letter to the Philippians is a blend of self-reflection by Paul, exhortations to rejoice, and warnings about an unnamed opposition. A theme that runs across the letter is a call for unity and selflessness. Paul offers a series of examples to imitate. He asks the Philippians to "be of the same mind" as that of Christ Jesus, then offers a reflection on the self-emptying of Christ. Phil 2:6–11 are typically presented in verse form in English translations because Paul adopts a poetic style at this point, perhaps incorporating an early Christ hymn. Notice the extremes in status reflected in the passage. Christ is described as moving from being in the "form of God" to taking on the "form of a slave" to being highly exalted by God. Paul's letter concludes with a reference to every knee bending at the name of Jesus. For his recipients, this reference likely suggested that they (and indeed all of the cosmos) were subject to a power other than Rome.

Basics on Philippians

I	Salutation	1:1–2	**Outline: exhortations for unity and selflessness**
II	Thanksgiving	1:3–11	
II	Body of the letter	1:12–4:20	
	A. Paul's self-reflection on his imprisonment	1:12–26	
	B. Calls for unity and models of selflessness	1:27–4:7	
	C. Acknowledgment of financial support	4:10–20	
III	Greetings and closing blessing	4:21–3	

The letter to the Philippians was likely written in the mid-50s CE. Earlier debates on the composition of the letter focused on the letter's abrupt shifts in tone and topic (for example, the shifts after 3:1 and 4:3). Some scholars have argued that these shifts were indications of a composite letter that combined parts of earlier letters that Paul wrote to the Philippians. However, many interpreters now read the letter as a single composition, perhaps with a digression to familiar topics. Note Paul's introduction to his warnings in Phil 3:2–3: "to write the same things is not irksome to me and for you it is a safeguard" (Phil 3:1b).   **Date and composition**

Other expressions in Paul's letter seem designed to relate even more closely to the specific setting of Philippi as a city with a history of occupation and colonization. For instance, Paul may have in mind the presence of Roman citizens intermingled with a majority of lower-status non-citizen inhabitants when he asserts that "our citizenship exists in heaven" (Phil 3:20). Similarly, the rest of that same verse – "from where we also await a savior, the Lord Jesus Christ" – may pertain to the Philippian setting. This is the only place in Paul's undisputed letters that he refers to Jesus with the term "savior." For the Philippians, this designation would be familiar from the many inscriptions honoring gods and the Roman emperor in Philippi and other Greco-Roman cities. Paul may offer an early example of how later writers, such as the author of the Gospel of Luke, made a point of identifying Jesus rather than the emperor as a savior.

Paul also uses terms related to the economic situation of Philippi. He regularly uses the language of the marketplace, which in the ancient world was language used by low-status merchants. The Roman elite used slaves or hired staff to conduct their business transactions. Marketplace language first occurs in the Christ passage, where Jesus does not "count" equality with God as something to be seized (Phil 2:6). Then, Paul uses economic language in a similar way with respect to his own status as a righteous "Hebrew born of Hebrews": "But whatever were gains to me, I counted as loss. Even more, I counted all things as loss compared to the exceeding value of knowing Christ my Lord," (Phil 3:7–8). Paul's use of these economic terms suggests the Christ group at Philippi would be familiar with such language, perhaps as merchants and low-status workers for whom counting gains and losses was part of daily life. We find further confirmation of the low-income status of the Philippians in Paul's words from another letter. In writing to the Corinthians, he says the following:

> We want you to know, brothers, of the gift of God that was given to the assemblies in Macedonia; that during a difficult testing under affliction, their abundant joy and abject poverty have overflowed in riches of generosity from them (2 Cor 8:1–2).

Here, Paul's reference to the "riches of generosity" refers to a collection that he took up as part of his ministry. I discuss this collection of funds further in later chapters. What interests us here is the description of the poverty of the Macedonian Christ-followers. Recall how Paul made a point of not accepting support from the Thessalonians, the other Christ group in Macedonia. His description of the Macedonians' poverty may explain why he refused their help.

That said, the last section of Paul's letter to the Philippians suggests that Paul does have some sort of financial relationship with the Christ group in Philippi. Indeed, Paul acknowledges their support, though in a guarded way; he offers a "thankless thanks," as some scholars put it. On the one hand, Paul "rejoices" in the Philippians' concern for him (Phil 4:10). On the other hand, he insists that he did not actually need the gift, did not ask for it, and would have been fine without it (Phil 4:11–13, 17). He again turns to marketplace language to argue that their financial support of him is actually a benefit to them: "Not that I seek the gift, I seek the profit that increases in your account" (Phil 4:17). Why this reluctance to offer a straightforward expression of gratitude? The answer likely lies in the cultural expectations regarding the patron–client relationships discussed in Chapter 1. Paul was aware that accepting support from the Philippians would put him on the dependent client side of the relationship. This would be an awkward situation for the founder of a group. It could make it more difficult, for example, for Paul to call on the community to imitate him in the way that he does (Phil 3:17). Nevertheless, Paul closes the body of the letter with the message that he is now "fully satisfied," having received the Philippians' gifts that were sent to him through a certain Epaphroditus. In other words, Philippians is a thank you letter, at least in part.

Overall, Paul's tone in this letter suggests a warm relationship with the Christ group in Philippi. Although he issues warnings in chapter three, nothing in the letter suggests that Paul is anxious about the conduct of this group. His calls to unity may point to some internal disputes, but Paul does not seem overly concerned about them. Even while he urges two women, Euodia and Syntyche, to be "of the same mind," Paul also describes the women positively as close co-workers. Their names, along with those of other co-workers of Paul, are "in the book of life" (Phil 4:2).

The reference to the book of life – that is, the book of those whom God will save – points again to Paul's apocalyptic worldview, this time as it is expressed to the Philippians. Paul writes of God bringing his work among them to completion "by the day of Jesus Christ" (Phil 1:6). In Phil 2:14–16, he uses apocalyptic imagery when he urges the Christ-followers to live blamelessly as children of God in the midst of a corrupt generation. The Philippians are to "shine like stars" in the world, a phrase that echoes astral imagery from other apocalyptic texts. For example, at the end of the biblical book of Daniel, those who lead others to righteousness will shine like the stars forever (Dan 12:3). Later in the letter, Paul reminds the Philippians that "the Lord is near," a temporal reference to the impending "day of Christ" (Phil 4:5; see 1:6; 2:16). As we saw in our study of 1 Thessalonians, Paul's work among the gentiles in Macedonia and elsewhere was premised on his expectation of an imminent day of divine judgment.

Paul's Letter to Philemon

FOCUS TEXT

We turn now to the focus text for this chapter. In this case, we will look at Paul's brief letter to Philemon. Focusing on this text will offer a good example of Paul's attention to rhetorical strategies in his writings. The letter also provides a striking example of the ongoing cultural influence of Paul's letters in later historical periods. This shortest letter of the Pauline collection is also the only undisputed letter of Paul that is addressed primarily to an individual rather than a community. Paul writes to Philemon as "my brother" and co-worker, while also addressing "sister" Apphia and "co-soldier" Achippus. Paul also addresses the *ekklesia* in "your (plural) house." Thus, despite the personal nature of the letter, Paul expects the letter to be read to the group of Christ-followers who meet in the household of Philemon. In this way, Paul ensures that his personal appeal to Philemon will become a more public event. The rest of the letter is addressed directly to Philemon, as indicated by the singular pronouns that begin in verse 4, as well as Paul's reference to "my brother" (v. 7). Overall, the brevity and content of the letter suggest the letter to Philemon is a surviving piece of Paul's business correspondence.

The letter follows the typical Pauline form of a Greco-Roman letter. Following the salutation (1–3), Paul writes words of thanksgiving (4–7), communicates his request in the body of the letter (8–22), then concludes with greetings (23–4) and a benediction (25). But while the structure of the letter is clear, its meaning is not. Paul writes in a cryptic style, carefully crafting his language to appeal to Philemon to do something regarding a person named **Onesimus**. The letter makes clear that Paul is sending Onesimus back to Philemon, presumably with the letter (12). Beyond that, interpreters have had to reconstruct the details that prompted Paul's letter.

At least since the fourth century CE, Onesimus was viewed as a slave who had run away from Philemon, perhaps stealing something from him as well. In this interpretation, Onesimus had come into service to Paul during Paul's imprisonment, but Paul was legally obliged to send the runaway Onesimus back to his owner, Philemon. Those who reconstruct the events in this way argue that Paul is appealing to Philemon to show clemency to a runaway slave. Other interpreters argue that Onesimus was not a fugitive at all, but perhaps a slave sent by Philemon to assist Paul. Paul may have become so attached to Onesimus, whom he describes as "my own heart" (12), that he chose to appeal to Philemon to free Onesimus. Still others have argued that Onesimus was not a slave but rather an estranged brother of Philemon who had been badly treated "*like* a slave" by Philemon (16). In response, Paul urges Philemon to once more treat Onesimus like a "beloved brother."

As mentioned at the outset, the occasion of the letter is difficult to determine because Paul writes in vague terms. Rather than ask directly, he relies on his rhetorical skills to hint at what he wants Philemon to do. For example, in several places, Paul uses wordplays involving the name Onesimus to make his point. In Greek, Onesimus means "useful" or "beneficial." Thus, Paul writes to Philemon, "Earlier [Onesimus] was *useless* to you, but now he is *useful* both to you and to me" (10). Toward the end of his appeal, Paul repeats this wordplay and adds another. Having already described Onesimus as "my own heart" (12), Paul reiterates, "Let me *benefit* from you in the Lord! Refresh *my heart* in Christ!" (20). Paul also displays an ironic wit in the letter. First, he makes a point of writing "I will repay" in his own hand, meaning he has not dictated the phrase to his secretary (19). The action is equivalent to writing an informal "I owe you" to Philemon. But Paul goes on to add, "I say nothing to you about owing me your own self." Of course, Paul has just reminded Philemon of that debt, presumably meaning his debt to Paul for bringing him a message of salvation. Paul assumes a position of authority over Philemon, thus appealing to Philemon's obedience (21). And in case Philemon is disinclined to obey, Paul suggests that he will soon be coming to Philemon in person (22). Paul concludes with a request for prayer from the group that meets with Philemon, still without offering a direct statement about what outcome he expects from his letter. At least, that is the case from our perspective because we do not know the events or people behind the letter. Paul must have presumed that Philemon would know exactly what Paul wanted of him.

The uncertainties surrounding the interpretation of Paul's letter to Philemon have had far-reaching implications. For instance, the letter was used on *both* sides of the nineteenth-century slavery debate in the United States. In the southern United States, Christian ministers used Paul's letters, including Philemon, to justify slavery and to teach slaves that it was their Christian duty to obey their masters. Meanwhile, northern abolitionists argued that Paul was asking for the freedom of Onesimus and thus supported an end to slavery. For example, an American minister named Albert Barnes described the following personal experience that changed his interpretation of Paul's letter to Philemon:

> About twelve or fourteen years [ago], as I was entering the gate of my church, to go into my study, early in the morning, a fine-looking coloured man, apparently about twenty-five or thirty years of age, met me, and told me that he was a runaway slave, from Maryland, and wished some assistance. Influenced by feelings which commonly prevailed at that time, and, as I then thought, in accordance with the Bible, and probably having [the] case of Onesimus in my eye, I endeavoured to show him the impropriety of his leaving his master, and to convince him that he ought to return. But I could make not the least impression on his mind, and all my arguments had no force in his view whatever. (From *An Inquiry into Scriptural Views of Slavery*. Philadelphia: Perkins & Purves, 1846, p. 324)

This experience led Barnes to ask whether anyone would choose to return to a state of slavery simply because they were asked to do so, even if asked by an authoritative figure from scripture such as Paul. Barnes goes on to offer his own detailed discussion of the letter to Philemon, raising many objections against those who interpret the letter as an endorsement of the institution of slavery. He concludes, "The principles laid down in this epistle to Philemon . . . would lead to the abolition of slavery. If all those who were now slaves were to become Christians, and their masters were to treat them 'not as slaves but as brethren beloved,' the period would not be far distant when slavery would cease." This was not the final word in the debate. Others continued to argue (against Barnes) that not only the letter to Philemon but the entire Bible demonstrates God's support of the institution of slavery.

This fraught history of the interpretation of Philemon is one example of how the letters of Paul were used – and continue to be used – as an authoritative source for contemporary cultural debates. It offers one example of the importance of having an informed academic understanding of the Pauline letters in their ancient context, if only, as in the case of Paul's letter to Philemon, to highlight the uncertainty about the occasion for the letter.

CHAPTER THREE REVIEW

1 Know the meaning and significance of the following terms discussed in this chapter:
- disputed and undisputed Pauline letters
- occasion (with respect to Paul's letters)
- Onesimus
- *parousia*

2 What evidence is there in 1 Thessalonians that Paul's mission was directed toward non-Jews?

3 What are Paul's expectations for the coming of the Lord? Why are some of the Thessalonians concerned about this impending event?

4 What are two different reasons that Paul wrote to the Philippians?

5 (Focus text: Paul's Letter to Philemon) Why is it hard to determine the situation that Paul addresses in his letter to Philemon? What other contemporary cultural debates can you think of where a New Testament writing has been used to support both sides of an argument? Do you think that the academic study of the Bible can help in these situations? Explain.

RESOURCES FOR FURTHER STUDY

For general studies of Paul and his letters:

Elliott, Neil, and Mark Reasoner, eds. *Documents and Images for the Study of Paul*. Minneapolis, MN: Fortress Press, 2011.

Fredriksen, Paula. *Paul: The Pagan's Apostle*. New Haven: Yale University Press, 2017.

Harrill, James Albert. *Paul the Apostle: His Life and Legacy in their Roman Context*. New York: Cambridge University Press, 2012.

Horrell, David G. *An Introduction to the Study of Paul (3rd edition)*. London: T&T Clark, 2015.

Marchal, Joseph A., ed. *Studying Paul's Letters: Contemporary Perspectives and Methods*. Minneapolis, MN: Fortress Press, 2012.

Porter, Stanley E. *The Apostle Paul: His Life, Thought, and Letters*. Grand Rapids, MI: Eerdmans, 2016.

Zetterholm, Magnus. *Approaches to Paul: A Student's Guide to Recent Scholarship*. Minneapolis, MN: Fortress, 2009.

For further studies of Thessalonians, Philippians, and Philemon:

Ascough, Richard S. *1 and 2 Thessalonians: Encountering the Christ Group at Thessalonike*. Sheffield, UK: Sheffield Phoenix Press, 2014.

Nasrallah, Laura. *Archeology and the Letters of Paul*. New York: Oxford University Press, 2019. See especially chapter four "On Poverty and Abundance: Philippi and the Letter to the Philippians."

Oakes, Peter. *Philippians: From People to Letter*. Cambridge: Cambridge University Press, 2001. Though dated in some respects, Oakes's work is useful for thinking about the economic situation of the Philippians.

Tamez, Elsa, Cynthia B. Kittredge, Claire M. Colombo, and Alicia J. Batten. *Philippians, Colossians, Philemon*. Collegeville, MN: Liturgical Press, 2017.

Reading Paul within Judaism: Galatians and Romans

4

Chapter Outline

Chapter Overview   61

Paul's Gentile Problem in Galatia   62

Paul on his "Earlier Life" (Gal 1:13)   64

Why and Why Not Circumcision in Galatia?   65

**Paul's Letter to the Romans: The Righteousness of God
in Relation to Jews and Gentiles**   69

**Focus Text: The Problem of Israel and the Place of the
Gentiles (Romans 9–11)**   75

Chapter Four Review   77

Resources for Further Study   77

Chapter Overview

This chapter focuses on two letters that point to a central issue that preoccupied Paul and other leaders in the Jesus movement: the relationship between Jews and gentiles in the Christ assemblies (fromv Greek, *ekklesia*; see Prologue for discussion of translation). In the letter to the Galatians, this issue surfaces with respect to the issue of male circumcision. Paul writes an entire letter to argue strongly against the practice for gentile men. In our time, a heated debate over the status of male genitals no doubt seems odd. However, because circumcision was a defining physical mark of Jewish identity for men, it was a central question as gentiles became part of the Jesus movement. In this chapter, I explore why Paul adopts an "anti-circumcision" position with respect to gentiles and why gentile Christ-followers would want to be circumcised in the first place. Paul's letter to the Romans also concerns questions of Jewish and gentile identity in the context of the Jesus movement. In Romans, questions such as the value of circumcision and the role of the law occur in the context of Paul's introduction of his gospel to the Christ group at Rome. This chapter also focuses on Paul's use of common rhetorical styles and scripture to support his case.

The New Testament: A Contemporary Introduction, First Edition. Colleen M. Conway.
© 2023 John Wiley & Sons Ltd. Published 2023 by John Wiley & Sons Ltd.

Paul's Gentile Problem in Galatia

READING

Read Paul's letter to the Galatians.

EXERCISE

Pay attention to indications of Paul's tone in the letter. Where and how does he communicate his agitation? Note also how he builds his argument. How does Paul establish his authority? Where does he use scripture to support his argument? What scriptural figures are important to him and how does he use them?

Galatia was not a city like Thessalonica or Philippi, but rather an entire Roman province in Asia Minor (modern-day Turkey). For this reason, the identity of Paul's intended recipients for the letter presents a puzzle. Part of the puzzle involves Paul's intriguing reminder to the Galatians that he first proclaimed the gospel to them because of a "weakness of the flesh" (Gal 4:13). Perhaps Paul never meant to stop in the region of Galatia, but illness or ailment necessitated a change in travel plans. Then, finding himself delayed, he began to teach in the area. In any case, the letter he writes back to the "Galatians" shows that he is not the only teacher who has influenced the group. Indeed, Paul feels compelled to begin his letter by making a case for his divinely authorized mission.

Basics on Paul's Letter to the Galatians

Outline: defining identity in Christ for the gentiles	I	Salutation and invocation of curse	1:1–10
	II	Body of the letter: the problem of circumcision for the gentiles	1:11–6:10
		A. Establishment of Paul's authority	1:11–2:14
		B. Argument against the circumcision of gentiles	2:15–4:31
		C. Instructions for a life of freedom in Christ	5:1–6:10
	III	Closing	6:11–18

Date and audience

The letter to the Galatians was likely written in the mid-50s CE. Scholars debate where the letter was intended to circulate. Some suggest Paul meant it to circulate in the cities of the southern part of the province (Antioch, Iconium, Lystra, and Derbe), which were inhabited by a Hellenized population. Others think the letter was directed toward the northern part of the province, where ethnic Galatians lived (descendants of the Gauls who invaded the territory in the third century BCE).

Paul opens his letter to the Galatians with an assertion: "Paul, an apostle, not from humans nor through humans but through Jesus Christ and God the father who raised him from the dead" (Gal 1:1). The Greek word *apostolos* means "messenger" or, more literally, "one who is sent out." As the Christian tradition develops, "apostle" will become a designation for Jesus's original disciples as featured in the gospel narratives. But in his letter to the Galatians, Paul uses *apostolos* in the more general sense of one who is commissioned for a task. In other words, claiming to have been made an "apostle" through Jesus and God is a way to claim divine authorization of his work.

Note also how in the opening lines of his letter, Paul omits his typical thanksgiving section to move straight to his confrontation with the Galatians. He expresses amazement at the Galatians for deserting him and calls curses down on those who are confusing and perverting the gospel of Christ (Gal 1:6–9) – and with this, Paul is just getting warmed up! Later in the letter, he calls the Galatians ignorant (Gal 3:1) and wishes that those who are leading them astray would cut themselves off from the Galatians (or, more sarcastically, would "castrate" themselves, Gal 5:12).

The issue that so disturbs Paul concerns circumcision. There are some in Galatia who have urged the gentile men in the Christ group to be circumcised. (It is worth pausing here to recognize that the entire debate in Galatians concerns male bodies. The only women mentioned in the letter are Sarah and Hagar, figures from the book of Genesis, who Paul puts to allegorical use in Gal 4:21–31.) We do not have more details about what group was advocating circumcision to the men in Galatia. Paul refers to the group only as "those of the circumcision" (Gal 2:12). They could be other gentile Christ-followers who had been circumcised with the understanding that exclusive devotion to the God of Israel required the mark of circumcision. Alternatively, they could be local Jewish leaders who expected new adherents to the God of Israel to be circumcised. They could also be other Jewish leaders within the Jesus movement who considered circumcision a requirement. In any case, Paul takes care to emphasize his mission to the gentiles as he begins his argument against circumcision for gentile Christ-followers.

For modern readers, it is difficult to understand *why* Paul is so vehemently opposed to circumcision for this group. His passionate objections seem more like assertions than argument; for example, he asserts that "if you are circumcised, Christ will not benefit you" (Gal 5:2). More graphically, he claims that circumcision would cut the gentiles off from Christ (Gal 5:4). Similarly, it may be difficult to understand why the Galatian men would *want* to be circumcised. Why would they perceive this physical ritual as necessary and beneficial? I explore both of these questions below. First, however, we need to dispel some long-held misperceptions of Paul, some of which stem from misleading translations of the Greek text.

The Question of Circumcision for Gentiles

The question of whether circumcision was required for gentiles who were interested in the Jewish traditions was not limited to early Christ-followers. According to the Jewish historian Josephus, a Jewish merchant named Ananias persuaded the Mesopotamian king Izates to "worship God according to the Jewish religion." Izates assumes that he also needs to be circumcised to fully practice Judaism. Ananias assures him otherwise, arguing that the king could worship God without being circumcised. God would forgive the omission, Ananias claims, because were Izates to be circumcised, his subjects might reject him due to his fondness of foreign rites. When a second Jewish teacher, Eleazar from Galilee, comes to the palace and finds the king reading the Torah, he offers an opposing opinion. Eleazar, who has a reputation for being "skillful in the learning of his country," argues that the king must not only read the law but also practice it. "How long will you continue uncircumcised?" he asks Izates. "But if you have not yet read the law about circumcision, and do not know how great impiety you are guilty of by neglecting it, read it now." At this, the king sends for a surgeon and does "what he was commanded to do" (Josephus, *Antiquities* 20.3–4). The story related by Josephus illustrates both the attraction of Judaism to some gentiles and the disagreements among Jewish teachers about whether circumcision was necessary for gentiles who devoted themselves to the God of Israel.

Paul on his "Earlier Life" (Gal 1:13)

Paul begins his argument against circumcision for gentile Christ-followers with an autobiographical account of his divine call to go to the gentiles. As part of this account, Paul writes, "For you have heard of my earlier conduct in *Ioudaismos*" (Gal 1:13). English translations typically translate this verse as something like "You have heard, no doubt, of my earlier life in Judaism" (see, for example, NRSV and NIV). Such English translations contribute to the misunderstanding of Paul as a convert from Judaism to Christianity, which is based on an anachronistic view of Christianity during Paul's lifetime. As you may recall from the Prologue of this book, in Paul's time, Christianity was not a distinct religion to which he or anyone else could convert. Moreover, Paul only uses *Ioudaismos* in Gal 1:13. Elsewhere, when Paul refers to his ethnicity, he calls himself a Hebrew (see Phil 3:5); when he refers to his own kin, he calls them Israelites (Rom 9:4). What, then, is he saying about his "earlier life"? This is a critical question to answer if we want to avoid misreadings of Paul as a convert from Judaism (see box "Changing Perspectives on Paul").

One clue comes from two Second Temple writings describing the Maccabean revolt (on the revolt, see Chapter 1). In these writings, *Hellenismos* is condemned (2 Maccabees 4:13), while *Ioudaismos* is praised and admired (2 Maccabees 2:21; 8:1; 14:38; 4 Maccabees 4:26). The contrast is revealing. In the context of a zealous advocacy for Greek customs on the one hand, *Ioudaismos* represents the zealous maintenance of practices like circumcision and dietary regulations on the other. Writing some two hundred years later, Paul speaks in a similar way of his earlier life, when he was advanced in *Ioudaismos* and more zealous for the "traditions of the ancestors" than his peers (Gal 1:13–14). In other words, in his earlier life, Paul was a fervid proponent of *the traditional practice of Jewish rituals within Judaism*.

If this is the case, then Paul's initial opposition to the Jesus movement was against practices that he thought contrary to proper Jewish practice. As for the question of gentile converts to Judaism, Paul's "earlier conduct in *Ioudaismos*" likely resembles the position of the Jewish teacher Eleazar depicted in Josephus's story of King Izates. Eleazar insisted that the king become circumcised to be recognized as one fully obedient to the Jewish law (see box "The Question of Circumcision for Gentiles"). Note that this explanation of Paul's "earlier life" makes sense of the otherwise confusing question he poses later in his letter to the Galatians: "If I am still preaching circumcision, why am I still being harassed?" he asks (Gal 5:11). What Paul means to say with this brief question could be phrased as follows: "Maybe you think that I am still preaching circumcision, but it is because I am no longer preaching circumcision that I am being harassed."

Why and Why Not Circumcision in Galatia?

As we have seen, Josephus's story of the gentile king Izates reveals competing perspectives within first-century CE Judaism regarding expectations for gentiles who devote themselves to the God of Israel. Like Izates, the Galatian gentiles were faced with conflicting instructions on whether they should adhere to the Jewish practice of circumcision. But they did not have the privileged position of a king. The issues at stake involve their status in their local communities. If the Galatians truly left behind their earlier practices, this would mean that they no longer offered sacrifices in local temples, no longer honored the emperor in imperial cult centers, and no longer paid homage to ancestral deities in their household shrines. Yet, without circumcision, the Galatian men were not full participants in Jewish customs. They may have felt themselves to be in a liminal position, no longer having the protection of their former gods but not certain they had gained favor with their new god. Perhaps the Galatians worried that this seemingly liminal situation, neither pagan nor Jewish, would result in negative social and economic consequences.

Meanwhile, Paul felt strongly that the Galatians should remain uncircumcised gentiles. One reason for his opposition was his understanding of gentile "nature." Note his terse statement in Gal 1:15: "We are by nature [*physis*] Jews and not gentile sinners." Paul's use of the Greek term *physis* here implies a contrast between the "natural" quality of gentiles (sinners) and the "natural" quality of Jews (not sinners). This view was in keeping with other ancient Jewish writers who characterized gentiles as fundamentally immoral. Paul's position is not simply that circumcision is unnecessary for gentiles but that, given their "nature," it will actually be detrimental to them. According to Paul, circumcision will "cut them off" from Christ (another play on words!) because it binds the gentiles to keeping the whole law of Judaism (Gal 5:3–4). Paul is not claiming that it is impossible for *anyone* to keep the whole law. Indeed, Paul saw himself as blameless regarding the law (Phil 3:6). Instead, he thinks that *gentiles* cannot possibly keep the whole law, beginning with the very act of circumcision. The Torah requires circumcision to take place on the eighth day after birth (Gen 17:12), a day long past for the Christ-followers in Galatia! This is why Paul thinks that gentiles must rely on faith in God rather than on circumcision. For Paul, their faith makes them descendants of Abraham and makes possible the gift of spirit (*pneuma*) (Gal 3:1–5).

A second reason that Paul insists the Galatians remain gentiles rather than be circumcised relates to his apocalyptic worldview. As discussed in Chapter 3, Paul's understanding of God's impending day of judgment included the idea that eventually gentiles would turn to belief in the God of Israel. For Paul, gentile Christ-followers must *remain* gentiles in order for them to represent this "gathering in" of gentiles as part of God's salvific work in the world (see, for example, Isa 66:18). Indeed, Paul may have understood his mission as one of identifying gentile groups who represented the coming in of the nations. I return to this point in the later discussion of Romans 9–11 (see the focus text below).

Although Paul makes several negative claims about the law, his argument against circumcision for gentiles is based on his interpretation of the Torah, which *is* the written law in Judaism. Indeed, Paul makes his method explicit: "Tell me, you who desire to be subject to the law, will you not listen to the law?" (Gal 4:21). Given this, it cannot be the law itself that is an issue for Paul. In what follows, I walk you through Paul's argument as an example of how Paul rereads scripture in light of his understanding of God working through Christ to "bring in" the gentiles.

At the heart of Paul's argument is the figure of Abraham, whose faithful response to God becomes an example of how faithful gentiles are considered righteous before God without circumcision (that is, as gentiles).

> Just as Abraham "had faith in God, and it counted as righteousness for him" [Gen 15:6], so, you know, those who have faith are the sons of Abraham. And the scriptures, foreseeing that God would justify the gentiles on the basis of faith, announced the good news to Abraham in advance, saying, "All the gentiles shall be blessed in you" [Gen 12:3]. For this reason, those who have faith are blessed with Abraham who had faith. (Gal 3:6–9)

Paul's reading of Abraham focuses on Genesis 15 because this allows him to argue that Abraham's faith was counted as righteousness *before* he was circumcised (an event that is not narrated until Gen 17:10–14). Paul then makes an interesting interpretive move. Using a typical Jewish method of interpretation, he pays special attention to grammatical form:

> Now the promises were made to Abraham and to his offspring; it does not say, "And to offsprings," as of many; but it says, "And to your offspring," that is, to one person, who is Christ.

When Paul writes, "it does not say. . ." the "it" refers to the Septuagint. In this Greek translation, Gen 17:7 uses the singular Greek word *sperma* (seed, or offspring) to refer to all of Abraham's descendants. But because the word is in the singular form, Paul asserts that *sperma* refers to a singular figure, Jesus Christ. It then remains for Paul to make the crucial link between Christ and the gentiles. He does so with baptismal imagery. With baptism, the gentiles have "clothed themselves" with Christ and thus "belong" to Christ (Gal 3:27). Most significantly, this belonging makes the gentiles become Abraham's "*sperma*" and "heirs according to the promise" (Gal 3:29). In this way, Paul interprets Genesis to show that baptized gentile Christ-followers are *not* in a liminal position. Like Jews, they are heirs to the promises of God.

Contemporary Voices: A Dalit Feminist Engagement of Gal 3:28

As part of Paul's baptismal imagery in Galatians, he offers an image of a unified community in which social boundaries like Jew versus Greek, slave versus free, and male versus female are no longer relevant (Gal 3:28). Readers of Paul draw varying conclusions regarding the value of Gal 3:28 as a resource for building a just community. On the one hand, Paul's recitation of oneness in Christ has been an inspiring text for Christians trying to build a just and equitable world. On the other hand, some readers wonder what exactly Paul means with his call to freedom and unity given the distinctions he makes between Jews and gentiles, slave and free, and male and female in other passages. Paul appears to dismiss social divisions in Gal 3:28 only to reinforce them in other places in his letters.

Surekha Nelavala's discussion of the hope and suspicion that she brings to the text helpfully illustrates some of the issues at stake (see Surekha Nelavala, "'My Story' in Intersection with Gal. 3:26–28," in *T&T Clark Handbook of Asian American Biblical Hermeneutics* (ed. Uriah Y. Kim and Seung Ai Yang; London: T&T Clark, 2019), 395–406). Nelavala identifies as a feminist Dalit-Indian biblical scholar. The term "Dalit," meaning crushed or oppressed, has been adopted as a self-designation of those perceived as "untouchable" within the caste system of India. Nelavala's social location offers an important perspective for the complexities of interpreting Gal 3:28 as a liberating text. She embraces a **liberation hermeneutic**, one that seeks "liberative elements in the texts of the Bible, to promote egalitarianism, fairness, and justice" (399). However, Nelavala's feminist Dalit-Indian perspective complicates the picture of oneness in Christ. What would happen, she asks, if someone from a lower social status than Paul, such as a low-status gentile woman or a slave, pronounced that all are one in Christ? Would the declarations of equality and oneness be welcomed by those in power? As Nelavala observes, those in power have more freedom to make liberative proclamations as if the erasure of social boundaries or border crossings were easy. Applying this critique to contemporary scholarship that sometimes romanticizes the concept of social border crossing, Nelavala writes that "it is important to be aware that it is not the same experience when the marginalized cross the borders to the center, or attempt to erase borders. Vengeance and violence are often the result because their action is deemed as trespassing" (403). Nelavala raises concerns about the language of "inclusion" that is offered too casually by those in power. In her words, "inclusion of the margins in oneness can be suffocating, and it could be a place of insecurity and fear unless extreme trust develops between the oppressor and the oppressed, or the privileged and the discriminated" (404).

Toward the end of his letter to the Galatians, Paul makes his typical shift to moral exhortation. Here, he draws on a tradition made famous by a Jewish teacher named Hillel – that the whole law can be fulfilled through one commandment: "You shall love your neighbor as yourself" (Gal 5:14; see Lev 19:18). Paul's description of how to fulfill the law offers more evidence that Paul's position against gentile circumcision is not a position against Jewish law. The rest of Paul's instructions include lists of vices and virtues of the sort that are commonly found in the writings of Greek and Roman moral philosophers (Gal 5:19–23). However, Paul does not conclude with these general moral instructions. Instead, he takes the stylus from his secretary to write in his own hand and criticize his opponents one last time (Gal 6:11–12). Paul's claim that his opponents advocate circumcision in order to avoid persecution "for the cross of Christ" reinforces the idea that circumcised gentiles would fit into a recognizable and thus less disturbing category.

Changing Perspectives on Paul

The critical interpretation of the letters of Paul has moved through multiple stages. While this is a long and detailed history, it is important to learn its basic outlines. This is true not only because it is a central aspect of the academic study of the New Testament, but also because past misreadings of Paul have contributed to violent expressions of supersessionism (the idea that Christianity has superseded or replaced Judaism). For the sake of simplicity, we will distinguish between the old perspective, the so-called "New Perspective," and the newest Paul within Judaism perspective.

The old perspective saw Paul as a Christian convert who had rejected Judaism as an overly legalistic religion. This way of interpreting the figure of Paul was deeply influenced by Martin Luther and other Protestant reformers in two ways. First, these reformers anachronistically projected their critique of the medieval Roman Catholic Church onto Second Temple Judaism. For example, Luther claimed that Roman Catholicism was legalistic insofar as one had to earn one's salvation by doing good. So, too, he found that Paul rejected Jewish legalism in favor of the Christian religion of grace. The second way that Luther influenced interpreters of Paul was made clear by a scholar named Krister Stendahl. In a highly influential article titled "Paul and the Introspective Conscience of the West," Stendahl showed how Luther and generations of scholars after him mistakenly imagined Paul as a person with a developed sense of the Western individual ego. They did not see Paul as the ancient Mediterranean Hellenistic Jew that he was. Luther turned Paul into a Christian with a troubled conscience, a man concerned with personal salvation (like Luther was!).

Stendhal emphasized that Paul was focused on the salvation not of *individuals* but of *groups* (Jews and gentiles). He also observed that Paul writes of his *call* to apostleship (1 Cor 1:1; Gal 1:15) but never refers to *conversion*. Paul does not exchange his Jewishness for a different religion called Christianity. In this way, Stendhl took an important step forward by reading Paul through the lens of Paul's Jewish identity. Other scholars added to this new way of interpreting Paul in relation to Judaism. E.P. Sanders produced a detailed study of ancient Judaism to show that its underlying premise was never legalism (or "works righteousness") but rather an idea that Sanders called "covenantal nomism" (Greek, *nomos* = law). That is, the Jews were chosen by God and his people on the basis of a covenant with God. They remained part of the covenant through obedience to the law that God gave to them. James Dunn contributed to the New Perspective on Paul by arguing that Paul's problem was with exclusivism rather than with legalism.

Paul wanted to include gentiles and not maintain an ethnically based exclusivism.

More recent work has contributed to this line of scholarship by proposing what is sometimes called "the radical New Perspective on Paul." This line of scholarship reinterprets Paul's position as fully *within* Judaism rather than standing *against* it. The Paul within Judaism perspective maintains not only that Paul was unequivocally Jewish but also that his message about gentiles was grounded in his agreement with other Jews of his time about the nature of Jewish and gentile identities. In particular, Paul and his contemporaries believed that Jews were defined as Jews by being born of other Jews – that is, quite literally by having Jewish bodies. We see this in Romans, for example, in Paul's use of the phrase "my kin according to the flesh" (Rom 9:3). As a result, Paul would not have thought it possible for "gentile sinners" (Gal 2:15) to become Abraham's descendants without a profound *physical* change in their entire bodies. In this sense, Paul considered being an heir of Abraham to be an ethnicity or a "kin" relation. Where Paul differed from at least some Jewish Christ-followers of his time was in his idea that uncircumcised gentiles could undergo a material change (an "ethnic" change) through their bodily reception of Christ's spirit (Greek, *pneuma*) in baptism (Figure 4.1). In its ancient Greco-Roman context, *pneuma* was understood as a fine, ethereal substance. That is, "spirit" was a material reality, a concept that is hard to grasp for twenty-first-century readers. According to Matthew Thiessen (see Thiessen, *Paul and the Gentile Problem*, in Resources for Further Study), Paul thought that gentiles who received this substance, the *pneuma* of Christ, would undergo a substantive bodily change that made it possible for them to become "a [physical] heir to Abraham." Thiessen uses a modern medical analogy to explain this idea: ". . .to Paul's mind gentile circumcision is mere cosmetic surgery compared to the holistic remedy of gene therapy that the infusion of Christ's *pneuma* into gentile flesh provides" (15). Again, if this seems strange to us in our twenty-first-century CE setting, this might be a sign that we are on the right track in understanding Paul within his first-century Hellenistic Jewish context!

FIGURE 4.1
Third-century CE wall painting depicting a baptism from the Catacomb of St. Callistus in Rome.

Paul's Letter to the Romans: The Righteousness of God in Relation to Jews and Gentiles

The letter to the Romans is Paul's longest letter and provides the fullest account of his understanding of the gospel. Paul has never been to Rome but says that he is planning to come after he has traveled to Jerusalem to deliver the money he has been collecting for the "holy ones" (Rom 15:25–6). Paul also seeks financial support for his plans to take his mission further westward to Spain (Rom 1:13; 15:23–4). He thus writes a lengthy letter to introduce himself and his gospel to the Romans. Paul's extended salutation in Rom 1:1–6 points to his sense of mission and to the fact that his teaching is directed toward gentile Christ-followers.

He writes of the apostleship he has received in order "to bring about the obedience of faith among all the gentiles on behalf of [Jesus Christ's] name, including you yourselves who are also called to belong to Jesus Christ" (Rom 1:5–6). Here Paul's thanksgiving section focuses more on himself and his desire to come to Rome to "reap some fruit" among the gentiles there, to whom he is eager to preach the gospel (Rom 1:8–15).

To prepare for that visit, Paul explains his gospel in Romans 1–8, returning to the themes of his letter to the Galatians: faithfulness to God, the example of faithful Abraham, the law in relation to the gentiles, and life in the spirit. In chapter nine, Paul shifts tone and writes personally about the anguish he feels regarding the unbelief of "Israelites," his own people "according to the flesh" (Rom 9:3). Soon after, Paul warns the gentiles in Rome against misplaced pride in their own relationship to God. These chapters suggest that the relationship between Jews and gentiles is very much on Paul's mind as he writes to the Romans. He may have been aware of tensions that existed between Christ-followers in the city.

Before exploring Paul's letter to the Romans further, we should recognize its importance for the development of Christian theology. Historically, Christian theologians have interpreted Paul's letter as a theological exposition about God's work through Christ, bringing about salvation to all of sinful humanity. While this has been a powerful interpretation for many Christians, it comes with problematic assumptions about Paul. For one thing, Paul was not a systematic theologian writing a Christian treatise. For another, as we have already seen, although Paul was Christ-follower, he was not a Christian in the modern sense.

Rather than treating Paul's letter as a theological treatise, then, I discuss it in light of Paul's mission to the gentiles and his apocalyptic expectations. This is not always easy to do. Even specialists in Paul find parts of the letter difficult to understand. One reason for this difficulty is Paul's use of ancient rhetorical devices in his argument. For example, in several places, Paul addresses an imaginary dialogue partner, called an **interlocutor**. The interlocutor raises questions about the argument so that Paul can offer further instruction. Paul borrows this instructional style, the **diatribe**, from Greek and Roman philosophical dialogues. Here is an example of the diatribe style from Rom 3:1–4 (NRSV):

INTERLOCUTOR: Then what advantage has the Jew? Or what is the value of circumcision?

PAUL: Much, in every way. For in the first place the Jews were entrusted with the oracles of God.

INTERLOCUTOR: What if some were unfaithful? Will their faithlessness nullify the faithfulness of God?

PAUL: By no means! Although everyone is a liar, let God be proved true, as it is written, "So that you may be justified in your words, and prevail in your judging."

Recognizing where Paul uses the diatribe clarifies some aspects of the letter to the Romans. Still, sometimes Paul's meaning is ambiguous. For example, in Rom 2:1–11, Paul attacks an unidentified "you" who judges others. Some interpreters think Paul's argument is with a type of arrogant Jewish teacher. Others propose that Paul's interlocutor is a gentile who has been circumcised and now "calls" himself a Jew (Rom 2:17). This seemingly minor debate about the identity of Paul's imagined "you" matters a great deal in the larger debate about how one interprets Paul's mission to the gentiles and his own position within (vs. against) Judaism.

Basics on Romans

Outline: Paul's letter to the Romans	I	Salutation and thanksgiving	1:1–15
	II	Body of the letter: Paul's gospel	1:16–15:13
		A. The revelation of God's justice for Jews and gentiles	1:16–4:25
		B. The roles of Christ, sin, law, and spirit	5–8

	C. The question of Israel and the place of the gentiles	9–11
	D. Instructions for life as a community of Christ-followers	12–14
III	Concluding matters with extended greetings	15:14–16:27

Date and audience

Romans is the longest and latest of the surviving letters of Paul, probably written toward the end of the 50s CE, perhaps 58 or 59. The letter is written to a community formed by someone other than Paul in a city to which he had not yet traveled. As with all his letters, Paul's focus is on his work among gentile Christ-followers (1:5, 13; 11:13). Some aspects of the letter suggest that he is aware that the mixed group of Jewish and gentile Christ-followers in Rome may be living in some tension with one another (14:1–15:13).

Read Romans 1–8.

READING

Try to follow the course of Paul's argument in the first chapters of Romans, keeping in mind the rhetorical devices discussed above. What is Paul's main claim about God? How does Paul talk about God's relationship with the Jews? With gentiles? What role does Abraham have in God's plan? Describe Paul's overall tone in Romans 8.

EXERCISE

Paul opens his letter with an unusually long salutation. The first seven verses form one long sentence into which Paul fits a description of himself, his gospel, and his mission (Rom 1:5). Paul then writes a lengthy thanksgiving section to delicately introduce his reason for his planned trip to Rome. He first says he wants to share a spiritual gift with the Romans in order to strengthen them, but then quickly balances his statement with a desire that they be "mutually encouraged by each other's faith" (1:12). Paul must be careful in asserting his authority over the Christ-followers in Rome. Someone else founded the group (we do not know who), so Paul cannot claim that he is their "father through the gospel" (see 1 Cor 4:15). Instead, Paul highlights his divine call to bring about the obedience of faith among all the gentiles and his eagerness to communicate his gospel to those in Rome. This is what he does, beginning with a thesis statement in Romans 1:16–17, where Paul announces that the gospel he preaches conveys God's power to save the faithful:

> For I am not ashamed of the gospel, for it is the power of God for salvation for all who have faith, to the Jew first and also the Greek. For the righteousness of God is unveiled/revealed (*apokalyptetai*) from faith to faith, just as it is written, the righteous one will live through faith.

Here, Paul is again thinking apocalyptically – that is, in terms of the unveiling of God's justice in the world. According to Paul, God's desire for right relations is being revealed through the continuing progress of faithful responses to God ("from faith to faith").

And while the justice of God is revealed for the faithful, the wrath of God is revealed against all impiety and injustice (Rom 1:18). Paul's description of faithfulness leading to salvation from God's wrath recalls his words in the earlier letter to the Thessalonians. In that letter, he praised the Christ-followers in Thessalonica for their faithful turning to God, and for their faithful anticipation of the coming of the resurrected Jesus (1 Thess 1:8–10). In both letters, Paul is consistent in his focus on gentile faithfulness to God as the key to their salvation.

In fact, Paul builds toward a reiteration of this main theme in Romans 3:28–30:

> For we hold that a person is justified by faith without works of the law. Or is God the God of Jews only? Is God not also the God of gentiles? Yes, also of gentiles since God is one; and he will justify the circumcised on the basis of faith and the uncircumcised through faith.

With this claim, Paul reveals the heart of his argument about the gentiles being made righteous before God through faith. Because there is only one God, Paul reasons, God must also be God of the gentiles. If that is true, gentiles must be able to enter into right relations with God without being circumcised – that is, without being Jewish. Paul concludes that both Jews and gentiles are justified through faith, while also quickly asserting that the law stands nevertheless (Rom 3:29).

Paul's use of the interlocutor opens the way for him to provide further instruction using the example of Abraham: "What then should we say was acquired by Abraham, our forefather according to the flesh?" (Rom 4:1). This question addresses the issue of genealogical kinship. The Jewish people are the flesh and blood descendants of Abraham, while the gentiles are not. As in Galatians, Paul's interpretation of Genesis 15 and 17 allows for Abraham to be the ancestor of those who are faithful and circumcised as well as those who are faithful apart from circumcision:

> Because of this, it is from faith, so that according to grace, the promise may be sure for all the offspring, not only to those of the law but also to those of the faith of Abraham (for he is the father of us all, as it is written, "I have made you the father of many nations").
> (Rom 4:16–17)

Paul's Rhetorical Use of Scripture

Ancient rhetoricians instructed their students to include appeals to authority in their persuasive arguments. For Paul, that meant frequent appeals to the authority of scripture. His regular quotations from the Septuagint (the Greek translation of the Hebrew Bible) as well as frequent allusions to biblical figures are meant to add weight to his words. Paul's heaviest use of scripture across his letters occurs in Galatians and Romans, the two letters that directly address the subject of gentiles in relation to Israel. He draws on scripture in nimble and sometimes surprising ways, employing the types of scriptural interpretation that were common in Second Temple Judaism. For instance, Paul uses **typological interpretation** in Rom 5:14, asserting that the figure of Adam from Genesis 2–3 is a "type of the coming one." Here, Adam prefigures the coming Christ by offering a contrast: one man's disobedience resulted in condemnation, while the other man's obedience led to justification (5:18–19). Paul also uses **allegorical interpretation** of scripture. This occurs in Galatians 4 in a surprising way. There, Paul argues that Sarah and Hagar, the mothers of Isaac and Ishmael in the Genesis narrative, represent two covenants. Twisting the Genesis account, Paul asserts that "Hagar is Mt. Sinai in Egypt," which he then associates with the present enslaved Jerusalem. Meanwhile, Sarah "corresponds to the Jerusalem above" and she (or it) becomes the mother of "us all," supposedly meaning all Christ-followers (Gal 4:26).

The allegorical interpretation of Sarah and Hagar is surprising coming from Paul because it casts a negative light on the tradition that Moses first received the law at Sinai. Indeed, his allegorical reading of Sarah and Hagar reminds us that some elements in Paul's letters remain puzzling. In any case, such examples of Paul's typological and allegorical interpretations illustrate the variety of ways that he and other ancient readers interpreted authoritative texts to persuade readers of their broader arguments.

At the same time that Paul explains God's salvation to Jews as well as gentiles in his letter to the Romans, he is preoccupied with another problem. More than once, Paul raises the question of his fellow Jews who have not expressed faith in Jesus as the messiah. For example, Paul's imagined interlocutor presses questions about Jewish unfaithfulness and what it implies about God's commitment to the Jews. "Will their faithlessness nullify the faithfulness of God?" (Rom 3:3). Not surprisingly, Paul vehemently denies this proposition. Later, in chapters 9–11, he will take up the question more fully.

Paul also anticipates that his emphasis on faith raises questions about the function of the law. He attempts to address such questions, but his unsystematic argument about the law is difficult to follow and sometimes seems contradictory. For instance, in Romans 2, Paul argues that God is impartial and will "repay each according to their deeds." He claims that God will repay evil with evil and good with good, distributing justice to the Jew first and also to the Greek (Rom 2:6–11). Moreover, doing good is equated with the law. As Paul puts it, "it is not the hearers of the law who are considered righteous by God, but the doers of the law who will be considered righteous" (Rom 2:13). Later in Romans, Paul affirms that "the law is holy, and the commandment is holy, just, and good" (Rom 7:12). At the same time, he states, "Therefore, all flesh before him will not be justified from works of the law, for through the law comes knowledge of sin" (Rom 3:20). Finally, as we have seen, Paul also argues that the law brings wrath (Rom 4:15).

Scholars have long struggled to bring together Paul's statements about the law in a coherent way. As I have already suggested, we can resolve some of these tensions (though not all!) if we read Paul's negative comments about the function of the law as *pertaining to gentiles*. Paul, like other Jewish thinkers of his time, saw the law as something that privileged Jews (who could obey it) and judged gentiles (who could not). Thus, when Paul asserts that "the law brings wrath," he has the gentiles in mind. Likewise, when he claims, "where there is no law then there is no violation," he likely means that if adult gentiles are not circumcised, then they do not violate the law's requirement for circumcision on the eighth day after birth (Rom 4:15).

On Paul and "Unnatural" Sex

In the late twentieth century, influenced in part by the AIDS epidemic and cultural debates about homosexuality, scholars undertook a series of historical studies on the Pauline texts that had been (and continue to be) weaponized against the LGBTQI community (1 Cor 6:9–11; Rom 1:25–27; 1 Tim 1:9–10). These historical studies showed that whatever sexual behavior Paul was including on his **vice lists**, it did not correspond to the same-sex relationships being debated in the contemporary context. One point that emerged from the historical critical studies of ancient sexuality is that ancient writers thought in terms of sexual acts rather than sexual identity. Sex was something one did, not a statement of who one was. A second point is that the elite men who wrote about sex assumed that sexual activity involved a passive partner and an active partner. These were gendered categories, with manliness connected to the active partner and unmanliness (or womanliness) to the passive partner. Paul may have been thinking in these terms when he writes of women who exchanged "natural use" for "use against nature" and men who abandoned the "natural use of women"

in their desire for other men. Here, I am using the literal meaning of the Greek word *chresis* (translated as "intercourse" in NRSV and NIV). The word "use" points to the ancient view of sex as an active partner's use of a passive partner. If Paul thought in these terms, then two women would be an "unnatural" coupling of two passive partners, and men's "naturally" active role in sex with women would be confused by a same-sex pairing.

We should also consider Paul's sexual references in the context of his larger argument. Along with listing what he considers to be "unnatural" sexual acts, Paul lists close to twenty other vices that the gentiles are "full of," ranging from disobedience toward parents to murder. This vice list points to Paul's main interest in Romans 1:18–32: offering a vivid picture of "godless" gentiles. But note that Paul's colorful condemnation of gentiles functions as a rhetorical trap in this larger argument. He will abruptly turn the focus on "you, whoever you are" who relishes in the judgment of the gentiles (Rom 2:1–11). (For examples of historical studies on the question of homosexuality in Paul, see Resources for Further Study.)

Paul is also convinced that God's cosmic transformation through Christ has solved the dilemma of the law for gentiles. This idea comes to a dramatic conclusion in Romans 8. Here, Paul reiterates his conviction that trust in God and the reception of the spirit of Christ make possible the inclusion of gentiles as heirs to God's promises (Rom 8:12–17). God's gift of the spirit through Christ means that faithful gentiles can also become righteous. For this reason, no one now can condemn the gentile Christ-follower, as they are counted among "God's elect" (Rom 8:33–4)! Note also that Paul's apocalyptic enthusiasm courses through this chapter. He contrasts the sufferings of the present times with the glory about to be revealed (Rom 8:18). He imagines the entire cosmos groaning in labor pains in anticipation of God's liberating salvation (Rom 8:22). Indeed, Paul ends the first part of his letter to the Romans on a rhetorical high point, celebrating the unbreakable relationship between God and God's people:

> For I am convinced that neither death, nor life, nor angels, nor rulers, nor things present, nor things to come, nor powers, nor height, nor depth, nor anything else in all creation, will be able to separate us from the love of God in Christ Jesus our Lord. (Rom 8:38–9 NRSV)

Following this exaltation, Romans 9 marks a stark shift in tone. However much Paul affirms the elect status of Christ-following gentiles, he also does not dismiss the long tradition of God's election of Torah-observant Israel that is at the heart of Israelite and Jewish tradition. On the one hand, he insists on God's impartiality (2:11). On the other hand, he asks, "Then what is the special advantage of the Jew? Or what is the usefulness of circumcision?" His answer is "much, in every way" (3:1–2). In chapters 9–11, Paul will take up at length the question of his Jewish kin who have not become Christ-followers.

The Problem of Israel and the Place of the Gentiles (Romans 9–11)

FOCUS TEXT

In Romans 9–11, Paul writes in a poignant and personal way, revealing his deep theological convictions about God's work with both Jews and gentiles. These chapters are arguably the climax of the whole letter, as they address the fundamental question of how God works to bring about salvation for all people. To reach his grand conclusion in chapter 11, Paul engages in creative rereadings of Hebrew scriptures. In this way, Romans 9–11 provide more evidence of the way Paul and other early Christ-followers freely reinterpreted their scriptural traditions in light of their belief in Jesus as the messiah.

Romans 9 opens with an intensely personal expression of Paul's feelings. The preceding section of his letter concluded with soaring words of praise (8:38–9). But as chapter 9 begins, Paul abruptly changes tone and speaks of his great sorrow and unceasing anguish on behalf of his own people. Affirming their status before God, he claims, "They are Israelites, and to them belong the adoption, the glory, the covenants, the lawgiving, the rituals, and the promises; to them belong the ancestors, and from them is the Christ according to the flesh" (9:4–5). These Israelites, according to Paul, are "his kin according to the flesh," and he goes so far as to wish that he himself would be cut off from Christ for their sake (9:3). The double mention of "according to the flesh" in these verses demonstrates how Paul has in mind an actual material connection to his fellow Jews. This fleshly, physical connection also matters for Paul in terms of their place in God's plan of salvation.

As Paul considers his fellow Jews who have not recognized Jesus as God's messiah, he is troubled by two things: (1) their lack of belief in Jesus as the messiah and (2) what their rejection of this claim says about God's broader plans. If God promised to be the God of Israel, and if these Israelites rejected the messiah sent from God while the gentiles did not, did God somehow make a mistake? Paul already anticipated this second problem in chapter 3. There, while listing the advantages of the Jewish people, he raised the question, "What if some do not believe? Will their unbelief put an end to the faithfulness of God?" (Rom 3:3). Chapters 9–11 are Paul's answer to this question. Using a series of different arguments, Paul insists that God's promises and justice remain steadfast. As he asserts early in the argument, "it is not as if the word of God had failed" (9:6).

To make this point, Paul draws on the Hebrew scriptures. In 9:6–13, his argument is based on the concept of God's election. The idea that God chooses the people of

Israel, a central idea in Hebrew scriptures such as Deuteronomy and the book of Hosea, becomes key to Paul's explanation of why some Jews believe that Jesus is God's messiah and others do not. Paul points out that the promise did not go to *all* of Abraham's children (9:7) but only to one genealogical line of descendants. According to Paul, God may choose whom God wants and "harden the heart" of others (9:18). In this way, Paul explains the lack of belief of some of his fellow Jews.

Next, Paul anticipates objections to this argument. You may already have thought of these yourself. If God is choosing mercy for some and not for others, how can anyone be blamed for a lack of faith? And how can it be just for God to choose some and not others? In responding to such objections, Paul alludes to the traditions of Job (Job 9:12) and Isaiah (Isa 29:16; 45:9), both of which suggest that it is inappropriate for a mere person to question the creator God. While this may not be a satisfying answer, Paul is not ultimately worried about questions of fairness or even about an individual's standing before God. He is not thinking about *individual* salvation at all, but rather of the place of Jews and gentiles in God's plan. Paul continues his argument with a creative rereading of passages from the prophet Hosea:

> I will call "not my people," "my people" and "not beloved," "beloved." And in the place where it was said to them. "You are not my people," there they will be called "sons of the living God." (Rom 9:25–6; see Hos 1:10; 2:23)

In Hosea's eighth-century BCE context, these passages refer to the estranged people of Israel with whom God restores a relationship. In his letter to the Romans, Paul draws on Hosea's words to offer scriptural authority for God's eschatological inclusion of the gentiles.

Before reaching his conclusion, Paul turns to the prophet Isaiah to introduce yet another explanation of what God is up to. He draws on Isaiah's concept of a "remnant" among Israel that God will save (Rom 9:27; compare Isa 10:21–2). In the context of the book of Isaiah, the "remnant" referred to exiles who would survive foreign attacks and live to see the restoration of Israel. Paul draws on the remnant idea to explain why only a small number of Jewish people have expressed belief in Jesus as the messiah. However, this argument does not ultimately satisfy Paul. He is not content with only a remnant of his people being saved. We see what troubles him as he reaches the high point of his argument in chapter 11. Paul begins with a direct question: "I ask then, has God rejected his people?" He quickly and firmly rejects the idea, using himself as an example – he is an Israelite and God has not rejected him (11:1)! Paul then takes another tack, suggesting that the role of the Jewish "stumblers" (those who do not yet trust in Christ) bears on the fate of the gentiles (11:11–12). It is God's initial hardening of some Jews that has allowed salvation to come to the gentiles. Paul's grand conclusion in chapter 11 is that God is working with *both* groups in ways that will bring about salvation to all of *Israel* (11:26).

It is important to see that Paul concludes this discussion with a direct address to gentiles, not Jews. He warns them not to become proud or feel superior because they are Christ-followers while some Jews are not. As gentiles, they are but a wild olive branch that, because of God's kindness, has been grafted onto the rich root that is Israel (Rom 11:17–20).

By reading Romans 9–11 as an address to gentiles about God's faithfulness both to them and to Paul's "kin according to the flesh," we see that he can no more condemn his people than he can give up on his belief in Christ. The centuries of scholarship that have read Paul's letter to the Romans as an expression of Paul's anti-legalism or anti-Judaism failed to take account of this climactic section of Romans, where Paul writes from his Jewish perspective. Of course, one can point to weaknesses in Paul's argument. He is struggling to make sense of his current reality, one that he does not fully understand. He describes the unbelief of many of his fellow Jews as "a mystery" and points to the inscrutable nature of God's ways (11:25, 33). In the end, what Paul reveals in Romans 9–11 is his firm conviction that the promises of God that were extended to Israel in the past remain steadfast, "for the gifts and the calling of God are irrevocable" (11:29).

CHAPTER FOUR REVIEW

1 Know the meaning and significance of the following terms discussed in this chapter:
   - allegorical interpretation
   - diatribe
   - interlocutor
   - liberation hermeneutic
   - typological interpretation
   - vice list

2 What is the difference between the old perspective on Paul, the New Perspective on Paul, and the Paul within Judaism perspective?

3 What is the major point of contention between Paul and some of the Christ-followers in Galatia? Explain the reasoning behind their differing positions regarding circumcision.

4 Why does Paul write to the Christ group in Rome?

5 (Focus text: Romans 9–11) What is Paul's main concern in Romans 9–11? What strategies does he use to make his case?

RESOURCES FOR FURTHER STUDY

On the New Perspective on Paul:

Dunn, James D.G. *The New Perspective on Paul (revised edition)*. Grand Rapids, MI: Eerdmans, 2008.

Sanders, E.P. *Paul and Palestinian Judaism: A Comparison of Patterns of Religion*. Philadelphia: Fortress Press, 1977.

Stendahl, Krister. "Paul and the Introspective Conscience of the West," Pp. 78–96 in *Paul Among Jews and Gentiles and Other Essays*. Philadelphia: Fortress, 1977.

On the Paul within Judaism perspective:

Eisenbaum, Pamela. *Paul Was Not a Christian: The Original Message of a Misunderstood Apostle*. New York: HarperOne, 2009.

Nanos, Mark D., and Magnus Zetterholm, eds. *Paul within Judaism: Restoring the First-Century Context to the Apostle*. Minneapolis, MN: Fortress, 2015.

Rodriguez, Rafael. *If You Call Yourself a Jew: Reappraising Paul's Letter to the Romans*. Cambridge: The Lutterworth Press, 2014.

Thiessen, Matthew. *Paul and the Gentile Problem*. New York: Oxford University Press, 2016.

For a collection of different perspectives on Paul and Romans:

Sumney, Jerry L., ed. *Reading Paul's Letter to the Romans*. Atlanta, GA: Society of Biblical Literature, 2012.

For more on Asian American biblical interpretation:

Foskett, Mary F., and Jeffrey Kah-Jin Kuan. *Ways of Being, Ways of Reading: Asian American Biblical Interpretation*. St. Louis, MO: Chalice Press, 2006.

Kim, Uriah Y., and Seung Ai Yang, eds. *T&T Clark Handbook of Asian American Biblical Hermeneutics*. London: T&T Clark, 2019.

For more on the New Testament and same-sex relations:

Brooten, Bernadette J. *Love Between Women: Early Christian Responses to Female Homoeroticism*. Chicago, IL: University of Chicago Press, 1998.

Dunning, Benjamin H. "Same-Sex Relations." Pp. 573–591 in Benjamin H. Dunning (ed.), *The Oxford Handbook of New Testament, Gender and Sexuality*. New York: Oxford University Press, 2019.

Marchal, Joseph A. "LGBTIQ Strategies of Interpretation." Pp. 177–196 in Benjamin H. Dunning (ed.), *The Oxford Handbook of New Testament, Gender and Sexuality*. New York: Oxford University Press, 2019.

Scroggs, Robin. *The New Testament and Homosexuality: Contextual Background for Contemporary Debate*. Philadelphia, PA: Fortress Press, 1983. A now-dated but representative example of historical analyses of Paul's references to "deviant" sexuality.

Conflicts with the Corinthian Christ Group

5

Chapter Outline

Chapter Overview	**79**
The Urban Setting of Corinth	**80**
Status Problems in Corinth	**83**
Conflicts over the Body and Sexuality in Corinth	**85**
Conflicts over Meat Consumption in Corinth	**87**
Disputing Ritual Practices in Corinth	**88**
Afflictions and Accusations in 2 Corinthians	**90**
Disputes Regarding the Collection for Jerusalem (2 Corinthians 8–9)	**92**
Paul's Self-Defense against Gendered Status Attacks	**93**
Focus Text: 2 Cor 11:16–12:13	**94**
Chapter Three Review	**95**
Resources for Further Study	**95**

Chapter Overview

This chapter examines Paul's communications with the Christ group in Corinth as an illustration of the far-reaching implications of the gentiles' new allegiance to Christ and the God of Israel. After introducing the ancient city of Corinth, I turn to the issues taken up in 1 Corinthians regarding social status, sexuality, marriage, eating habits, and new ritual practices. The surviving letters from Paul's Corinthian correspondence suggest that the Christ group (or groups) in Corinth were divided over such issues. They also appear to have been divided over the question of Paul's authority over them. This chapter explores the disputes between Paul and the Corinthians and what they tell us about the life of gentile Christ-followers in Corinth.

The New Testament: A Contemporary Introduction, First Edition. Colleen M. Conway.
© 2023 John Wiley & Sons Ltd. Published 2023 by John Wiley & Sons Ltd.

The Urban Setting of Corinth

The surviving correspondence from Paul to the Christ-followers in Corinth offers a chance for time travel. More than any other writing in the New Testament, the letters known as First and Second Corinthians (typically written as 1 and 2 Corinthians) offer a glimpse of the early stages of a newly formed Christ group living in a prospering city in the Roman empire. Once again, I begin with a discussion of the city of Corinth, encouraging you to imagine the history and life setting of the people to whom Paul's gospel message appealed.

In Paul's time, Corinth was a bustling cosmopolitan city located just south of a narrow isthmus connecting the Greek Peloponnese peninsula to the mainland. Yet just two hundred years before Paul, the city lay in ruins. In 146 BCE, the Roman Republic sent armies to Corinth in order to quell Greek resistance to Rome's growing regional power. The resulting battle proved disastrous for Corinth, as the Roman army plundered and almost completely destroyed the city. Corinth stayed this way for another hundred years until Julius Caesar rebuilt it as a Roman colony. According to the geographer Strabo, the original Roman colonists were mostly wealthy freedpersons and businesspeople. This would make sense if Julius Caesar meant to take economic advantage of Corinth's location. Roman Corinth included a large amphitheater, a large Roman-style forum, and many restored temples devoted to the gods and goddesses of the Greek and Roman pantheons. One prominent temple was built on the Acrocorinth, a large rock overlooking the city. This large temple was devoted to the city's patron goddess, Aphrodite. The city was also home to large temples devoted to Apollo (Figure 5.1) and the healing god Asclepius. Surviving ruins from the Asclepius temple include evidence of spacious dining rooms. Like any Greco-Roman city, there were temples to many other gods as well.

By Paul's time, Corinth had rapidly grown in wealth and prominence and served as the capital of the Roman province of Achaia. The city's location near the isthmus between the Greek mainland and the Peloponnese peninsula meant that it was near two ports on two seas and thus benefited from a lively trade market (Figure 5.2). This market, along with the Isthmian Games, a biennial athletic and musical competition, brought a steady supply of immigrants and visitors from across the Mediterranean world. By the first century CE, the city was growing in wealth and was home to a diverse population, including a Jewish community attested by the Jewish writer Philo of Alexandria.

The cosmopolitan context of Corinth is reflected in the diversity and disputes that occupy Paul and the Corinthian assembly. Together, 1 and 2 Corinthians tell the story of a difficult relationship with at least some of the Corinthians – a relationship filled with periods of suspicion, challenges to Paul's authority, hurtful exchanges, and pleas for reconciliation on Paul's part. In the following discussion, I explore the nature of these disputes, including the perspectives of both Paul and the group to whom he writes. The issues at stake in Corinth concern social and economic status, conceptions of the body, and disputes over ritual practices such as the following:

- whether and how the Corinthians should discipline errant community members (1 Corinthians 5)

FIGURE 5.1
Ruins of the Temple of Apollo in Corinth in front of the Acrocorinth.

FIGURE 5.2
Doorways of shops in ancient Corinth.

- taking other Christ-followers to court (1 Corinthians 6)
- what and where Christ-followers could eat (1 Corinthians 8–10)
- what a new identity in Christ meant for sexual practices (1 Corinthians 5–7)
- what a new identity in Christ meant for existing or future marriages (1 Corinthians 7)
- how men and women's heads should look when praying and prophesying (1 Corinthians 11)
- how the ritual of "speaking in tongues" should be practiced in the group (1 Corinthians 12–14)
- whether there is such a thing as resurrection from the dead (1 Corinthians 15)

As we explore some of these issues in the coming pages, keep in mind that we have only Paul's perspective on the disputes. Also, we should not assume that there was a single "Corinthian" perspective. We know that Paul objected to divisions among the Christ-followers in Corinth, and perhaps they never thought of themselves as a single assembly at all. For this reason, I will often refer to "some Corinthians" in the discussion that follows as a reminder that Paul was not writing to a unified group.

The Composition of the Corinthian Correspondence

The Pauline letter collection includes two letters to the Corinthians, titled 1 and 2 Corinthians. However, clues from these letters point to a more extended series of communications between Paul and the Corinthians. In 1 Cor 5:9, Paul refers to a past letter that he had written to Corinth. Then in 1 Cor 7:1, Paul indicates that he is responding to a letter that some Corinthians wrote to him. In 2 Corinthians, Paul mentions another letter that he wrote "with many tears" (2 Cor 2:3–4) and describes this letter as painful for the group in Corinth (2 Cor 7:8–12). Moreover, Paul mentions several past and future visits (1 Cor 2:1; 4:19; 16:5; 2 Cor 2:1; 12:14; 13:1, 10) and writes of envoys being sent back and forth (1 Cor 1:11; 4:17; 16:10–11, 15; 2 Cor 7:6, 13; 8:6, 16–24). Given this record of ongoing exchanges between Paul and the Corinthians, why do we now have only two letters?

One answer to this question is that 1 and 2 Corinthians contain parts of several letters. This theory is based on the letters' sudden shifts in tone and topic, especially in 2 Corinthians. In the first part of 2 Corinthians, Paul offers a self-defense and appeal for reconciliation that ends on a note of rejoicing and confidence (see, for example, 2 Cor 7:13–16). But later, in 2 Corinthians 10–12, Paul is again on the defensive, adopting a sarcastic tone that differs sharply from his tone in 2 Corinthians 1–7. In addition, chapters 8 and 9 contain two separate appeals for a donation to the Jerusalem group (2 Cor 8:1–15; 9:1–15).

Given this evidence, 2 Corinthians may contain fragments of several letters from Paul to Corinth. For example, 2 Corinthians 10–12 may be part of the so-called "tearful letter" that Paul mentions twice (2 Cor 2:3–4). Scholars who favor such theories of composition have proposed as many as five different letters from Paul to Corinth that are now contained in fragments across 1 and 2 Corinthians. Meanwhile, other scholars rightly note that there is no ancient manuscript evidence supporting a theory of compilation. An alternative explanation of Paul's shifts in tone is that he composed the letters over an extended period of time. Without new evidence, whether the surviving letters combine parts of other letters will continue to be a point of scholarly debate.

Status Problems in Corinth

Read 1 Corinthians 1–4.

READING

A major theme of these chapters is divisions in the community. What clues can you find about the causes for these divisions? Identify at least one place where Paul uses sarcasm to communicate his point. What attitude of the Corinthians does he critique?

EXERCISE

News about contending factions of Christ-followers in Corinth first came to Paul through a message sent by a woman named Chloe (1 Cor 1:10–11). Like the figure of Lydia discussed in Chapter 2, Chloe was likely a woman with financial means who was part of Paul's network. The reference to her "people" (in Greek, more literally "those of Chloe") probably refers to her slaves. Initially, Paul describes the divisions with slogans that point to competing allegiances in the Jesus movement, such as "I am with Paul" or "I am with Apollos" (1 Cor 1:12). We do not know on what basis such allegiances were formed, but Paul's comments in chapters 1–4 suggest that the divisions were related to social and economic status. Consider the following statements:

- ". . . not many of you were wise according to human measures, not many of you powerful, not many of you well-born." (1 Cor 1:26)
- "Do not deceive yourself. If any among you think they are wise in this age, they should become a fool in order to become wise." (1 Cor 3:18)
- "Already you are full! Already you are rich! Without us, you reign as kings!" (1 Cor 4:8)
- "We are fools for the sake of Christ, but you are wise in Christ. We are weak, but you are strong. You are held in honor, but we in disrepute." (1 Cor 4:10–11)
- ". . . some of you have become arrogant." (1 Cor 4:18)

Paul's assertion that not many in the assembly were "well-born" suggests that, like the Christ groups in Thessalonica and Philippi, most of the Christ-followers in Corinth were low in socioeconomic status. However, Paul's qualifying phrase that "not many" were of high birth suggests that some of the group had a higher social standing than others. Meanwhile, the way that Paul links wisdom, power, and being "well-born" reveals the ancient cultural assumptions regarding socioeconomic status. Such status differences appear to undergird many of the Corinthians' conflicts among themselves and with Paul. For this reason, Paul devotes the first section of his letter to undercutting ideas of social privilege, especially claims of superior knowledge.

Paul grounds his argument in the following statement: "The message about the cross is foolishness to those who are perishing, but to us who are being saved it is the power of God" (1 Cor 1:18). Soon after, he tells the Corinthians of his earlier decision to proclaim to them only "Jesus Christ and him crucified" – that is, to focus his preaching on Christ's crucifixion – rather than preaching the mystery of God using distinguished words or wisdom (1 Cor 2:1–2). Paul's salvific news centered on a crucified messiah would sound ridiculous to most people in the first century CE; as Paul puts it, the cross would represent "a stumbling block for Jews and foolishness for Greeks" (1 Cor 1:23). Crucifixion was a punishment that Rome reserved for slaves or traitors. For Paul, however, the "foolishness" of the cross becomes a way to undercut Corinthian claims of status. He uses the fact of the cross to argue that God chooses "what is foolish in the world," not only the cross but also the foolish, weak, and lowborn, to shame the wise and strong (1 Cor 1:27–8). Such a claim may have offered a boost to the low-status Corinthians in the midst of group quarrels. Paul aligns himself with the lower-status group by contrasting the social status of the apostles of Christ with the seemingly high-status Corinthian Christ-followers. As apostles, he and his co-workers are hungry, thirsty, poorly clothed, beaten, and homeless. They have become like the scum of the world (1 Cor 4:11–13).

Meanwhile, Paul also draws on status categories in a more typical way to elevate himself and exert his authority over the quarreling Corinthians. In Paul's view, the Corinthians are acting like infants who are not yet ready to be fed solid food (1 Cor 3:1–3). He then explicitly asserts patriarchal authority over them: "You have countless teachers in Christ, but not many fathers, for in Christ Jesus I begot you through the gospel" (1 Cor 4:14–15). Paul uses his claim of fatherly status to issue a threat against the arrogant members. "What do you wish?" Paul asks, "should I come with a stick or with love and a gentle spirit?" (1 Cor 4:21). In short, in order to contend with conflicts over status between the Corinthians, Paul asserts his own status over all of them.

Basics on 1 Corinthians

Outline: divisions and disputes in Corinth	I	Salutation and thanksgiving	1:1–9
	II	Body of the letter: contending with the Corinthians	1:10–16:12
		A. Divisions and Paul's authority	1:10–4:20
		B. Issues of sexuality and marriage	5:1–7:39
		C. Eating food sacrificed to idols	8–10
		D. Problems with rituals and worship	11–14
		E. Disagreements over resurrection	15:1–58
	III	Concluding matters and greetings	16:1–21

Date and audience Paul started the Corinthian community around 50–52 CE. He writes to an economically diverse group with competing ideas about how they should live given their new identity as Christ-followers. Paul repeatedly challenges expressions of status and privilege, arguing that the Corinthians should relate to each other in ways that build up the group.

Conflicts over the Body and Sexuality in Corinth

Read Corinthians 5–10.

READING

List the different topics that Paul raises in this section. Note that many English translations (for example, the NRSV and the NIV) use quotation marks to indicate where it seems that Paul is quoting the Corinthians, perhaps from a letter they wrote to him (see, for example, 1 Cor 6:12–13; 7:1, 8:1). As you track Paul's argument and instructions, pay attention to places where Paul restates a Corinthian position. (It is possible, of course, that scholars are wrong about the Corinthian "slogans," as they are often called; Paul may be simply stating his own positions. You might consider how this alternative would change Paul's meaning.)

EXERCISE

As Paul moves on to other issues that have been reported to him (1 Cor 5:1), he turns first to instances of what he describes as *porneia*. Paul uses this word in a general sense to mean immoral sexual practices. In the first case, a man is having sex with his stepmother (1 Cor 5:1–13). Perhaps what disturbs Paul most about this situation is the response from the Christ-followers in Corinth. He notes that rather than mourning the conduct, they are "arrogant" about it (1 Cor 5:2). In the second case, Paul responds to some Corinthians who are having sex with prostitutes (1 Cor 6:16). We do not have the Corinthian's explanation of their sexual conduct, but Paul appears to be quoting their general position with statements like "all things are lawful for me" and "food for the stomach and the stomach for food" (1 Cor 6:12–13). Given the subject matter, the latter statement is best understood as an indirect way of claiming that sex is for the body and the body is for sex. Such claims could be coming from members of a higher-status group who think that they have license to act as they wish. This Christ group may think that having been infused with the *pneuma* of Christ, they have been elevated to a state of existence where the material body is inconsequential. Note that later in the letter, Paul will argue against some in Corinth who say there is no bodily resurrection from the dead. Such a position would indicate another reason the Corinthians do not share Paul's concern about the body (1 Cor 15:12)

Whatever their reasoning, Paul soundly rejects their behavior, insisting that what the Corinthians do with their bodies is directly relevant to their spiritual state. Using the same formulation as the food/body analogy, Paul counters, "the body is not for *porneia*, but for the Lord, and the Lord for the body" (1 Cor 6:13b). He follows with a string of arguments designed to convince the Corinthians of the physical body's ongoing significance in relation to their new status as Christ-followers: the body will be raised like Christ's body was raised; the body is a part of Christ; the body is a temple for the Holy Spirit that dwells within it (1 Cor 6:14–19). Paul's use of temple imagery in the Corinthian context would bring to mind the many temples in Corinth. Perhaps Paul meant to encourage the Corinthians to regard their own spirit-infused bodies with the reverence they once had for their city's temples. In any case, Paul's need to assert such arguments indicates the gap between his understanding of the body and that of the Corinthians.

Contemporary Voices: Queering Paul's Letters

In the twenty-first century, queer theory has offered a way to move beyond the twentieth-century debates about Paul and homosexuality (see Chapter 4). Queer theory challenges perspectives that claim heterosexuality is "natural" while non-heterosexual relations are "unnatural." Queer theorists resist the binary of homosexual versus heterosexual altogether, arguing that this socially constructed binary does not reflect the fluid nature of human sexuality. In addition, these theorists describe the varied ways in which the dominant culture polices and regulates human sexual expression.

Midori Hartman's reading of 1 Corinthians 5 offers an example of the use of queer theory for biblical interpretation (see Midori E. Hartman, "A Little *Porneia* Leavens the Whole: Queering Limits of Community in 1 Corinthians 5," in *Bodies on the Verge: Queering the Pauline Epistles* (ed. Joseph A. Marchal; Atlanta: Society of Biblical Literature Press, 2019), 143–63). In 1 Cor 5:2, Paul condemns the Corinthian Christ group for boasting about a member who is having sex with the "woman of his father." Hartman argues that Paul's use of the term *porneia* and his instructions for the expulsion of this person are a form of communal policing. Hartman questions Paul's assumption of malicious intent on the part of the Corinthians. Whereas Paul sees their response to the sexual conduct as an arrogant violation of norms (1 Cor 5:1–2), perhaps the Corinthians see it differently. In her words,

> . . .here is another reading, on the other side of the coin from the one Paul offers: one person's idea of pride might in fact be excitement, joy and liberation. What if the *ponēros* relationship is one interpretation of the new freedom to live outside social constructions determined by a world that already minoritizes and excludes [the Corinthians] on the basis of their affiliations to the Christ movement? (152)

Hartman's point is not to weigh in on the morality of having sex with one's stepmother. In truth, we know little about the situation that Paul was condemning. Rather, she uses queer theory to call attention to Paul's insistence on community policing on the basis of an imagined purity. Hartman asks, "aside from the relationship between the *ponēros* and 'his father's woman' who else falls into this category of sexually immoral persons who must be excised? Or, perhaps more worryingly, who might find themselves slotted into this category at some later date, given Paul's reticence to define *porneia*?" (157). For more on queer biblical interpretation of the New Testament, see Resources for Further Study.

At 1 Cor 7:1, Paul addresses additional matters raised in his correspondence with the Corinthians. He states: "it is good for a man not to touch a woman." Whether Paul is here quoting a statement by the Corinthians (as many scholars assume) or asserting his own position, he affirms a life of sexual renunciation. Such ascetic aspirations would be a radical form of sexual self-control that Greek and Roman writers described as a characteristic of manly behavior. In other words, even an interest in celibacy may have been driven by status insofar as sexual renunciation indicated superior control over one's body.

Far from dismissing the Corinthian aspiration for a celibate lifestyle, Paul wishes that *everyone* could be like him: unmarried and self-controlled. Still, he apparently doubts the Corinthians' ability to sustain such sexual self-control, framing his own manly achievement as a particular gift from God (1 Cor 7:7–8). For this reason, Paul concedes to the necessity of marriage because of (again) *porneias* (sexual immoralities). As he puts it, "it is better to marry than to burn," meaning to be consumed by sexual desire (1 Cor 7:9).

Both the Corinthian interest in celibacy and Paul's seeming lack of interest in marriage for reproduction were at odds with Roman cultural expectations. Emperor Augustus introduced legislation that encouraged marriage and reproduction. Unmarried men could be penalized for being celibate beyond a certain age. Similarly, women were subject to penalties if they did not remarry after being widowed or divorced. Married couples could lose a portion of their inheritance if they had no children. The point of such legislation was to encourage the household structure that was understood to be the foundation of a strong empire. In contrast, Paul's countercultural view of marriage and celibacy is best viewed in light of his apocalyptic expectations. As a general principle, he sees no point in changing one's position or status in life "in view of the present crisis" (1 Cor 7:26). He thus exhorts his readers to "each live in the way that the Lord assigned, each as God called" (1 Cor 7:17). Paul applies this principle more specifically to Jews and gentiles (1 Cor 7:18–19), to virgins (1 Cor 7:25–6), to the married and the unmarried (1 Cor 7:27, 32–4), and to widows (1 Cor 7:39). The one exception may be the slave, who Paul seems to suggest should use an opportunity to gain freedom should it arise. Otherwise, Paul argues, one's social status will soon be irrelevant because "the time is short" and "the form of this world is passing away" (1 Cor 7:29, 31). Such statements illustrate how Paul's apocalypticism shaped his mission and potentially the lives of new Christ-followers who were influenced by his message. All that said, we do not know the degree to which the Corinthians adhered to Paul's teaching on sexuality.

Conflicts over Meat Consumption in Corinth

Chapters 8–10 turn to another topic raised by some of the Corinthians. In this case, the issue is not sexual practices but disagreements about what food they can eat. Paul opens the discussion in the same way he introduced issues of sexuality and marriage. He names the topic, "Now concerning food sacrificed to idols," and then appears to quote a Corinthian statement, "all of us possess knowledge" (1 Cor 8:1). The point of contention concerns whether the Corinthians should eat meat that has been ritually given in sacrifice to a deity. The issue is not simply one of diet or even religious practice. From the Corinthian side, the question concerns their basic social and civic relations. To flourish and have important contacts in an urban center such as Corinth, one needed to be a member of a **voluntary association**, perhaps a trade guild or a cult devoted to a Greek or Roman deity. Recall that large temple complexes, like the one dedicated to Asclepius in Corinth, typically included dining facilities where groups could gather. The meat served at such social gatherings would be meat that had been offered in sacrifice to the deity to whom the temple was dedicated. Even meat that was sold in the marketplace to serve in private homes was often meat that had been offered in sacrifice. To refrain from attending these meals would have major implications for social and economic relationships in Corinth.

The position of some Corinthians reflected in 1 Cor 8:1 illustrates their confidence on this issue. What they know appears to be what Paul taught them about their former religious practices and their newly adopted one – namely, that "there is no idol in the world" and that "there is no God except one" (1 Cor 8:4). Both statements relate to central teachings in Judaism (see Exod 20:1–6; Deut 6:4–9). Some of the Corinthians reason, logically enough, that if there are no other real gods besides the one true God, then the sacrificial nature of the food is insignificant. They suggest that no harm can come from eating the meat, nor from participating in the social events connected to the meal. "Food will not make us present to God. We will not lose an advantage if we do not eat, nor gain one if we do" (1 Cor 8:8).

Paul again approaches the problem in terms of claims of superiority. He warns against claims of knowledge that inflate one's sense of importance. Instead of relying on knowledge to elevate oneself over others, Paul encourages conduct based on a love that reinforces group identity (1 Cor 8:1). Later in his argument, Paul again evokes the Corinthians' words, "All things are lawful," only to refute them with "not all things are beneficial," by which he means helpful to others. Paul envisions a setting where some Christ-followers who are less confident about their new belief in only one god ("the weak") are misled by the behavior of the "knowledgeable" group. Thinking that those who eat the meat are honoring other deities, these "weak" believers "stumble" back to the worship of other gods (1 Cor 8:9–10). Given this scenario, Paul argues that he will never eat meat so as not to bring harm to a "brother" (1 Cor 8:13).

Later in the argument, Paul anticipates objections, pointing to the social complexity of the issue. He first allows that one can eat meat sold at the market (apart from a temple setting) without inquiring about its origins – that is, whether or not it was sacrificial meat. He also offers a concession for private dinner parties, advising the Corinthian Christ-followers to eat whatever they are served without asking about the nature of the meat. However, if someone at the dinner party makes a point of stating "This has been offered in sacrifice," one should refuse the meat "out of consideration for the one who has informed you." With this, Paul returns to his original argument that one should take care that others are not misled by one's conduct. Paul's general principle undercuts concerns about high social status: acting for the benefit of others must take precedence over personal advantage (1 Cor 10:24, 31–2).

Disputing Ritual Practices in Corinth

Two more examples from 1 Corinthians point to Paul's resistance to some in Corinth who were ranking themselves above other Christ-followers. The first concerns the practice of the Lord's supper. Paul bluntly states his displeasure with their current practice: "I do not praise you because when you come together it is not for the better but for the worse" (1 Cor 11:17). Paul's description of some of the Corinthians' conduct again suggests that the factions in the Corinthian assembly are based on socioeconomic status. If Paul's account is accurate, the Corinthians of higher status were proceeding as they normally would when coming together for a meal. They would gather earlier than those of lower socioeconomic status because they had more leisure time. Paul suggests that the higher-status Corinthians then ate and drank together, seemingly to excess, while others who came later went hungry (11:21–2). Such a scenario would be entirely in keeping with Greek and Roman status distinctions at public assemblies. The poor of the group would be relegated to the distant seats and not given food to eat. Paul rejects such conduct and admonishes some of the Corinthians for showing contempt for the assembly of God and for shaming those who have nothing.

Paul's instructions regarding the problem may not go as far in confronting status distinctions as we might hope. He twice reminds the higher-status Christ-followers that they have homes where they can eat, suggesting they should keep their social eating and drinking as private affairs apart from the assembly (11:22, 34). Note that as part of Paul's response, he reminds the Corinthians of the ritual words of the Last Supper that he had "handed on" to them (11:23–6). In so doing, he distinguishes between gathering for ritual meals, for which the Corinthians should "wait for one another," and the social eating and drinking that they were accustomed to in their daily lives.

The last example of status consciousness affecting life in the assembly concerns gathering for ritual worship. In this case, some in the Corinthian Christ group have elevated speaking in tongues over other gifts. In the ancient Roman context, this practice was likely privileged above others because it was viewed as divinely inspired esoteric speech. The very fact that it was beyond human comprehension, compared to the practice of preaching or prophesying, would signal its special status. While Paul recognizes the significance of speaking in tongues (he claims he does it best of all!), he returns once more to his principle of love-based conduct that reinforces group identity. Indeed, he suggests that prophecy is better because it *can* be understood and interpreted to build up the assembly. Thus, Paul is consistent in challenging the higher-status group not to act as though their social status affords them privilege over others in the assembly. He pushes back against expressions of privilege that he sees as immoral or destructive to the group. "See that this authority of yours," he argues "does not cause the weak to stumble" (1 Cor 8:9).

There are additional issues in 1 Corinthians that I leave for further study. The examples above show the degree to which the Corinthians' new identity as Christ-followers affected basic life questions regarding sexuality, marriage, food, social gatherings, and ritual practice. Throughout the letter, Paul moves between reprimanding and instructing the group on these and other issues. Given the competing factions in Corinth, he must have had some concerns about how his intervention on these topics would be received. To pursue this question, I turn to 2 Corinthians.

Women, Paul, and the Jesus Movement

Evidence that women were active members of the Jesus movement is scattered throughout Paul's undisputed letters. In Romans 16, Paul names 28 different people in his list of greetings. Paul means to show his broad network, perhaps reinforcing his credentials before his visit to Rome. But Paul's list of greetings also shows that women were prominent figures in the early Christ assemblies. Among the co-workers that Paul names, nine are women. Paul first commends Phoebe, whom he also identifies as a *diakonon* of the assembly at Cenchreae, a town near Corinth. The Greek word indicates a position that involves offering service or ministry to others. Paul also says that Phoebe was a benefactor to him and to others (Rom 16:1–2), suggesting that she provided financial assistance. Paul then names Prisca as a co-worker who risked her life for him (Rom 16:3). Tryphena and Tryphosa are described as "workers in the Lord," and Mary and Persis both "worked hard" (Rom 16:6, 12–13). Paul also gives special recognition to Andronicus and Junia, a man and woman who were "outstanding among the apostles" and who were "in Christ" before he was (Rom 16:7).

Paul's reliance on women is also evident in 1 Corinthians, where he refers to Chloe's account of the situation in Corinth (1 Cor 1:11). Paul assumes that women pray and prophesy in the Christ assembly. He also considers celibacy to be an option for women in a culture that had legal incentives for women to marry and bear children as well as penalties for those who remained single (1 Cor 7:34).

All that said, Paul also assumes without question a social hierarchy that places men above women. He insists that women should cover their heads when they pray or prophesy, in a meandering argument that includes appeals to nature, propriety, and custom (1 Cor 11:2–16). Then there is the question of 1 Cor 14:33b–36, where women are forbidden to speak at all in the assembly. Here, Paul states that women are to submit to their husbands and learn only at home because it is shameful to speak in the assembly. It is difficult to see how Paul could both give instructions to women about praying or prophesying in the assembly and also say that they are to be silent. For this reason, many scholars think 1 Cor 14:33b–36 was inserted by a scribe with an interest in curtailing women's activities in the assembly. Notably, the location of these verses differs among ancient manuscripts; in some manuscripts, the material in verses 34–45 comes after verse 40. I return to differing perspectives on women in the Jesus movement in the next chapter. As for Paul, it is safe to say that while he seems to have imagined a new creation in Christ that included "oneness" as a feature (Gal 3:28), this did not affect what he thought was "proper" for women in the present age.

Afflictions and Accusations in 2 Corinthians

READING

Read 2 Corinthians 1–7.

EXERCISE

What clues can you find about what has occurred since the writing of 1 Corinthians?

In 2 Corinthians 1–7, Paul infuses his rhetoric with words of suffering, affliction, grief, and consolation. For example, some form of the Greek word *lupe*, meaning grief or pain, occurs 17 times. Paul writes of his own grief, of someone who has grieved him, and especially of the grief on the part of the Corinthians. It seems that a series of difficult events took place between Paul and some of the Corinthians after he sent the letter we studied above. Paul indicates that he made a painful visit to Corinth (2 Cor 2:1) during which someone publicly insulted him. Paul refers to this unnamed person as "the one who caused grief" (2 Cor 2:5). According to Paul, rather than make another painful visit, he wrote an earlier letter to the Corinthians with an anguished heart "through many tears," perhaps because they did not come to Paul's defense in the situation or reprimand the offender (2 Cor 2:4). However, by Paul's account, his "letter of tears" caused the Corinthians to grieve and to punish the person (2 Cor 2:6; 7:8–12). According to Paul, he felt regret about the Corinthians' grief over his earlier letter (2 Cor 7:8), although he no doubt exaggerates his experience when he writes of feeling "utterly crushed" and "despairing of life," as though (as the Greek wording suggests) he had sentenced himself to death (2 Cor 1:8–9). Now, after this painful episode, Paul writes in a conciliatory way, urging the group to forgive the one who caused grief (2 Cor 2:7–8) and to be reconciled with him. "Our heart is wide open to you," he writes, ". . .open wide your hearts also!" (2 Cor 6:11b–12).

Besides dealing with the consequences of the painful visit and his tearful letter, Paul's rhetoric in 2 Corinthians 1–7 includes expressions of hardship, assertions of confidence in God's power, defensive comments about his own conduct, and insinuations about his opponents. All of these rhetorical elements are intended to persuade the Corinthians of Paul's trustworthiness and secure their confidence in his authority. That he must write such a conciliatory letter suggests that Paul remains unsure of his standing among them.

Basics on 2 Corinthians

I	Salutation and blessing	1:1–11	**Outline: Paul's defense and appeals for reconciliation**
II	Seeking reconciliation and offering a self-defense	1:12–13:10	
	A. Defense of conduct and ministry toward the Corinthians	1:12–6:10	
	B. Appeal to the Corinthians for reconciliation	6:11–7:16	
	C. Appeal for financial donations for the Christ group in Jerusalem	8:1–9:15	
	D. Additional defense of Paul's apostolic work	10:1–13:10	
III	Concluding greetings and benediction	13:11–12	

The heightened tension reflected in parts of the letter and Paul's call for reconciliation suggest 2 Corinthians was written after 1 Corinthians, probably between 54 and 57 CE. Despite questions about the composition of 2 Corinthians, including whether it is one letter or contains fragments of several, one recurring theme is that God's power and wisdom paradoxically manifest themselves in human weakness. **Date and theme**

Paul's defensive comments begin early in the letter. He insists that he has behaved in a sincere and straightforward way (2 Cor 1:12) and denies that he vacillated about his travel plans (1 Cor 1:15–23). A few chapters later, he claims that he does not walk around in crafty ways, distorting the word of God (2 Cor 4:2). Paul also feels the need to argue that his gospel is not "veiled" except to unbelievers (2 Cor 4:3).

At the same time, Paul subtly contrasts his missionary work with that of others. When he asserts that he is "not a peddler of God's word," he implies that those who accept financial support from the Corinthians *are* selling the word of God. Similarly, when Paul observes that he does not require a letter of recommendation, he distinguishes himself from those who do (2 Cor 2:17; 3:2). Reading between the lines of Paul's defense, we can imagine other teachers in the Jesus movement, or perhaps other types of religious specialists, coming to Corinth with letters of recommendation and accepting payment for their services.

At four points in 2 Corinthians, Paul uses a **hardship catalogue** as part of his argument (2 Cor 4:8–9; 6:4–5; 11:23–32; 12:10). Such lists of afflictions were common features in the writings of Greek and Roman moral philosophers, who argued that the ability to withstand suffering was a sign of moral virtue. Like the moral philosophers, Paul certainly means to showcase his ability to endure suffering with his use of hardship catalogues. But instead of focusing on his own virtue and self-sufficiency, Paul shifts the focus to God's power to bring life (2 Cor 4:10–14; 5:11–15). Paul's afflictions also play a central role in his vehement self-defense against his opponents, as we will discuss with respect to the focus text later in the chapter.

Disputes Regarding the Collection for Jerusalem (2 Corinthians 8–9)

As we have seen, Paul's missionary work among the gentiles included soliciting financial donations to support the "saints" in Jerusalem, who were likely also the "poor" mentioned in Gal 2:10. 2 Corinthians contains an extended request for a contribution from the Corinthians (or perhaps two different requests; see box "The Composition of the Corinthian Correspondence"). Paul first offers the example of the Macedonian assemblies in Thessalonica and Philippi who, he claims, "begged" to contribute to the collection, even beyond their financial means (2 Cor 8:3–4). Paul also uses the example of Jesus Christ, arguing that Christ "became poor" for the Corinthians' sake (2 Cor 8:9). As part of his appeal, Paul feels compelled to defend his handling of the funds. He argues that "No one should blame us" and adds that "We intend to do what is right," presumably referring to his use of the money (2 Cor 8:20–1). A second appeal starts at 2 Corinthians 9, where Paul again stirs competition with the Macedonian assemblies and warns the Corinthians of feeling shamed in front of them (2 Cor 9:1–5). Taken together, Paul's defensive posture, his appeal to the Corinthians' sense of honor, and his repeated evocation of the Macedonians who gave enthusiastically despite their poverty suggest that some of the Corinthians were reluctant to donate.

These extensive appeals may again point to some of the Corinthians' higher status and wealth. Paul's difficulties with this group are especially evident in the contentious final chapters of 2 Corinthians.

Paul's Self-Defense against Gendered Status Attacks

2 Corinthians 10–13 shifts dramatically in tone from the preceding chapters of the letter. Many scholars believe these chapters come from a separate letter that Paul wrote to defend himself against opponents who were challenging his leadership among the Corinthians. Paul never mentions these opponents by name but labels them "false apostles" and, sarcastically, "super-apostles." Both designations imply that Paul's opponents considered themselves to be leaders in the Jesus movement (even if he did not). Paul's language points to a sort of "turf war" between Paul and others. He claims his authority over the Corinthians by asserting that he was in Corinth first, adding that he did not go beyond the area that God assigned to him and does not claim credit for others' work (2 Cor 10:13–16).

Paul's sarcastic self-defense also suggests that his opponents are attacking Paul in ways that undercut his masculine status. This would be a particularly personal challenge in a culture that privileged masculinity. Such gender-coded attacks are evident, for example, in the claim that Paul was humiliating himself among the Corinthians (2 Cor 10:1; the Greek term *tapeinos*, often translated as "humbled," has a negative connotation of acting in a servile way). The point is made even more strongly as Paul quotes his opponents: "For they say, 'his letters are weighty and strong, but his bodily presence is weak, and his speech contemptible'" (2 Cor 10:10). Because Greek and Roman standards of masculinity called for strong bodies and refined speaking abilities, these are gender-coded attacks on Paul's manliness.

As we will see, Paul counters these gendered attacks through the sort of reversal we have seen him employ already in 1 Corinthians, but now with respect to his own weak body. But first, Paul engages in his own gendered attack by raising questions about the masculine status of some of the Corinthians. In 2 Cor 11:1, Paul prepares the way for an extended play on words. He twice asks the Corinthians to "bear with" him using the Greek verb *anechein*, which conveys a sense of putting up with or enduring something difficult. Next, Paul again evokes his role of father to the Corinthians (see 1 Cor 4:15), but this time he likens the Corinthians to his virginal daughter whom he has betrothed to Christ. After this, Paul draws on first-century CE Jewish interpretations of the biblical Eve to suggest the Corinthians may be led astray as Eve was. At this point, Paul uses the same verb, *anechein*, to observe that Corinthians "endure it," that is, submit themselves to someone who offers them another Jesus, spirit, or gospel. In this way, Paul writes of the Corinthians' openness to other teachers in terms of sexual promiscuity, casting the Corinthians in the role of the woman. Paul will use the same verb again in his "fool's speech."

2 Cor 11:16–12:13

Within Paul's extended self-defense in 2 Cor 10–12, he writes what has come to be known as a "fool's speech." The reference to the fool comes from ancient Greek and Roman comedies, where the fool played a slapstick role. Paul's claim that he is "speaking as a fool" (2 Cor 11:16) casts his boasting in the realm of the ridiculous. In fact, we might read Paul's boasting as a parody of the boasting Paul claims his opponents perform. Playing the fool allows him to brag about his own credentials while mocking the boasting of his opponents at the same time. Directly addressing some of the Corinthians, Paul returns to his wordplay, "for you all gladly put up with fools, being wise yourselves" (2 Cor 11:19). And he will use it a final time, again with an open challenge to their masculinity: "You all put up with it when someone enslaves you, cons you, takes advantage of you, is condescending, or strikes you in the face" (2 Cor 11:20). Being accused of acting submissively when he is with the Corinthians in person, Paul here argues that it is the Corinthians who are debasing themselves – indeed, emasculating themselves – with respect to the so-called "super-apostles."

At 2 Cor 11:21, Paul begins "speaking like a fool," that is, daring to boast like his opponents do. In Paul's first set of boasts, he compares his credentials to the ones his opponents apparently boast about. Like them, Paul is a Hebrew, an Israelite, and a descendent of Abraham (2 Cor 11:22). From there, Paul moves to boasting about his credentials as a minister of Christ (all the while insisting that in doing so, he speaks as one "out of his mind"). Here, Paul includes another hardship catalogue, this one intended to prove that he is a better minister of Christ than his opponents. Including this list of afflictions as a subject for boasting is unusual because Paul focuses on ways that his body has been violated by others. In the ancient world, such bodily violations would not be a cause of bragging. The extended details about the number of imprisonments, floggings, beatings, and stonings that Paul has suffered could function both as a mocking parody of his opponents' boasting of their afflictions and as a way to highlight his own willingness to suffer on behalf of the gospel. Such bodily violations also illustrate how Paul shares in Christ's own bodily violations. Indeed, Paul has already prepared the Corinthians to consider certain forms of weakness to be signs of God's power and strength. The second half of the catalogue illustrates Paul's attention to rhetorical flair. He offers a rhythmic repetition of *kindunois*, "in danger," in listing the threats from his "own people," "the gentiles," and "false brothers." According to Paul, he willingly faces danger from all sides.

Following the hardship catalogue, Paul moves quickly to his final boast, finishing with an experience that would be viewed as exceptional. As Paul puts it, "I will go on to visions and revelations of the Lord." Once again, Paul tries to avoid the appearance of boasting about himself, even while doing just that. Here, he writes in the third person about "knowing a man" who was transported to the "third heaven" and "caught up to paradise." Paul does not provide a description of what he saw in these visions and revelations. Instead, he accentuates the mystical quality of the experience. He does not know whether he was in or out of his body. He does report hearing words that no person is permitted to speak (2 Cor 12:1–4). In this sense, Paul continues to have it both ways, insisting that he is not going to boast about these revelations even though they were exceedingly great (Greek, *hyperbole*). Moreover, Paul notes that the outcome of these amazing revelations was that he was given "a thorn in the flesh" to keep him from feeling above others (2 Cor 12:7). With this, Paul may be referring to some type of physical impairment. If so, implicit in Paul's claim is that his bodily impairment is a sign of his special status rather than an indication of his inferiority to the so-called "super-apostles."

Paradoxically, given all the focus on weakness, Paul ends his fool's speech with claims of power and strength. He first shares the divine response he received to his prayers that the thorn would leave him: "My grace is enough for you, for power is completed (or "perfected") in weakness" (2 Cor 12:9). Thus, boasting ever more of weakness, Paul ends his speech with one final catalogue of afflictions, before concluding: "for when I am weak, then I am strong." That is to say that in the end, Paul does not abandon the rhetoric of strength and power. Nor does he lift up weakness as a virtue or end in itself. Instead, weakness becomes a paradoxical display of strength.

CHAPTER FIVE REVIEW

1 Know the meaning and significance of the following terms discussed in this chapter:
   - hardship catalogue
   - voluntary association
2 List at least three issues that Paul addresses in 1 Corinthians. Explain both the Corinthian position and Paul's response.
3 Scholars differ over whether Paul was "good" for women. What do you think? Give evidence from Paul's letters to support your position.

4 In general, what does the Corinthian correspondence show us about life in the urban settings of the Jesus movement? What was challenging for the Corinthians? What was challenging for Paul?
5 (Focus text: 2 Cor 11:16–12:13) What does Paul want to accomplish with his "fool's speech"? What does he boast about and why? Do you think this would be an effective response to the gendered attacks from his opponents? Explain.

RESOURCES FOR FURTHER STUDY

Lull, David John. *1 Corinthians*. St. Louis, MO: Chalice Press, 2007.

Minor, Mitzi. *2 Corinthians*. Macon, GA: Smyth & Helwys, 2009.

Wire, Antoinette Clark. *2 Corinthians*. Collegeville, MN: Liturgical Press, 2019.

For more on queer biblical interpretation:

Hornsby, Teresa J., and Ken Stone, eds. *Bible Trouble: Queer Reading at the Boundaries of Biblical Scholarship*. Atlanta, GA: Society of Biblical Literature, 2011. A collection of essays that are theoretically dense but provide a good example of diverse ways that queer theory can inform biblical interpretation.

Moore, Stephen D. "Queer Theory." Pp. 95–116 in Benjamin H. Dunning (ed.), *The Oxford Handbook of New Testament, Gender, and Sexuality*. New York: Oxford University Press, 2019.

Guest, Deryn, Robert E. Goss, Mona West, and Thomas Bohache, eds. *The Queer Bible Commentary*. London: SCM Press, 2006.

Claiming Pauline Authority: Later Trajectories of Pauline Traditions

6

Chapter Outline

Chapter Overview	97
Ancient Pseudonymity and the New Testament Writers	98
Three Deutero-Pauline Letters: 2 Thessalonians, Colossians, and Ephesians	99
Conforming to Roman Imperial Values: The New Testament Household Codes	104
More Deutero-Pauline Letters: 1 and 2 Timothy and Titus	105
The Paul of Legend: The Acts of Paul and Thecla	108
From Local Letters to Scriptural Authority	109
Chapter Six Review	111
Resources for Further Study	111

Chapter Overview

In this chapter, I step outside of the chronological framework of this textbook to discuss writings from the late first century and second century CE that draw on Paul's authority in diverse ways. These later Pauline trajectories include the disputed letters in the Pauline letter collection as well as a later legend that developed about a woman named Thecla and her interest in Paul. The chapter begins with a discussion of the ancient practice of **pseudepigraphy**, that is, writing in someone else's name. From there, I discuss the **Deutero-Pauline letters** (another designation for the six disputed letters) showing how they differ from undisputed letters. 2 Thessalonians offers a different apocalyptic framework than 1 Thessalonians. Colossians and Ephesians do

The New Testament: A Contemporary Introduction, First Edition. Colleen M. Conway.
© 2023 John Wiley & Sons Ltd. Published 2023 by John Wiley & Sons Ltd.

not address specific issues in a community, but instead offer a more general image of a cosmic Christ. Finally, the Pastoral Letters focus on bringing order to the assembly and showing basic conformity to Roman values, especially with respect to the household.

Ancient Pseudonymity and the New Testament Writers

To begin, we should first note that the disputed Pauline letters are not the only examples of pseudepigraphy in the New Testament. The letters attributed to James, Peter, and Jude are also cases of unknown authors writing in the name of an authoritative figure in the Jesus movement. This practice of false authorial attribution only increased in the second century CE and beyond. Examples of Christian pseudepigrapha (writings with falsely attributed authors) include a number of gospels attributed to authoritative figures such as Peter, James, Thomas, and Mary. There was even a series of letters purportedly written between Paul and the Roman writer Seneca.

To modern sensibilities, the literary practice of writing in someone else's name is problematic. Some scholars deal with the problem of pseudonymous writing – or forgery, to use a more provocative term – by arguing that it did not occur. They try to make the case that Paul, Peter, James, and Jude actually wrote the documents that claim their authorship. This is a difficult argument to sustain. For example, one has to explain how an uneducated Galilean fisherman like Peter was capable of writing at all, let alone writing in the sophisticated Greek prose that occurs in 1 Peter. In the case of the disputed Pauline letters, the argument requires an explanation for why Paul radically changes his writing style. It also requires extending Paul's life, as I will explain below. Alternatively, some scholars acknowledge that several New Testament writings were written pseudonymously but argue that the practice was considered acceptable in certain circumstances. For example, these scholars might argue that if a student of Paul wrote a letter in Paul's name, it was a way of honoring Paul as a teacher.

More recent scholarship on what ancient people actually wrote about forgery reveals a keen awareness and disapproval of the practice. Note, for example, that the author of 2 Thessalonians warns readers not to be shaken or alarmed by a letter written "as though from us" (2 Thess 2:2). Issuing such a warning was a common way that pseudonymous writers tried to make their work appear authentic. In the case of the Pastoral Letters, the author goes to even greater lengths to conceal his literary deception. In 2 Timothy, the author asks for his cloak and books, and "especially the parchments" (2 Tim 4:13). Including personal details like these (which Paul does not do in the undisputed letters) was another common practice of pseudonymous authors. In this case, the mention of books and parchments links with Paul's reputation as a literate writer.

There were many reasons why ancient writers would falsely attribute the authorship of their work. Some authors may have considered their writings to be extensions or elaborations of the earlier work of others and thus extended the authorial attribution as well. In some cases, the author may have hoped to gain a broader audience by having a well-known figure attached to the work. Other writers likely claimed the authority of a prominent figure to give more weight to their argument, especially concerning contentious topics. For example, this chapter will show how Paul's authority was used to promote two different positions regarding women's celibacy. In the midst of a diverse Jesus movement, pseudonymous writers may have engaged in literary deceit in the belief that their action was divinely sanctioned for the purpose of advocating a correct teaching.

Research and debate continue regarding the ancient practice of pseudepigraphy and its function(s) in the early stages of the Christian tradition. Since the actual authors of these writings are lost to us, there is much that we may never know. In some ways, the ongoing scholarly debate about Pauline authority for these six letters is odd because nearly all of the books in the Bible are by unknown authors. For the communities that read the New Testament as scripture, the Deutero-Pauline letters have canonical authority whether or not they were written by Paul. Nevertheless, because some of the content of the disputed letters is controversial – indeed, outright disturbing for many contemporary readers – some interpreters stress their "non-Pauline" character. Still, given Paul's less-than-consistent comments in the undisputed letters, it makes sense that later writers with diverse positions might understand their work as an extension of Paul's ideas.

Three Deutero-Pauline Letters: 2 Thessalonians, Colossians, and Ephesians

Read 2 Thessalonians.

READING

What ideas in this letter seem similar to what you have read in the undisputed letters of Paul? What different ideas do you notice? Hint: Compare 1 Thess 4:13–5:1–5 and 2 Thess 2:1–12. What problem does the author address in 2 Thess 3:6–15?

EXERCISE

For more than a hundred years, scholars have questioned whether Paul wrote 2 Thessalonians. There remains no consensus on the issue. Structurally, only this letter and 1 Thessalonians have a second thanksgiving, an unusual feature for a Greco-Roman letter. This feature's inclusion in 2 Thessalonians could be the result of an author imitating the structure of 1 Thessalonians. Another possible clue that someone other than Paul wrote 2 Thessalonians is the way the author insists that he is, in fact, Paul. He asserts, "I, Paul, write this greeting with my own hand. This is the mark in every letter of mine; it is the way I write (2 Thess 3:17). Meanwhile, Paul calls attention to writing in his own hand in only three of the undisputed letters (1 Cor 16:21; Gal 6:11; Philemon 19).

Basics on 2 Thessalonians

Outline: instructions on the *Parousia*	I	Salutation and thanksgiving	1:1–12
	II	Body of the letter	2:1–3:15
		A. Instructions about Jesus's coming	2:1–12
		B. Second thanksgiving	2:13–16
		C. Exhortation to pray and to avoid idleness	3:1–15
	III	Concluding blessings and greetings	3:16–17

Date and audience

The letter denies rumors that the Day of the Lord has already arrived and instructs its readers on events that must occur before that day. The date of the letter's composition is difficult to determine. If the letter was not written by Paul, it likely addresses a later generation around the end of the first century CE.

The main arguments against Pauline authorship concern the letter's different representation of the Day of the Lord compared to 1 Thessalonians. As we saw in Chapter 3, Paul expected this day to come during his lifetime. In 1 Thessalonians, he vividly describes a meeting in the air with the Lord and urges the Christ group to be vigilant because Jesus could return at any moment (1 Thess 4:15–17; 5:1–7). In contrast, in 2 Thessalonians, the author does not mention being present for the events that are described, even as he assures the readers that certain events will signal the *parousia*. There must first be "the apostasy" and the revealing of the "lawless one" (2 Thess 2:1–12). The Greek term *apostasia* (translated as "rebellion" in the NRSV) suggests a defection from God and from the group. The text implies that this will occur because of the self-exaltation of the lawless one, who declares himself to be God (2 Thess 2:4). The author may be referring to the Roman emperor, given the reference to this figure being worshiped and seated in a temple. In any case, the description of certain events that must occur before the Day of the Lord differs from 1 Thessalonians, which describes that day as coming unexpectedly, like a thief in the night, and suddenly, like a woman going into labor (1 Thess 5:1–3).

Toward the end of the letter, the author turns to internal problems. Some in the group are living in a disorderly way. These members are apparently not working but instead meddling in the affairs of others. The author's suggestion that these people "should not eat" likely means that the disorderly people should be excluded from group meals. As discussed in Chapter 5, shared meals were a common part of voluntary associations in Greco-Roman cities; these associations were groups resembling worker's guilds. Scholars who argue that 2 Thessalonians was written by Paul suggest that the group's problems were a result of Paul's initial emphasis on the imminent coming of the Lord. Some members may have stopped working in anticipation of this day. Even if we cannot ultimately determine the letter's authorship, whoever wrote 2 Thessalonians appears to address circumstances specific to a local group. This is not the case in Colossians and Ephesians, which I turn to now.

Scholars have long observed the many parallels between Colossians and Ephesians. Compare the texts listed below to see these similarities.

READING

What are some different ways of explaining these parallels? How does this evidence inform your thinking about the authorship of these two letters?

EXERCISE

Ephesians	*Colossians*
1:1–2	1:1–2
1:15–16	1:3–4, 9
3:2–3	1:25–6
4:22–4	3:5–12
5:18–20	3:16–17

I discuss Colossians and Ephesians together because their parallel content suggests some type of literary relationship between them. Most likely, the author of Ephesians drew on Colossians (which may have been his own earlier letter) to write a longer, generalized letter about gentile conduct. The general nature of Ephesians is further attested by the fact that some ancient manuscripts of the letter do not refer to Ephesus in the opening address. In these manuscripts, the opening salutation is more generally to "the saints who are also faithful in Christ Jesus."

Along with common language, Colossians and Ephesians also share a similar writing style that differs from that of Paul's undisputed letters. The sentence structure is more complex, and the vocabulary differs substantially. While this is most apparent in the Greek text, these letters' long, complex sentences stand out even in English translations. For example, in the Greek text, Ephesians 3:1–7 is one long sentence that the translators of the NRSV manage to convey in two sentences that are still quite lengthy. Ephesians and Colossians also use many words that do not appear in the undisputed Pauline epistles. Note, for example, the repeated references to "the heavenly places" that appear only in Ephesians (Greek, *tois epouraniois*; Eph 1:3, 30; 2:6; 3:10; 6:12). These types of observations are what scholars mean when they refer to the different writing style of Ephesians and Colossians compared to the undisputed letters.

Another indication that these two letters are pseudonymous is that they seem to reflect a later stage of the development of the Jesus movement than we see in the undisputed letters. For instance, when Paul writes to the Corinthians about laying a foundation, he goes on to say that the "foundation is Jesus Christ" (see 1 Cor 3:10–11).

The letter to the Ephesians adds another layer of authority to this foundation, claiming that the "household of God" is built upon the foundation of the apostles and the prophets, with Christ as the cornerstone (Eph 2:20). The reference to the apostles as part of the foundation suggests that more time has passed since Paul was busy defending his own apostolic credentials and fighting with the so-called "super-apostles."

Both Colossians and Ephesians refer to Christ as the head over the body – that is, the *ekklesia* – suggesting a hierarchal structure with a ruling authority (Col 1:18; Eph 5:23). In contrast, Paul uses the body metaphor in 1 Corinthians to claim that God has given honor to the indispensable weaker parts and to argue for mutual care among members of the body (1 Cor 12:12–26). Further, whereas Paul uses the term "body" to refer to a specific Christ group (1 Cor 12:27), Colossians and Ephesians emphasize a universal and unified "body" of Christ assemblies (Eph 4:4–16; 5:23; Col 1:18).

Also, compared to Paul's focus on the anticipated appearance of Christ for a day of judgment, the letter to the Colossians describes Christ in ways that link him to the creation of the cosmos. According to the author, Christ is "the image of the individual God, the firstborn of creation," who "is before all things, and in him all things hold together" (Col 1:15–16). These descriptions recall the figure of Wisdom in the Hebrew scripture and some Second Temple texts. While we will see a similar association between Christ and Wisdom in the gospels (especially John 1:1–4), it is not typical of the undisputed letters of Paul. In addition, the claim of Christ's supremacy over the entire cosmos in Col 1:15–20 goes beyond anything we read in Paul's undisputed letters.

Finally, the letter to the Ephesians refers to the unification of Jews and gentiles in a way that runs counter to Paul's view in the undisputed letters. Consider the following verses:

> For he is our peace, the one who in his flesh has made both into one and broken the dividing wall, that is, the hostility, nullifying the law with commandments and ordinances, in order that he might create in him one new humanity from two, making peace, and might reconcile both in one body for God through the cross, killing the hostility with it. (Eph 2:14–16)

This rather literal translation highlights several ideas that conflict with Paul's statements in the undisputed letters. First, Paul rejects the idea of the law being nullified (Rom 3:31). Second, he insists on both Jews and gentiles maintaining their identity as the circumcised and uncircumcised. For Paul, bringing in the gentiles *as* uncircumcised gentiles is a critical part of his apocalyptic expectations. In contrast, the author of Ephesians leaves behind the use of the terms "gentile," "circumcised," and "uncircumcised" (Eph 2:11). The passage's references to "one body" and a "new humanity" appear to dissolve the distinction between Jews and gentiles. Taken together, all such differences raise questions about the Pauline authorship of Ephesians and Colossians.

Basics on Colossians

I	Salutation, thanksgiving, and prayer for wisdom	1:1–14	**Outline: a**
II	Body of the letter	1:15–4:6	**cosmic Christ**
	A. Praise of the cosmic Christ who reconciles	1:15–23	
	B. Paul's mission to the gentiles	1:24–2:5	
	C. Warnings against false teaching and practice, call to virtue	2:6–3:17	
	D. Commands for hierarchical household duties	3:18–4:1	
III	Final exhortations, closing greetings, and blessing	4:2–18	

Colossae was a town in the Roman Province of Asia with a sizable Jewish population. The letter to the Colossians is the only place that it is mentioned in the New Testament. According to Colossians, the Christ group in the town was founded by Epaphras (Col 1:7; see also Philemon 23), and Paul had never traveled there (Col 2:1). The letter combines general warnings against being captivated or led astray "through philosophy or empty deceit" (Col 2:8) with exhortations to live virtuously in light of having "received Christ Jesus the Lord" (Col 2:6).

Theme

Basics on Ephesians

I	Salutation, extended blessing, and prayer for wisdom	1:1–23	**Outline: exhortation**
II	Body of the letter	2:1–6:20	**for unity in Christ**
	A. Gentiles' new life in Christ	2:1–22	
	B. God's revelation to Paul and Paul's prayer	3:1–21	
	C. Exhortations for ethical conduct	4:1–5:20	
	D. Commands for hierarchical household duties	5:21–6:9	
III	Final exhortations, closing greetings, and blessing	6:10–24	

Ephesus was a major city in Asia Minor that became a center for developing Christianity. According to the Acts of the Apostles, Paul lived and worked there for three years. Nevertheless, most scholars think that Paul did not write the letter to the Ephesians. The writing may have been meant to circulate generally to Christ groups in Asia Minor (present-day Turkey). One main theme is the proper conduct of gentiles who had joined the Jesus movement. Another concerns the unity of gentiles and Jews in the assembly. If it was not written by Paul, Ephesians probably dates to the late first century CE, decades after Paul's death.

Date and theme

Conforming to Roman Imperial Values: The New Testament Household Codes

Another reason that scholars think that Ephesians and Colossians reflect a later period in the Jesus movement concerns their exhortations about household management. Both letters contain instructions to live according to typical Roman standards of hierarchal household management. Scholars refer to these sections as **household codes** (Col 3:18–4:1; Eph 5:21–6:9). Two more of these codes appear in Titus and 1 Peter. All of the New Testament household codes align closely with the Roman household structure, urging the submission of wives to husbands, children to parents, and slaves to masters. Similar codes appear frequently in Greek and Roman writings, and the authors of Ephesians and Colossians do encourage behavior that aligns with certain Greco-Roman cultural values. It may be that by the time these texts were written, Christ-followers were increasingly drawing attention as a distinct group apart from Judaism. At a time when new cultic practices were regarded with suspicion, embracing traditional cultural values could make these Christ groups appear unremarkable and non-threatening.

Whatever their function in ancient times, the use of the household codes in the Deutero-Pauline letters has contributed to a long history of patriarchal patterns of the oppression of women, slaves, and children. There are a great many contemporary Christians who consider scripture to be authoritative but also do not think women must "submit" to their husbands and certainly do not condone slavery. How, then, should one deal with the scriptural household codes? Christian interpreters attempt to alleviate this tension in different ways. Some argue (1) that the codes are not written by Paul and (2) that they move the Jesus movement in a culturally conforming direction that Paul never intended. Others say that this was a widely accepted social structure in the ancient world, though not in our time. Still others highlight the mutuality of the New Testament household codes, arguing that in this way the codes undercut the hierarchal structure of Roman culture. The New Testament household codes do advocate some behavior modification for the men who hold power over others – husbands are encouraged to love their wives (Col 3:19; Eph 5:33) and treat their slaves justly and fairly (Col 4:1). Moreover, the role of the masters is relativized by references to the "master in heaven" (Col 4:1; 6:9), a move that extends the patriarchal hierarchy to a heavenly Father. Finally, for some Christian communities, the codes present no difficulties because these communities continue to advocate patriarchal structures in their churches and homes.

Another problem with the ancient household codes is that they narrow one's identity to a single role that ignores the complexity and fluidity of actual life. The framework assumes an ancient household where one was either a husband or a wife, a parent or a child, a master or a slave. But of course, the truth is that all people, ancient and contemporary, are a mix of multiple intersecting identities (recall the earlier discussion of intersectionality in the Prologue and Chapter 1). For example, in a Roman household, a woman could be a wife, mother, daughter, and master at the same time. Moreover, this problem is further complicated by the various identities one might have outside the household.

A petition for freedom presented in 1774 by a group of enslaved people to the province of Massachusetts provides a powerful historical example of the usefulness of attending to intersecting identities when reading the New Testament household codes. Whereas slaveholders routinely turned to the verses in the household codes that advocate the slave's obedience to the master, the petition draws on the whole of the household codes. In the opening line, the authors of the petition identify themselves as "a Grate Number of Blackes of this Province who by divine permission are held in a state of Slavery within the bowels of a free and christian Country." Having evoked the Christian foundation of the colonizers of North America, the petitioners turn to the Pauline household codes to make their case for freedom. They ask several questions:

> How can a slave perform the duties of a husband to a wife or parent to his child . . . How can the wife submit themselves to there husbands in all things. How can the child obey thear parents in all things.
> (Quoted in Lisa Bowens, *African American Readings of Paul: Reception, Resistance, and Transformation*. Eerdmans, Grand Rapids, MI: 2020, p. 22.)

While their argument did not challenge the basic hierarchical structure of the household codes, it did point to the fact that enslaved Africans were more than slaves: they were part of their own families comprised of husbands, wives, and children. The petitioners argued that the institution of slavery, which separated slaves from their families, made it impossible for them to fulfill scriptural duties related to the aspects of their identities that slavery denied. Despite this scripturally based argument, it took six petitions and several lawsuits for the Massachusetts colony to abolish slavery in 1783.

More Deutero-Pauline Letters: 1 and 2 Timothy and Titus

1 and 2 Timothy and Titus are short letters. Read through them in their entirety with Paul's undisputed letters in mind.

READING

Where do you see similar ideas? What stands out to you as different? What seems to be the main concern of the author of these letters?

EXERCISE

The other three disputed letters, 1 and 2 Timothy and Titus, are called the **Pastoral Letters** because they offer instructions regarding the conduct of leaders and members of the Jesus movement. (The word "pastoral," related to shepherding, in this sense means guiding and caring for the community of Christ-followers). Most biblical scholars agree that these three letters were not written by Paul but probably by the same author writing in Paul's name, likely in the early second century CE. These letters are unique in that they are written to one person, sharing an opening formulation from Paul to "my genuine (or 'beloved') child." In the undisputed letters, Paul identifies Timothy and Titus as his close companions and co-workers (see, for example, Rom 16:21; 1 Cor 4:17; 2 Cor 8:23). The author of the Pastoral Letters draws on this close relationship, writing as if he were Paul instructing trusted colleagues in Christ. 1 Timothy and Titus are similar in their focus on false teaching and institutional order. In some sections, 2 Timothy reads like Paul's parting words at the end of his life.

Both 1 Timothy and Titus assume a level of organization in the assembly that did not exist when Paul was carrying out his mission to the gentiles. Both letters list the proper traits for bishops and deacons as if these are established leadership positions (1 Tim 3:1–13; Titus 1:7–9). Moreover, both 1 Timothy and Titus express repeated concern for "sound doctrine," and all three Pastoral Letters call out various types of false teaching. The author of 1 Timothy refers to those who "forbid marriage and require abstinence from foods" (1 Tim 4:3), suggesting that his opponents are promoting an ascetic lifestyle. In Titus, the author worries about "many unrestrained, empty talkers and deceivers" who are "upsetting whole households" (Titus 1:10–11). His special attention to "those of the circumcision" and to "Jewish myths" suggests the author's opposition to expressions of Jewish mysticism among Christ-followers. Later, he urges his readers to "avoid stupid controversies, genealogies, dissensions, and quarrels about the law" (Titus 3:9). None of this allows much insight into who or what exactly the writer was opposing. Nevertheless, we can see that the diversity of thinking among Christ-followers that we saw reflected in the undisputed Pauline letters continued into the second century CE.

Apart from the concern about false teaching, most of the focus of the Pastoral Letters is on the proper conduct of group members in the context of the household hierarchy. The familiar themes from Paul's letters regarding faithfulness, the relation of gentiles and Jews, and the coming of the Lord are nowhere in view.

Basics on 1 Timothy

I	Salutation and greeting to Timothy	1:1–2
II	Body of the letter: instructions to Timothy	1:3–6:19
	A. Warnings against false teachings	1:3–11
	B. Examples of faith and faithlessness	1:12–20
	C. Instructions for life and order in the assembly	2:1–6:19
III	Closing blessing	6:21b

Basics on 2 Timothy

I	Salutation and greeting to Timothy	1:1–2
II	Thanksgiving for Timothy	1:3–7
	Body of the Letter	1:8–4:18
	A. Call for and examples of shared suffering rather than shame	1:8–2:13
	B. Warnings and strategies to avoid false teachers	2:14–4:5
	C. Paul's personal reflections	4:6–18
III	Closing greetings and blessing	4:19–21

Basics on Titus

I	Salutation to Titus	1:1–4
II	Body of the letter: Titus's commission for work in Crete	1:5–3:14
	A. Titus's commission to appoint elders in Crete	1:5–16
	B. Commission to teach sound doctrine and promote household order	2:1–3:11
	C. Final instructions regarding Paul's travel plans	3:12–14
III	Closing greetings and blessing	3:15

The Pastoral Letters differ in their attitude toward women compared to the ambivalent attitude Paul expresses in the undisputed letters (see box "Women, Paul, and the Jesus Movement" in Chapter 5). All three of the letters claim that women should be submissive and silent in the assembly. Consider the following examples. In 1 Timothy, men are instructed how to pray (1 Tim 2:8), while women are instructed how to dress and style their hair in a modest way (1 Tim 2:9). While Paul expresses opinions about the Corinthian women's hair while they prayed or prophesied (1 Cor 11:2–16), the Pastoral Letters go further: no woman is permitted to teach or have authority over a man; "she is to keep silent" (1 Tim 2:12; recall the discussion of 1 Cor 14:33b–36). The author also evokes the story of Adam and Eve to imply that all women are transgressors (see Genesis 2–3). This misreading of the Genesis garden story contributes to a long and distorted history of interpretation that places the blame for human transgression on Eve alone (1 Tim 2:13–14; compare 1 Cor 5:12). Rather than promoting celibacy, the "Paul" of this letter claims that women will be saved through childbearing (1 Tim 2:15). And instead of recognizing the contributions of women to the work of the Jesus movement, 2 Timothy portrays women as "silly" and "overwhelmed by their sins and all kinds of desires" (2 Tim 3:6). Further, as mentioned above, Titus contains a hierarchal household code that instructs older women to train young women to be self-controlled, pure, and kind household workers who are submissive to their husbands (Titus 2:4).

In these ways, the Pastoral Letters move the Jesus movement in the direction of cultural accommodation. The instructions in 1 Timothy demonstrate this interest most explicitly: "I urge, therefore, first of all, that requests, prayers, petitions, and thanksgivings be made for all people, for kings and for all who are in high positions, so that we may live a peaceful and quiet life in all piousness and dignity" (1 Tim 2:1). Of course, the "kings" and others in high positions are the Roman emperor and his appointees.

Alongside this push for accommodation and perhaps assimilation to Roman culture, we find a few faint echoes of the countercultural aspects of Paul's undisputed letters. In 2 Timothy, the author evokes Paul's experience of imprisonment, as well as his call not to be ashamed but instead to join him in suffering for the gospel (2 Tim 1:8). Further, while much of the ethical instruction in the Pastoral Letters is typical of ancient Greco-Roman moral exhortation, the arena for living an orderly life is not a Roman household but the "household of God, which is the *ekklesia* of the living God" (1 Tim 3:15). Finally, because these writings are instructions, they are not reflections of what was actually occurring in the Christ groups. That is, the letters are not descriptive but prescriptive. The author hopes to convince his audience to conform to the set of values reflected in the text, most likely in light of alternative, competing positions among the Christ groups. We have evidence of such a competing position from another Pauline trajectory: a second-century CE legend featuring Paul and a woman named Thecla.

The Paul of Legend: The Acts of Paul and Thecla

The Acts of Paul and Thecla is not a pseudepigraphal writing. Rather, it is an example of early Christian **apocrypha.** Earlier in this book, I discussed the technical sense of the Greek word "apocrypha": the collection of books that were included in the Septuagint but are not part of the Hebrew writings in the Jewish Tanakh and Protestant Old Testament (see Prologue and Chapter 1). In addition to this meaning, the word is also used in a more general sense to describe later writings that were popular among early Christians but did not become part of the New Testament canon.

The Acts of Paul and Thecla is one such text. It relates a story about a young aristocratic Roman woman named Thecla. She is engaged to marry a man named Thamyris who comes from another prominent family. However, the marriage plans go awry when Paul travels to their town. Thecla sits in her window and overhears him from a nearby house. In part, the story imitates Greek romance novels from this period. Thecla's reaction to hearing Paul's preaching is to be overcome with desire. What follows is Thecla's mother's report to Thamyris when he comes to see Thecla:

I have a strange [new] report to tell you, Thamyris. For three days and three nights Thecla has not risen from the window, but is staring intently, as if at some happy spectacle, and is thus exposed to this foreign man who is teaching deceptive and subtle words; it's a real wonder to me how the modesty of such a girl is overwhelmed so grievously.

Thamyris, this man is stirring up the city of the Iconians, and your Thecla as well, for all the wives and the youth are going in to him, and they are being taught by him because, "it is necessary," he says, "to reverence only one god and to live purely." And even my daughter is stuck like a spider to the window by his words, being seized by a strange desire and a fearful passion. For the girl just stares and is transfixed by the things he says. Go and speak to her, for she is engaged to you!

(Modified from Hayes, Leslie K. The Acts of Thecla: Introduction, Translation, and Notes. The Claremont Graduate University. ProQuest Dissertations Publishing, 2016. 10099662. 230, 232.)

The rest of the story goes on to tell of Thecla breaking her marriage engagement and of her persistent efforts to follow Paul. At one point, Paul suggests that a woman as beautiful as Thecla will not be able to withstand temptation. The account of Thecla includes many trials that she miraculously survives, including death by fire and wild beasts. Though Paul himself will not baptize her, Thecla eventually baptizes herself by leaping into some water. At one point, Thecla dresses like a man, following the pattern of other stories of early Christian women that include episodes of gender shifting. Eventually, Thecla lives out her chaste life in a cave, where she instructs other women who come to her about God. The end of her life comes as she miraculously escapes yet another sexual attack, thus maintaining her virginity for 90 years.

The Acts of Paul and Thecla shows the diversity of thought among Christians in the second century CE and beyond. Far from teaching that women will be saved through childbearing, the Paul of legend advocates a life of chastity for women. Thecla emerges as a heroine who leaves behind the Roman values of marriage and family to travel with Paul. Given the Pauline legend's emphasis on chastity, some scholars argue that the Pastoral Letters were written as a direct and opposing response. Whether or not this was the case, the ideas around marriage, chastity, and women's positions in the Jesus movement reflected in the Pastoral Letters and the story of Thecla are certainly at odds. Finally, we should note that the cultural figure of Thecla lived on after the character's death at the end of the legend. Evidence of her ongoing popularity extends across the fourth and fifth centuries in both Asia Minor and Egypt in literary and material artifacts attesting to the cult of Saint Thecla (Figure 6.1).

From Local Letters to Scriptural Authority

With this, we come to the end of this introduction to the Pauline letters. We have focused especially on the occasional nature of the undisputed letters – that is, the particular situation of the urban Christ groups to whom the letters are written and Paul's interests in writing to them. However, at some point in the second century CE, Paul's letters

FIGURE 6.1

Wall painting of Paul and Thecla discovered near Ephesus (sixth century CE). The painting is evidence of the popularity of Thecla and of the cult devoted to her. Thecla is depicted as having a greater stature than Paul and with the same raised teaching hand. However, her eyes and upraised teaching hand have been scratched out by some later person in an effort to silence and blind this authoritative female figure in the early church.

were published together as a collection. Paul himself might have begun this process by gathering some of his letters for publication. This would be possible because letter writers regularly had their secretaries make copies of their own letters before sending off the original letter. Later, followers of Paul added to the collection until all 13 of the letters that are now in the New Testament were published together. One notable part of this process is a comment made by the author of the pseudonymous letter 2 Peter:

> So also our beloved brother Paul wrote to you according to the wisdom given to him, speaking as he does in all of his letters about these things. In them are some things that are hard to understand, and the ignorant and unstable twist their meaning, as they do with other scriptures, to their own destruction. (2 Peter 3:15b–16).

The fact that the author puts all of Paul's letters in the same category as "other scriptures" suggests the collection has reached an authoritative and sacred status. We can also appreciate the observation that some things in Paul's letters are hard to understand! In any case, once the letters were published as a collection, their "occasional" nature began to recede from view. Readers were no longer interested in the circumstances of why Paul wrote what he did to Christ-followers in different cities. Instead, interpretations of the letter collection began to focus more generally on the letters' contributions to Christian theology. While these letters have become a treasured resource for the Christian church, the "Christianizing" of Paul's letters has historically come with a cost. Reading Paul as if he had rejected his own Jewish identity has contributed to antagonism toward Jews.

Similarly, reading the household codes discussed in this chapter as the inspired word of God has contributed to centuries of oppression for those enslaved by Christian owners and for women living under the oppression of patriarchy. Reading the letters in their context and analyzing how the Pauline letters continue to be used to include and exclude certain groups of people, remain important parts of the academic approach to the New Testament.

CHAPTER SIX REVIEW

1 Know the meaning and significance of the following terms discussed in this chapter:
   - apocrypha
   - Deutero-Pauline letters
   - household codes
   - Pastoral Letters
   - pseudepigraphy
   - The Acts of Paul and Thecla

2 How does 2 Thessalonians differ from 1 Thessalonians? What similarities do you see? Given this evidence, do you think the letter was written by Paul?

3 What are some of the reasons that scholars think Colossians and Ephesians were not written by Paul?

4 Why might the author of the Pastoral Letters be focused on issues of order in the assembly? What links are there between these letters and the undisputed letters?

5 In what ways was the Acts of Paul and Thecla countercultural in its ancient context? Do you think Paul would approve of the legend? Explain your answer with evidence from Paul and from the Acts of Paul and Thecla.

RESOURCES FOR FURTHER STUDY

Huizenga, Annette Bourland. *1–2 Timothy, Titus*. Collegeville, MN: Liturgical Press, 2016.

Levine Amy-Jill, with Marianne Blickenstaff, eds. *A Feminist Companion to the Deutero-Pauline Epistles*. London: T&T Clark, 2003.

Tamez, Elsa, Cynthia B. Kittredge, Claire M. Colombo, and Alicia J. Batten. *Philippians, Colossians, Philemon*. Collegeville, MN: Liturgical Press, 2017.

For additional reading on pseudepigraphy, the following two works represent two sides of a debate on how best to understand the ancient practice of writing in another person's name:

Baum, Armin D. "Content and Form: Authorship Attribution and Pseudonymity in Ancient Speeches, Letters, Lectures, and Translations – A Rejoinder to Bart Ehrman," *Journal of Biblical Literature*, 136 (2017) pp. 381–403. https://doi.org/10.15699/jbl.1362.2017.200369

Ehrman, Bart D. *Forgery and Counterforgery: The Use of Literary Deceit in Early Christian Polemics*. Oxford and New York: Oxford University Press, 2013.

The Gospel of Mark: Suffering and Trauma under Imperial Rule

7

Chapter Outline

Chapter Overview	**113**
The Jewish War (66–70 CE)	**114**
Clues to the Dating and Context of the Gospel of Mark	**115**
The Story of Jesus in the Gospel of Mark	**118**
The Rising Popularity of Jesus and Rising Conflict with the Authorities	**118**
Teaching and Misunderstanding "on the Way"	**122**
Mark's Suffering Messiah	**126**
An Enigmatic Ending	**129**
Focus Text: Mark 12:1–12	**130**
Chapter Seven Review	**132**
Resources for Further Study	**132**

Chapter Overview

In this chapter, I resume the chronological framework of the textbook, moving back to describe events that occurred after the ministry of Paul and before the writing of the New Testament gospels: the Jewish War and the destruction of the Jerusalem Temple by Rome. This chapter focuses on how these historical events are reflected in the major themes of the earliest canonical gospels. The Gospel of Mark tells the story of a messiah who must be rejected, suffer, and die. At the same time, it depicts Jesus's closest followers as struggling to understand or accept this idea. I show how these themes work together to address Christ-followers during a time of instability and crisis. The chapter begins with an overview of that time.

The New Testament: A Contemporary Introduction, First Edition. Colleen M. Conway.
© 2023 John Wiley & Sons Ltd. Published 2023 by John Wiley & Sons Ltd.

The Jewish War (66–70 CE)

As we saw in Chapter 2, toward the end of the first century BCE, Herod engaged in a massive building program designed to gain favor from his subjects and from his Roman benefactors. We saw how a tour of Jerusalem during Herod's time would have offered much to impress the traveler. But a traveler to Jerusalem decades later would have encountered a very different sight. Instead of gazing on the architectural achievements of Herod's reign, after 70 CE the traveler would have found broken city walls, the Jerusalem Temple looted and ravaged by fire, and much of the city destroyed by war. All of this would have been the result of the **Jewish War**, which began with a Jewish revolt against Rome in 66 CE.

As you may recall, the end of Jewish independent rule came with the invasion of Palestine by the Roman general Pompey in 63 BCE. By 6 CE, Rome had reorganized Judea and the surrounding regions into a larger Roman province. This change to provincial status meant that Rome now had direct rule over the region through "prefects," or governors, appointed by the Roman Senate. These prefects, including Pontius Pilate of the gospels, were notorious for both their incompetence and their brutality. Living under such inept rulers led to increasing unrest among the local Jewish community, culminating in an armed revolt against Rome in 66 CE.

The Jewish rebels had some initial success, managing to occupy the Temple and even mint their own silver coins in the first year of the revolt (see Figure 7.1). But by 70 CE, the Roman army had Jerusalem in the grip of what would become a protracted siege. According to the Jewish historian Josephus, this was a time of great suffering for the inhabitants of Jerusalem. He writes of widespread starvation in Jerusalem and deadly struggles for what food remained. Those who left the city in search of food were captured by the Romans and crucified outside the city walls. Of these, Josephus states, "so great was their number, that space could not be found for the crosses nor crosses for the bodies"

FIGURE 7.1
Silver shekel minted about 67 CE during the Jewish revolt. The inscription in archaic Hebrew recalls the Zion theology of the ancient past, stating "Jerusalem the Holy."

FIGURE 7.2
The pillaging of the Jerusalem Temple depicted on the Arch of Titus, which still stands in Rome and commemorates Titus's triumph over the Jewish revolt.

(see Josephus, *Jewish War* 5.451). Eventually, in an effort led by the Roman general Titus, the Roman army breached the walls of Jerusalem and destroyed most of the city, including plundering and burning down the Temple (see Figure 7.2). For the Jewish people, this was a devastating end to the rebellion against Roman imperial rule. With the city and Temple destroyed and large numbers of the population either dead or scattered to other regions, it may well have seemed like the end to the Jewish people (see Figure 7.3).

Clues to the Dating and Context of the Gospel of Mark

Although it is unlikely that the Gospel of Mark was written in Jerusalem, there are indications that the tragic events that occurred in the city from 66 to 70 CE helped shape this author's story of Jesus. In particular, Mark 13 has clear links to the Jewish War with Rome. The Markan Jesus's description of increased suffering through war, famine, and betrayal in Mark 13 matches the experience of those besieged within the walls of Jerusalem. (Recall that the term "Markan Jesus" is used to distinguish this gospel's presentation of Jesus from the historical Jesus and from the depiction of Jesus in other gospels.) These historical connections suggest a date for the Gospel of Mark close to 70 CE. Notice especially the reference to "the desolating sacrilege set up where it ought not to be" (Mark 13:14). This is an allusion to Dan 11:31, which evokes an earlier violation

FIGURE 7.3
"Judaea Capta" coin minted in Rome to commemorate victory over the Jewish rebels. The seated woman represents conquered Judea. Depicting a defeated opponent as a woman was a common means of humiliation in the Roman world.

of the Temple by a foreign presence, the Seleucid king Antiochus IV (see Chapters 1 and 2). Notably, the narrative is interrupted at this point by a direct address to the reader ("let the reader understand"). In other words, the audience of the gospel is supposed to interpret the allusion in light of events occurring in their own time.

Basics on the Gospel of Mark

Outline: Mark's story of Jesus as the suffering messiah			
	I	Rising popularity of Jesus and rising conflict with authorities	1:1–8:21
	II	Transition: passion predictions and instructions about the demands of discipleship	8:22–10:52
	III	Predictions fulfilled: the suffering messiah	11:1–16:8

Location and audience

There is no certainty about who wrote the gospel or where it was written. Church tradition has associated the gospel with the disciple Peter, claiming that Mark was Peter's "interpreter" and suggesting that Peter related these stories to Mark while he was in Rome. Many have questioned this traditional association, finding little evidence in the gospel that it is narrated from Peter's point of view. Some have theorized that the gospel was written closer to Jerusalem, perhaps in northern Galilee or Syria. At points, the narrative seems to assume a lack of familiarity with Jewish customs (7:3–4), leading some to argue that the author had primarily a gentile audience in mind or was himself a gentile Christ-follower.

The reference to Daniel also highlights the apocalyptic flavor of Mark 13. Indeed, scholars often refer to this chapter as Mark's "little apocalypse." Its presence is another indication of the influence of Jewish apocalypticism on the Jesus movement. Along with the reference to increased suffering comes the expectation of divine intervention that will reward the faithful who have endured (Mark 13:13). In addition to war and famine, the description of suffering includes persecution from synagogue and governmental authorities and hatred because of Jesus's name (Mark 13:9, 13). There is no evidence of widespread persecution of Christ-followers as early as 70 CE, but we do have reports of isolated incidents. The best-known of these is the report by the first-century CE Roman historian Tacitus, which describes Nero's persecution in Rome of a group that the populace called Christians (in Latin, *chrestianos*). According to this account, Nero used the Christians as a scapegoat for a devastating fire that swept through Rome in 64 CE (see box "Tacitus's Account of Nero's Persecution of Christians in Rome" in Chapter 12). The references to persecution in the Gospel of Mark may allude to this specific event, or they may refer more generally to increased antipathy toward Christ-followers as their growing numbers drew more attention from local authorities.

Markan Priority

Scholars use the phrase **Markan priority** to refer to the consensus opinion that the Gospel of Mark, the shortest of the four canonical gospels, was written before the other canonical gospels. Readers of the gospels did not always think this was the case. Until the nineteenth century, the Gospel of Matthew was thought to be the earliest gospel, while the Gospel of Mark was viewed as an abbreviated version of Matthew. But this theory requires an explanation for why the author of Mark would omit significant sections of the Gospel of Matthew. For example, the Gospel of Mark does not have any stories about Jesus's birth and resurrection. It begins with the story of Jesus's baptism as an adult and concludes without any scenes featuring the resurrected Jesus. Although one could imagine a writer who knew the Gospel of Matthew or Luke deciding to compose a shorter story of Jesus, it is harder to explain why such a writer would conclude that accounts of Jesus's birth and resurrection should be left out of his narrative. Observations like these have led scholars to posit that Mark was written before the other gospels. The author seems to have collected oral traditions about Jesus – stories about what he did and said – and combined them into an extended written narrative. Some scholars argue that the author built on an early written account of Jesus's suffering and death, a **passion narrative**, by adding stories about Jesus's ministry. That may be true, but we do not have any certain evidence of a pre-Markan passion narrative. For now, it is enough to understand the idea of Markan priority: the Gospel of Mark, written several decades after Jesus's death, appears to be the earliest of the biblical gospels. The theory of Markan priority is a first step in answering the question of how the canonical gospels are related, a question we discuss in more detail in the next chapter.

The Story of Jesus in the Gospel of Mark

With this evidence for the dating and context of the gospel in mind, I turn to the story itself. The Markan narrative unfolds across two main parts that are linked by a transition section. The first part of the gospel (Mark 1:1–8:21) tells the story of Jesus's miracle-working ministry, resulting in his increasing popularity among the crowds. This growing popularity among the people is juxtaposed with accounts of growing conflict with the Jerusalem authorities. The transition section (Mark 8:22–10:52) features Jesus traveling to Jerusalem from the northern region of Caesarea Philippi. On the way, the Markan Jesus tries to prepare his disciples for his coming trial and crucifixion and to instruct them in the ways of discipleship. For their part, the disciples continue a pattern of misunderstanding Jesus that is already evident in the first section. The transition section also prepares the gospel audience for a shift from the miracle-working Jesus of the first section to the stark picture of the suffering messiah featured in the second part of the gospel. This second part (Mark 11:1–16:8) focuses on Jesus's final days in Jerusalem, during which his predictions of his suffering and death are fulfilled.

The Rising Popularity of Jesus and Rising Conflict with the Authorities

READING   Read Mark 1–4; 8:1–21.

EXERCISE   Pay attention to what the Markan Jesus says and does in these chapters. How do the crowds respond to Jesus in the opening chapters? Where do you see signs of conflict between Jesus and the authorities? What are the conflicts about?

Chapters 1–8 of the gospel tell the story of the rapidly rising popularity of Jesus juxtaposed with the increasing conflict between Jesus and the Jewish authorities. The first words of the Markan Jesus take the form of a proclamation: "The time is fulfilled, and the kingdom of God has come near, repent and believe in the good news" (Mark 1:15). The first chapter of the gospel then depicts Jesus in the full range of activities that will make up his ministry in the rest of the narrative: calling disciples (Mark 1:16–20), teaching (Mark 1:21–2), casting out demons (Mark 1:23–6, 32–4, 39), and healing the sick (Mark 1:29–34, 40–2). Jesus seems to move quickly through these activities, especially because of the frequent use of the Greek word *euthus*, "immediately." This word occurs so often in this chapter, and in the first half of the gospel more generally, that English translations typically find different ways to render the term to avoid repetitiveness (see, for example, 1:10, 12, 18, 20, 21, 23, 28, 29, 30, 42, 43; also 2:8, 12; 3:6; 4:5, 15, etc.). The repetition of the word may indicate the author's limited Greek skills. Even so, the frequent references to Jesus acting "immediately" gives an impression of fast-paced activity that corresponds to Jesus's rapidly increasing fame. One reason given for Jesus's appeal is that he speaks with authority or power (Greek, *exousia*), in contrast to the scribes (Mark 1:22, 27). By the end of the chapter, the Markan Jesus is so popular that, as the narrator reports, "he was no longer able to go into a town openly . . . and people came to him from all directions" (Mark 1:45).

Mark 2 introduces the other dynamic at work in the first section of the gospel: the local authorities' increasing hostility toward Jesus. The story of the paralyzed man (Mark 2:1–12) begins as a healing story that again highlights the popularity of Jesus. The house is so full of people that those bringing the man to be healed by Jesus have to lower the man through the thatched roof (Mark 2:3–4). But the healing story soon hints at the conflict to come as the "scribes from Jerusalem" appear on the scene. The Jerusalem scribes are portrayed as "questioning in their hearts" and accusing Jesus of blasphemy (Mark 2:6–7). By chapter 3, the two themes of popularity and opposition are closely linked. After Jesus performs another healing, this time on the Sabbath, the Pharisees conspire with the Herodians about how to destroy him (Mark 3:6). Meanwhile, the very next scene shows the Markan Jesus so overwhelmed by crowds from all over Palestine that he must get into a boat on the lake to avoid being crushed (Mark 3:7–8). The juxtaposition of these two themes in the early part of the gospel produces an image of the fervent expectations around this miracle-working healer on the one hand and the lurking threat from his opponents on the other.

Here, it is worth pausing over the identity of Jesus's opponents in this gospel. They are typically identified as the scribes, Pharisees, and chief priests (for example, Mark 2:6; 3:22; 7:1; 8:31; 10:33; 11:27). Past scholarship has often assumed that these figures represented religious authorities on the written and oral Torah of Judaism, arguing that Jesus challenged these authorities in the interest of a more spiritual and humane interpretation of tradition. In the next chapter, we will return to the question of who the Pharisees actually were compared to the gospel portrayals of this group. Here, we focus on the often-unrecognized *political* dimension of the depiction of the Markan Jesus's opponents. A key to understanding this political element is the fact that Roman imperial power was exercised through local elite men. As discussed in Chapter 2, Rome could not control its vast empire through military strength alone. Instead, Roman commanders enlisted the support of local leaders who stood to benefit from cooperating with Rome. This is how the Jerusalem scribes would have functioned toward the end of the Second Temple period. They would have either worked in the Temple or been employed in government administration. In either case, they would have been perceived as working closely with Roman authorities.

In the Gospel of Mark, the scribes are depicted as authorities on scripture and tradition (Mark 9:11; 12:28, 32–3). Nevertheless, the Markan Jesus describes them as men who love public recognition and prestige but are vicious toward the disadvantaged

(Mark 12:38). Note also that the scribes are repeatedly described as coming from Jerusalem, the seat of Roman power in Judea (Mark 3:22; 7:1). Given these descriptions, it is intriguing that in Mark's gospel, Jesus's ministry begins in Galilee, the place where the Jewish revolt against Rome began. Moreover, the gospel ends with an exhortation for the disciples to return to Galilee to find the risen Jesus (Mark 16:7).

In this gospel, then, Jerusalem is the origin of the opposition to Jesus and the place where he is ultimately executed by Rome. In contrast, Galilee is the region where the revolt against Rome began, the point of origin for Jesus, and the place where he will appear to his disciples after he has been raised from the dead. A critique of Jerusalem and its leaders is evident throughout the gospel. Note that this critique pertains to more than religious matters. The gospel also offers a political critique of the way these leaders cooperated with Rome to maintain their local authority.

An Exorcism of Rome?

An allusion to Roman power (and its imagined demise) is found in the story of the demon-possessed man in Gerasene (Mark 5:1–20). In the story, Jesus arrives by boat in "the region of the Gerasenes" and encounters a demon-possessed man living among the tombs. Unlike other exorcism stories in the gospel, Jesus demands to know the name of the demon. The response, "My name is Legion," is the first clue that this exorcism may be more than a healing story (5:9). "Legion" is the term for a Roman cohort of soldiers. Caesar's tenth legion, which took part in the Jewish War and was then stationed in Jerusalem, had an image of a boar on its standards. In the story, the demon named Legion begs to be permitted to enter a herd of pigs, which then runs into the sea and drowns (5:12–13). The story contains other military terms as well. For example, the Greek term for "herd," which refers to the group of pigs, is a term that was used to refer to military recruits. Two verbs used in the story, *epetrepsen* (he permitted) and *hormesen* (they charged), are both typically used in a military context. These are subtle allusions, and not every scholar is convinced that the author had Rome in mind. To be sure, the story serves equally well as an example of Jesus's battle with Satan at the ushering in of God's reign on earth. The story may well convey both the idea of an exorcism of Rome and Jesus's battle with Satan. These two interpretations would not have been mutually exclusive for ancient readers.

Another theme that emerges quite early in the gospel concerns the identity of Jesus. In several places, the Markan Jesus makes clear that he wants to keep his identity hidden from others. Scholars have labeled this aspect of the Gospel of Mark "the **messianic secret**." Although the most striking examples of this theme will occur in the transition section (Mark 8:22–10:52), the secrecy motif is already evident in some of the early healing and exorcism stories in Mark 1–7. For example, the Markan Jesus urges those he has healed not to speak to anyone about it (Mark 1:43–4; 5:43; 7:36; see also 8:26). Similarly, Jesus silences the demons "because they knew him" (Mark 1:34; 3:11–12). We will return to this puzzling aspect of the gospel in the next section.

Related to the theme of Jesus's identity is the characterization of the disciples as followers who repeatedly misunderstand Jesus and his teaching. The first indication of the disciples' lack of comprehension appears in Mark 4. There, Jesus quotes a passage from Isaiah 6:9–10 to answer a question about why he teaches in parables:

> To you has been given the mystery of the kingdom of God, but for the ones on the outside, everything comes in parables; in order that "seeing, they may see but not perceive, and hearing, they may indeed hear, but not understand; so that they may never turn and be forgiven." (Mark 4:11–12)

Contemporary readers are often surprised by this passage. They do not expect Jesus to say that he teaches in parables so that outsiders are kept on the outside with no chance of forgiveness. Given this explanation, it is even more startling when the Markan Jesus asks the disciples: "Do you not understand this parable? Then how will you understand all the parables?" (Mark 4:13). Does this mean the disciples are on the outside?! It may be reassuring that the Markan Jesus goes on to explain the parable to them (Mark 4:14–20). Indeed, the narrator later reinforces the point that Jesus "privately explained everything to his own disciples" (Mark 4:34). Still, they do not seem to benefit from these explanations. Instead, the narrative soon turns again to the disciples' lack of understanding and also the claim that their "hearts were hardened" (Mark 6:52). This phrase is used frequently in the story of Exodus, where God hardens the Egyptian Pharaoh's heart (Exod 4:21; 7:3, 13; 8:15; 9:12). In a later scene, the Markan Jesus associates the disciples' hardened hearts with the same words that he used to describe those on the "outside" in chapter 4:

> And he ordered them, saying, "Look! Watch out for the yeast of the Pharisees and the yeast of Herod." They discussed it together, saying, "We have no bread." And perceiving it, Jesus said to them, "Why are you discussing that you have no bread? Do you not yet perceive or comprehend? Have your hearts been hardened? Having eyes, do you not see? Having ears, do you not hear?" (Mark 8:15–18; compare 4:12)

This scene ends with a final question from Jesus lingering in the air, unanswered: "Do you still not understand?" (Mark 8:21). By this point in the narrative, the ancient gospel audience themselves may not have understood what the Markan Jesus expected the disciples to "see" and "hear." They may have felt confused about what they were supposed to understand as Christ-followers. But tapping into this sense of confusion may be part of the point. Given the traumatic **destruction of the Second Temple** and the loss of the war against Rome, Christ-followers may have felt uncertain about the movement they had joined. Perhaps their initial trust in Jesus as God's messiah had included a hope for the restoration of Israel and its release from Roman occupation. Instead of experiencing such a release, the events of 70 CE demonstrated the unyielding power of Rome. For some, the devastating results of the Jewish revolt against Rome likely raised questions about whether Jesus was actually the longed-for messiah.

Contemporary Voices: The Syrophoenician Woman and the Politics of "Sass"

In Mark 7:24–30, Jesus travels north to Tyre, a mostly gentile region where a Syrophoenician woman (that is, a woman of Greek origin) asks him to cast a demon out of her daughter. Jesus responds negatively, using an expression that prioritizes Jewish "children" over gentile "dogs" (Mark 7:27). The woman responds with a clever expression that moves Jesus to change his mind: "Sir, even the dogs under the table eat the children's crumbs" (Mark 7:28).

Mitzi Smith offers a **womanist interpretation** of this Markan story (see Mitzi J. Smith, "Race, Gender, and the Politics of 'Sass': Reading Mark 7:24–30 Through a Womanist Lens of Intersectionality and Inter(con)textuality," in *Womanist Interpretations of the Bible: Expanding the Discourse* (Eugene, OR: Cascade Books, 2018), 95–112). Womanism "prioritizes and highly values black women's epistemology (ways of knowing), agency, experience, lives, and

artifacts, rather than accepting them as peripheral to white feminist thought" (96). From this perspective, the woman "talks back" or uses "sass" to call out Jesus's dismissive attitude toward her and her sick daughter. As Smith explains, "Sass is when the oppressed name, define, call out, and sometimes refuse to submit to oppressive systems and behaviors" (97). Smith powerfully links the "talking back" or "sass" of the Syrophoenician woman with the long tradition of Black women who have spoken out against oppression. In her words, "The story of the Syro-Phoenician woman shows that sass can call our attention to and challenge unjust, biased, and oppressive traditions, laws, and expectations. The power of sass can reveal and question the destructive forces at work in or against our communities" (109). For more on womanist biblical interpretation, see Resources for Further Study.

Teaching and Misunderstanding "on the Way"

READING

Read Mark 8:22–10:52.

EXERCISE

What are some general themes of Jesus's teaching in this section? What does he teach about himself? What does he teach about discipleship? How do the disciples respond?

The central section of the gospel responds to such confusion. From 8:22 to 10:52, the Markan Jesus travels with his disciples from the northern city of Caesarea Philippi southward to Jerusalem (see Map 7.1). At this point, the rapid pace of the narrative slows down and the focus shifts to Jesus's instructions to his disciples. To that end, the narrative reports several conversations between Jesus and his disciples that occur "on the way."

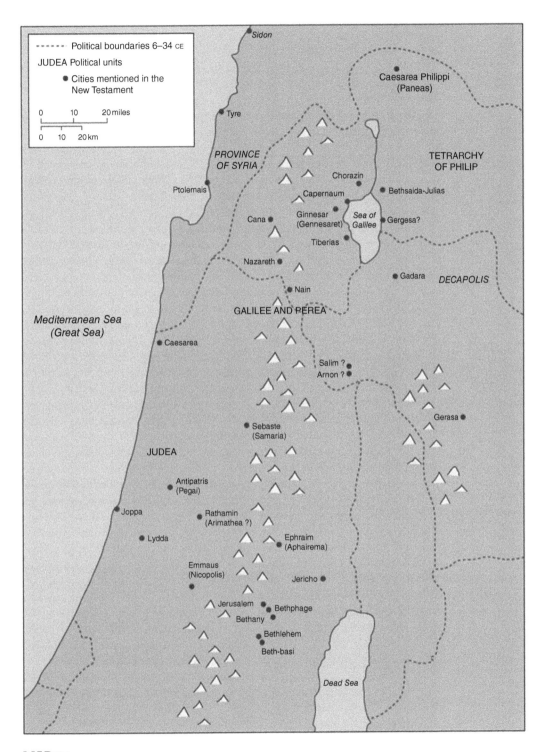

MAP 7.1

Palestine in the first century CE. Redrawn from Bart Ehrman, *The New Testament: A Historical Introduction to the Early Christian Writings* (3rd edition). Oxford: Oxford University Press, 2004, page 73.

This phrase indicates both their shared journey to Jesus's deadly confrontation with the authorities and "the way" of discipleship that Jesus teaches. The section continues themes that emerged in the first part of the gospel regarding Jesus's identity and mission and the portrayal of the disciples. In fact, the question of the Markan Jesus's identity and the repeated misunderstandings of the disciples become even more accentuated.

Note first how the author creatively frames this part of the gospel with two healing stories. The first healing story, Mark 8:22–6, is unusual because Jesus must try twice to successfully heal the blind man. After the first attempt, the man reports that he has limited vision: "I see people, but I see them as trees that are walking" (Mark 8:24). Only after Jesus's second try can the man see clearly (Mark 8:25). The story's setting suggests its symbolic significance. It comes just after Jesus's sharp questioning of the disciples' lack of understanding and just before an extended section of instruction. This placement implies that disciples are like the blind man – it will take a determined effort on Jesus's part to help them see clearly. Indeed, coming at the beginning of the teaching section, the story suggests that understanding Jesus may be a gradual and initially difficult process not just for the disciples but also for the audience of the gospel. Notably, another healing takes place at the end of the teaching section. This time, a blind beggar from the roadside calls to Jesus asking to see again (Mark 10:47–8). Jesus tells him that his faith has healed him, and significantly, the man who can now "see" immediately follows Jesus "on the way." In other words, at the end of the transition section, the narrative provides an example of a new disciple with newly acquired vision.

What are the disciples (and the gospel audience) supposed to understand as a result of the Markan Jesus's instructions? The section communicates two main ideas: the experience of suffering that awaits Jesus in Jerusalem and what it will take to be Jesus's disciple. A distinctive pattern across chapters 8–10 encourages the gospel audience to define their own discipleship in relation to the suffering, death, and resurrection of Jesus. Three times, the Markan Jesus predicts what is to happen to him when he arrives in Jerusalem (Mark 8:31; 9:31; 10:33–4). Each of these **passion predictions** ("passion" is from the Latin *passus*, "to suffer") is followed by some type of misunderstanding on the part of the disciples. In the first instance, Peter rebukes Jesus (a verb used elsewhere only for Jesus's "rebuking" of the demons). Jesus rebukes Peter in return, exclaiming, "Get behind me, Satan! You are not thinking of the things of God, but of the things of humans" (Mark 8:33). The implication is that Peter is not willing to hear of Jesus's suffering and death, which Jesus describes as the "things of God." The second passion prediction is followed by a report of an argument among the disciples about who among them is the greatest (Mark 9:33–4). The third prediction is followed by a request from James and John that they be given seats of honor beside Jesus "in his glory" (Mark 10:35–7). In each case, the disciples' response to Jesus's description of his suffering and death involves their misplaced hopes of achieving greatness with Jesus. All three times, the disciples' misunderstanding provides Jesus with an opportunity to instruct them in the ways of discipleship. Each time, in different ways, Jesus informs his companions that to follow him means to put aside greatness in favor of suffering and service. Followers of Jesus are to deny themselves, take up their crosses, be last of all, and be slaves of all (Mark 8:34–5; 9:35; 10:42–5).

Finally, this central section includes two significant passages regarding the secrecy motif in the gospel. The first passage relates a climactic moment in the Markan narrative when Jesus asks his disciples, "Who do you say that I am?" (Mark 8:27). Peter responds to Jesus's question about his identity with the statement, "You are the Christ" (Mark 8:29). (The Greek word *christos* means anointed one, translating the Hebrew word messiah.) This is the first time in the gospel that anyone has attributed this title to the Markan Jesus, and his response is emphatic: they are not to tell anyone about him (Mark 8:30). Jesus's command to secrecy at this point is why scholars have named the secrecy motif the "messianic secret." The second important passage related to the messianic secret occurs in Mark 9. Jesus takes Peter, James, and John with him up a mountain, where they see him transformed, wearing dazzling white clothes and talking with Moses and Elijah. A voice from a cloud pronounces, "This is my son the beloved. Listen to him" (9:7). After this extraordinary experience, the Markan Jesus once again warns the disciples "not to tell anyone about what they had seen until after the Son of Man had risen from the dead" (Mark 9:9). This verse may be the most significant clue to the meaning of the secrecy theme. It suggests that before moving too quickly to a glorified image of Jesus, one must first understand that as God's anointed one, Jesus will suffer and die.

More on the Messianic Secret

The messianic secret emerged as a scholarly puzzle with the 1901 publication of William Wrede's book of the same title. Wrede noticed a number of elements in Mark's narrative that contributed to a theme of secrecy around Jesus's messianic identity: Jesus's silencing of the "unclean spirit" (1:25), his commands to tell no one about his healings (1:43–4; 3:11–12; 5:43), and his order to the disciples "not to tell anyone about him" (8:30). In addition to identifying and connecting these various aspects of the text, Wrede theorized that this "messianic secret" did not originate with the historical Jesus. Instead, the motif developed as a way to explain why Jesus was not recognized as the messiah during his lifetime. In short, for Wrede, the secrecy theme in Mark's gospel is literary and apologetic rather than historical.

While Wrede's theory gained prominence in the early twentieth century, scholars eventually recognized that it did not adequately explain the evidence of the gospels. For example, it does not account for why the Markan Jesus does not *always* command secrecy and silence (see Mark 5:19–20). Nor does it explain the cases where the command to silence is *not* kept (Mark 1:40–5). To date, there is no theory that accounts for all of the elements of the gospel that have been grouped under the idea of the messianic secret.

As mentioned above, the teaching section concludes with a healing story that suggests that Jesus's instructions will contribute to the formation of new disciples with new understanding. In truth, as the story continues, those closest to Jesus do not exhibit such clear vision. There is still betrayal and denial to come. Nevertheless, Mark 8:22–10:52, framed as it is by stories of people gaining their sight, seems designed to help open the eyes of the gospel audience to the idea of a suffering messiah. The conclusion to the gospel then puts the image of such a messiah directly before them.

Mark's Suffering Messiah

The last section of the gospel is traditionally called the passion narrative because it relates the story of Jesus's suffering. It is the earliest surviving written narrative about Jesus's trial and crucifixion. As mentioned earlier, because these chapters present a sustained narrative as compared to the episodic quality of the first section of the gospel, some have hypothesized that the author used an earlier written account of the passion as a source. Whether the source was written or oral, the author relied on traditional interpretations of the last days of Jesus in writing his account. A close reading of the Markan passion narrative shows how thoroughly the story was shaped by texts from the Hebrew scriptures, especially passages from the biblical prophets and psalms. The narrative shows how early believers reread the scriptures in light of their experience of Jesus and then told the story of Jesus in light of these new scriptural interpretations. In addition to this process, we can also see the familiar Markan themes in this final section of the gospel: the conflict with the Jerusalem authorities, the disciples' failure to understand Jesus, and especially the idea of the suffering messiah.

The link between the passion narrative and the Hebrew prophetic tradition is already present in Jesus's "triumphal" entry into Jerusalem on a colt secured by his disciples (Mark 11:1–10). The procession appears to be an enactment of the following text from the prophet Zechariah:

> Rejoice greatly, O daughter Zion! Proclaim, O daughter Jerusalem! See, your king comes to you. He is just and one who saves, showing clemency and mounted on a donkey, that is, on a new colt. He will cut off the chariot from Ephraim and the horse from Jerusalem; and the bow shall be destroyed, and he shall command peace to the nations. He will rule from sea to sea, and from the river to the ends of the earth. (Zech 9:9–10)

In Zechariah, this prophecy concerns God's defeat of Israel's enemies followed by a royal procession of the victorious king into the capital city, Jerusalem. In the gospel, the crowd prepares a royal processional way for Jesus, welcoming him as a king. Their words of acclamation come from Ps 118:25–6. "Hosanna! Blessed is the one coming in the name of the Lord! Blessed is the coming kingdom of our father David! Hosanna in the highest!" (Mark 11:9–10). With these words, the gospel shows the crowd symbolically welcoming Jesus into Jerusalem as the anointed king who will bring peace to the city. Given this, the Markan Jesus's entry into the Jerusalem Temple is anticlimactic. He goes in, looks around, and then leaves because (as the text explains) it was already late (Mark 11:11). Even after the long trip to Jerusalem, Jesus and his disciples do not stay in the city but go back to the village of Bethany to spend the night. Perhaps this is a way that the author distances Jesus from Jerusalem and the Temple – he will not even stay inside the city walls. This idea is confirmed by Jesus's actions in the Temple on the following day.

Mark 11:12–21 is an example of Markan **intercalation** (see box "Intercalation, or the Markan 'Sandwich'"). In this seemingly odd account, the Markan Jesus curses a fruit-less fig tree because he is hungry, even though it is not the season for figs (11:13). He then enters the Temple again, this time causing a massive disturbance, overturning tables and driving out those who are buying and selling animals for Temple sacrifices. By way of explanation, the Markan Jesus cites a passage from Isaiah: "Is it not written, 'My house will be called a house of prayer for all the nations'? But you have made it a cave of ban-dits" (Mark 11:17; see Isa 56:7). The implication is that the Temple is infested with corrupt practices and Jesus's actions are a protest against this corruption. After the Markan Jesus leaves the Temple, the fig tree is once again the focus, as the disciples notice that it has completely withered to its roots (11:20). On the surface, the combination of the fig tree and the Temple makes little sense. Why would Jesus curse a tree for not having fruit when it is not the season for fruit? And what does a fig tree have to do with Temple corruption?

As with the entry into Jerusalem, the key to understanding this scene is found in the prophetic literature. In the Hebrew Bible/Old Testament, the eighth-century proph-ets linked corruption with the downfall of Israel and Judah. Now, the same type of prophetic critique is introduced at a time when Jerusalem is suffering through the after-math of a war with a dominant foreign power. In this case, Hos 9:10–16 appears to be the backdrop for Jesus's actions. In the Hosea passage, Israel is first identified as "the first fruit on the fig tree, in its first season" (Hos 9:10). As the text continues, it describes Israel's corruption and the resulting judgment from God: "Because of the evilness of their deeds, I will throw them out of my house" (Hos 9:15). The oracle in Hosea closes with a description of the stricken Israel: "The root is dried out. It will no longer bear fruit" (Hos 9:16). The Gospel of Mark uses the same pattern as the book of Hosea to express judgment against corruption: a fig tree with reference to its season, an expulsion from God's house/Temple, and a reference to a barren fruit tree. By evoking the figure of the corrupted and rejected fig tree/people in Hosea, the gospel writer suggests that Jesus's confrontation with the Temple authorities is in keeping with earlier prophetic expressions of God's judgment.

Intercalation, or the Markan "Sandwich"

Historically, biblical scholars have debated whether the author of Mark simply strung a series of stories about Jesus together or gave attention to narrative struc-ture. Those who argue that the author was intention-ally structuring a literary work point to places in the gospel where one story is framed by another. Scholars have called this literary device intercalation, or more descriptively, Mark's "sandwich" structure. The fig tree/Temple episode is one example of Markan interca-lation, but there are others. Mark 5:22–43 relates two healing stories: a request for healing for a synagogue leader's daughter frames an account of a lone woman who surreptitiously seeks Jesus's healing power. In this case, the intercalation increases narrative tension because the diversion created by Jesus's encounter with the woman allows enough narrative time to pass for the leader's daughter to die. Other examples of the sandwich structure include Mark 3:21–35; 6:7–30; and 14:53–72. Read these and consider how the interwoven stories comment on each other.

Other details of the passion narrative are also influenced by the Jewish scriptures, especially Isaiah and the Psalms. For instance, the Markan Jesus's silence during much of his trial recalls the servant songs of Isaiah (Mark 14:61; 15:4–5; compare Isa 53:7). Similarly, details drawn from Psalms 69 and 22 are used to fill out the description of Jesus's suffering. Just as Ps 69:4 speaks of false accusations, the gospel writer describes the opponents of Jesus bearing false witness against him (Mark 14:56). The detail of bystanders giving Jesus sour wine (Mark 15:36) echoes the description of the psalmist being given vinegar to drink (Ps 69:21). The reference to the soldiers casting lots for Jesus's clothes (Mark 15:24) recalls the psalmist's experience in Psalm 22 (Ps 22:18), and the bystanders' mockery of Jesus (Mark 15:31–2) is like the mockery of the psalmist by others (Ps 22:7–8). Finally, the Markan Jesus quotes Psalm 22 directly at the moment of his death (Mark 15:34), a point to which we will return.

A Glimpse of Life under Roman Occupation

One Markan conflict story is especially revealing in light of the reality of Roman occupation and the difficulties it posed for local residents of Judea. In this case, the Pharisees and Herodians try to trap Jesus with a politically charged question: "Is it lawful to pay a poll tax to the emperor?" (the Greek word used for tax, *kensos*, is singular and refers to a tax on every person; Mark 12:14). The tax in question was first imposed on the region when it became a province of Rome in 6 CE. At that time, resistance to the tax was mounted by a certain Judas (not the disciple of Jesus), who called on others to refuse to pay the tax (see Josephus, *Jewish War* 2.8.1 §117–18). In the Gospel of Mark, the opponents' question about paying tribute to Caesar is another iteration of the centuries-long dilemma: Israel was called on to pay tribute to a foreign nation even though doing so was understood as paying tribute to a foreign god. In other words, Jewish people had to weigh their commitment to obeying Torah regulations against the demands of their foreign rulers. There appears to be no good answer to the question asked of Jesus; "yes" would signal compliance to Rome, displeasing those who wanted to resist Roman occupation, while "no" would make Jesus a traitor in the eyes of Rome. However, the Markan Jesus's pronouncement cleverly avoids either a yes or a no. Asking his opponents to produce a coin that bears the emperor's image, Jesus retorts: "The things of the emperor give to the emperor, the things of God give to God" (Mark 12:13–17; see also Matt 22:15–22; Luke 20:20–6). Thus, one point of this conflict story is to demonstrate the rhetorical cleverness of the Markan Jesus as he bests his opponents. But the story also illustrates life under Roman occupation. The telling of this story around 70 CE would resonate with the situation of a conquered people and the pressing question of whether one should resist paying tribute to the emperor.

In addition to linking with the scriptures in these ways, the story of the Markan Jesus's arrest, trial, and crucifixion is shaped by themes introduced earlier in the gospel. Indeed, the two themes from the first part of the gospel – the growing popularity of Jesus and his increasingly deadly opposition – move toward a climax. We saw earlier how Jesus is enthusiastically welcomed by crowds into the city of Jerusalem. But this kingly procession is followed by a series of stories of conflict between Jesus and the Jerusalem authorities and their attempts to "trap him in what he said" (Mark 12:13). The relationship between the two themes is further evident in the dilemma expressed by Jesus's opposition: "The chief priests and the scribes were looking for a way to arrest Jesus by stealth and kill him; for they said, 'Not during the festival, or there may be a riot among the people'" (Mark 14:1–2).

What gives way, in the gospel story, is Jesus's popularity. As the narrative counts down days until the Passover (and Jesus's crucifixion), the adoring crowd that flocked to Jesus in Galilee, as well as the "many" who laid cloaks on the ground as he entered Jerusalem, fade from view. Instead, the last thing we hear from the crowd is its clamoring for Jesus's crucifixion (Mark 15:11–14).

Even worse, the Markan Jesus's own disciples fail him miserably in his time of need, continuing the theme of the disciples' misunderstanding and failure that emerged in the first half of the narrative. As Jesus approaches his death, he predicts the impending betrayal of one of his disciples (Mark 14:18–21), abandonment by all of them (Mark 14:27), and the denial of Peter (Mark 14:30). Although the disciples protest these predictions, all of them come to fruition (Mark 14:44–5, 50, 66–72). None of Jesus's followers or family is present in his final hour. The women followers are closest, but even they watch from far away (Mark 15:40). Most telling, however, are the Markan Jesus's final words, a quote from Psalm 22: "My God, my God, why have you abandoned me?" (Mark 15:34). The gospel provides no answer to this question.

An Enigmatic Ending

Another puzzling aspect of the gospel concerns its closing scene. The Gospel of Mark has no stories of Jesus's appearance after his resurrection from the dead. Instead, Mark 16:1–8 relates the story of the empty tomb. To be sure, this story is intended to convey to the reader that Jesus "has been raised," as the young man in white reports to the women. What is surprising is the women's response to his words. Although they are asked to go and tell the others to meet the risen Jesus in Galilee, the narrator reports that the women say nothing to anyone, for they are terrified (Mark 16:8). At this point, according to the oldest surviving manuscripts, the gospel ends.

Therein lies the problem. Why would a gospel writer end his story with the failure of devoted yet terrified women? The scribal activity around the gospel's ending suggests that at least some early Christ-followers were troubled by this abrupt ending. There were two different endings added to the gospel by later scribes. One, the "shorter ending," has the women fulfilling the command, then concludes with language unfamiliar to the Gospel of Mark about Jesus's "sacred and imperishable proclamation of eternal salvation." In a longer addition, a scribe added a series of resurrection appearances, some of which are found in other canonical gospels. But these two added endings to the gospel only reinforce the problem of the original ending. Some scholars note that ancient manuscripts often suffered damage and argue that a more complete ending of Mark was lost when part of the original manuscript broke off. Others, however, think that this is precisely how the author intended the gospel to end. These interpreters focus on the potential impact of the ending on the audience. Perhaps the fear of the women matches the audience's own fear in a time of political turmoil. The ending may be a way of empathizing with this emotion. Alternatively, the silent women may act as literary foils for the audience, presenting a negative example of discipleship that the audience can surpass if they boldly spread the gospel to others. As the narrative form of the gospel allows for multiple interpretations, the gospel is truly open-ended.

Mark 12:1–12

We conclude with a closer look at a parable that conveys several of the gospel's themes: the parable of the vineyard in Mark 12:1–12. In fact, Mary Ann Tolbert has called this parable a "plot synopsis" of the gospel. It is a sharp indictment of the Jerusalem leaders. The context of the parable is a challenge to the Markan Jesus's authority in which the chief priests, scribes, and elders ask him directly, "By what authority are you doing these things? Who gave you this authority to do them?" (Mark 11:28). Jesus first responds with a question concerning the authority of John the Baptist that the Jerusalem leaders are at a loss to answer (Mark 11:29–33). He then tells the parable.

The parable begins with an allusion to Isa 5:1–7, another parable of judgment. However, as we will see, the focus of God's wrath is different in the Markan parable. Both texts begin with the careful preparation of a vineyard. In Isaiah 5, the vineyard allegorically represents Israel and Judah, which yielded wild rather than cultivated grapes despite God's care. That is, the two kingdoms produced corruption instead of justice, thus incurring God's judgment. The image of Israel and Judah as a vineyard gone wrong is also used by Jeremiah (2:21), Ezekiel (19:10–14), and Hosea (10:1).

In Mark 12, however, the problem is not with the vineyard itself. Instead, the critique is directed toward the tenants who are charged with caring for the vineyard. The tenants kill the many slaves who are sent to collect produce from them. In the Markan parable, these "slaves" likely represent the line of prophets who have been sent by God and rejected. The tension of the parable rises as the vineyard owner decides to send his "beloved son," assuming that the tenants would not dare to kill him. The "beloved son" is an obvious reference to Jesus (see Mark 1:11; 9:7). The tenants do not hesitate to kill the beloved son so that they will gain the son's inheritance. So, too, in the Gospel of Mark, the Jerusalem authorities plan for the death of Jesus. In this way, the parable of the vineyard serves as a prediction of Jesus's death as well as an indictment of the authorities who seek to kill him. Notably, the parable elicits sympathy for the vineyard owner – the one who wields power – rather than for the tenant workers who rebel against his authority. Indeed, in this version of the parable, the audience is intended to approve of the punitive actions of the vineyard owner, who "will come and destroy the tenants and give the vineyard to others" (Mark 12:9 NRSV).

In the political and religious context of the gospel, this reappropriation of the Isaiah's vineyard prophecy operates on multiple levels. In Isaiah's vineyard story, it is God (through Assyria) who brings destruction upon Israel, the vineyard. In the Markan parable, the vineyard owner/God is coming to destroy not the vineyard but its tenants. In the larger context of the gospel, these tenants represent the elite Jewish leadership. Their destruction in the parable corresponds to what happened historically: Rome brought destruction on Jerusalem, decimating its leaders and devastating what was once the center of power in the region. In this way, the gospel alludes to Rome as the agent of God's wrath that carries out God's judgment against the elite men (the chief priests, scribes, and elders) responsible for the death of Jesus. Indeed, the parable suggests that the destruction of Jerusalem and the Temple, and the resulting loss of authority for the Temple priests and scribes is God's just punishment for their unjust behavior. The parable goes on to suggest that the vineyard will be given to others as part of this divine intervention.

Past interpretations of the parable, influenced by supersessionist interpretations of Christianity, saw these "others" as the gentile church of emerging Christianity. In this misreading of the parable, Judaism was destroyed and God's people were now the gentile Christian church. However, as we have seen, it is not Israel/the vineyard that is destroyed in Mark's version, but the leaders/tenants. The "others" to whom the vineyard will be given in the parable represent the new, faithful Christ-followers who will replace the corrupt leaders (who were in power, in part, because of collaboration with Rome). One possible reading of the Markan parable, then, is that God is working in mysterious ways, using Rome to destroy the Temple because it was a source of economic exploitation that was corrupted by authorities who cooperated with Rome. The parable suggests that the Temple's destruction made possible the emergence of a new leadership for a renewed Israel, a community that will be a place of prayer for all the nations (Mark 11:17). Here, we should note the mixed portrayal of Rome in the gospel. It is both an oppressive enemy and, in this case, a destructive agent of God. This is another example of the ambivalent attitude that often results between the colonizer and the colonized. Rome is the ever-present dominant power, whether seen as a political oppressor or as a deliverer of divine justice against other, more localized opponents.

The parable concludes with a scriptural citation, this time by way of direct quotation. The Markan Jesus asks, "Have you not read this scripture: 'The stone that the builders rejected has become the cornerstone; this was the Lord's doing, and it is amazing in our eyes'?" (Mark 12:10–11; see Ps 118:22–3). The link between Jesus and various "stone sayings" appears to be an early and well-established tradition (see Rom 9:32–3; Eph 2:20; Acts 4:11; 1 Pet 2:4–8). The gospel writer draws on the stone tradition here to shift the focus from the judgment of Jesus's opponents to the vindication of God's "beloved son." Thus, the parable tells the whole story of God's work in Jesus Christ: the sending of the son, his rejection and crucifixion, and eventually – with this stone saying – the resurrection by which he will become the "cornerstone" of the new community of Christ-followers.

Finally, note that in this case, "those outside" have no difficulty understanding that the parable is told against them (Mark 12:12). This parable differs, then, from the earlier explanation about why Jesus teaches in parables. The opponents of Jesus *do* hear and understand this parable. Perhaps the ancient audience was meant to draw a similar lesson: that in spite of the present dismal circumstances, God is still working in the world, in the midst of Roman occupation and perhaps even *through* Roman occupation, to restore the people of God.

CHAPTER SEVEN REVIEW

1 Know the meaning and significance of the following terms:
   - destruction of the Second Temple
   - intercalation
   - Jewish War
   - Markan priority
   - messianic secret
   - passion narrative
   - passion prediction
   - womanist interpretation
2 Why do scholars typically date the Gospel of Mark to around 70 CE?

3 What are some possible reasons why the author portrayed the disciples as repeatedly misunderstanding Jesus?
4 How does the presentation of Jesus in the Gospel of Mark fit with the historical circumstances at the time the gospel was written?
5 (Focus text: Mark 12:1–12) What is the difference between Isaiah's use of vineyard imagery and the use of the vineyard in the Markan parable? How does our understanding of the parable's meaning change if we read it with an awareness of Rome's destruction of the Second Temple and Jerusalem?

RESOURCES FOR FURTHER STUDY

Beavis, Mary Ann. *Mark*. Grand Rapids, MI: Baker Academic, 2011.

Black, C. Clifton. *Mark*. Nashville, TN: Abingdon Press, 2011.

Carter, Warren. *Mark*. Collegeville, MN: Liturgical Press, 2019.

Collins, Adela Yarbro. *Mark: A Commentary*. Philadelphia, PA: Fortress, 2007.

Leander, Hans. *Discourses of Empire: The Gospel of Mark from a Postcolonial Perspective*. Atlanta, GA: Society of Biblical Literature, 2013.

Tolbert, Mary Ann. *Sowing the Gospel: Mark's World in Literary-Historical Perspective*. Minneapolis, MN: Fortress Press, 1989.

For further study of womanist biblical interpretation:

Bryon, Gay L., and Vanessa Lovelace, eds. *Womanist Interpretations of the Bible: Expanding the Discourse*. Atlanta, GA: Society of Biblical Literature, 2016.

Junior, Nyasha. *An Introduction to Womanist Interpretation*. Louisville, KY: Westminster John Knox Press, 2015.

Smith, Mitzi. *Womanist Sass and Talk Back: Social (In)justice, Intersectionality, and Biblical Interpretation*. Eugene, OR: Cascade Books, 2018.

The Gospel of Matthew: Defining Community in the Wake of Destruction

8

Chapter Outline

Chapter Overview	**133**
The Synoptic Problem	**134**
The Structure of the Gospel of Matthew	**136**
The Matthean Jesus and Jewish Tradition	**138**
The Matthean Jesus, Righteousness, and Torah Obedience	**140**
The Matthean Jesus, Wisdom, and Torah	**142**
Matthew's Apocalyptic Vision and the Kingdom of Heaven	**143**
The Matthean Polemic against the Pharisees	**146**
Focus Text: Matt 25:31–46	**150**
Chapter Eight Review	**152**
Resources for Further Study	**153**

Chapter Overview

When the gospel writers tell their stories of Jesus, they do so on the other side of the destruction of the Jerusalem Temple by the Romans. Whereas the Gospel of Mark reflects a time of suffering, fear, and uncertainty in the immediate aftermath of this event, the Gospel of Matthew addresses the early stages of community rebuilding and redefinition a decade or more later. Once again, a foreign imperial power had destroyed a major symbol of Jewish religious and cultural identity. This meant that the Jewish community was once more facing threats to their very survival as a distinctive group in the midst of a powerful imperial presence. In this historical context, the Gospel of Matthew encourages Christ-followers to maintain their connection to the other major symbol of Judaism in the first century CE – the Torah. This chapter will show how the gospel links Jesus to the Torah in multiple ways. It also details another strategy of group survival adopted by the author: vilifying one's perceived opponents. Before beginning the study of the Gospel of Matthew, I discuss a theory adopted by

The New Testament: A Contemporary Introduction, First Edition. Colleen M. Conway.
© 2023 John Wiley & Sons Ltd. Published 2023 by John Wiley & Sons Ltd.

scholars for the academic study of the gospels. Understanding this theory is crucial for interpreting the story of the Matthean Jesus.

READING

Using either your Bible or *Gospel Parallels*, compare the passages listed below. For now, our interest is not in the meaning of these passages. Instead, focus only on their content. To make this work easier, you can use this useful website for comparing the gospels: http://sites.utoronto.ca/religion/synopsis

- **Healing of the Paralytic: Mark 2:12; Matt 9:1–8; Luke 5:17–26**
- **Stilling of the Storm: Mark 4:35–41; Matt 8:23–7; Luke 8:22–5**
- **A House Divided: 3:23–30; Matt 12:25–37: Luke 11:17–23**

EXERCISE

What do you observe from doing these comparisons? What questions do you have as a result?

The Synoptic Problem

If you did the exercise above, you no doubt noticed that the gospels of Matthew, Mark, and Luke are very similar in many places. In fact, some of the gospels' material has identical wording. A close look across these three gospels would also show how individual stories often follow the same sequence. Because these three gospels are similar enough that such comparisons are possible, they are called the **synoptic gospels**. This term means that one can "see" (optic) the gospels "together" (syn). The Gospel of John is not so easily compared. Many of its scenes are unique among the gospels and for this reason, it is not counted as a synoptic gospel.

As we saw in the last chapter, the Gospel of Mark is widely considered to be the earliest canonical gospel. How, then, do the other canonical gospels relate to this earliest one? Did the other gospel writers know about the Gospel of Mark? If so, did they have a copy of it? Did they build on the Gospel of Mark to write their own gospels? Such questions define what scholars call the **synoptic problem**. Understanding the consensus solution to this problem is foundational to the academic study of the gospels.

Because the gospels of Matthew and Luke parallel the Gospel of Mark in many places, most scholars think that the authors of Matthew and Luke used the earlier gospel as a source for their own. At the same time, evidence like the differing birth and resurrection accounts in Matthew and Luke suggests that their authors did not know of each other's work. Instead, it appears that each author had a copy of the Gospel of Mark that they incorporated in their own gospels to different extents. The author of Matthew incorporated about ninety percent of the Gospel of Mark in his narrative, whereas the author of Luke used about half of it. The two authors also edited this source differently to suit their own thematic purposes, as we will see in our discussion of each of these two gospels.

So far, so good: we know of one source for the gospels of Matthew and Luke. But knowing of this one source does not explain all the similarities and differences that we see when doing a close comparison of the gospels. The gospels of Matthew and Luke share

Two-Source Hypothesis

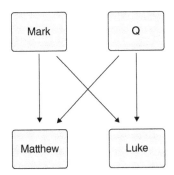

FIGURE 8.1
A diagram of the synoptic relationships.

many sayings of Jesus that are *not* in the Gospel of Mark. The famous teaching of Jesus known as the "beatitudes" or "blessings" is an example of this type of shared material (compare Matt 5:3–12 with Luke 6:20–3). What is striking about this material is that the authors often use identical wording. This would be surprising if they were recording material that they had heard. Instead, scholars posit that the two authors had access to another written source that was a collection of Jesus's sayings. This hypothetical source is commonly referred to as **Q**, an abbreviation of the German word for source, *Quelle*.

Putting these two ideas together, we arrive at what is known as the **two-source hypothesis** (or two-source theory; see Figure 8.1). The theory provides a convincing solution to the synoptic problem: the authors of Matthew and Luke each independently incorporated parts of the Gospel of Mark and parts of Q into their narratives. In both cases, the authors also revised and expanded their sources to shape their own stories of Jesus. We can easily study how the authors adapted the Gospel of Mark. It is harder to know how they worked with Q since we do not have a copy of the source.

More about the Q Document

The theory that a now-lost collection of Jesus's sayings was used as a source for the gospels has been the scholarly consensus for more than one hundred years. Evidence that Q was a written source rather than an oral one includes the near-identical wording of much of the material shared between Matthew and Luke, as well as the similar sequencing of sayings; these features would be unlikely if the sayings had been transmitted orally. Also, the fact that the sayings shared between Matthew and Luke are identical in *Greek* is significant. As Jesus's native tongue was Aramaic, it is hard to account for identical Greek renderings of his sayings unless they were written down. In addition, the discovery of the Gospel of Thomas in 1945 lent more evidence to the theory. The Gospel of Thomas, found in Egypt along with a collection of other early Christian writings, is a list of sayings of Jesus. While it is not Q, the existence of this separate written collection of sayings supports the idea that such collections existed in the early days of the Jesus movement. Some scholars have posited detailed reconstructions of the hypothetical Q document, but others are skeptical that such a project is possible.

One last piece of the solution to the synoptic problem remains. Passages such as the birth narratives and resurrection accounts show that the gospels of Matthew and Luke also contain stories and sayings of Jesus that are unique to each of these gospels. Scholars have designated this type of material **Special M** and **Special L** passages.

The position I have detailed in this section has been the consensus in gospel studies for more than a century. This two-source solution to the synoptic problem has proved enormously influential for the academic study of the gospels. The solution provides a way of understanding how the gospel writers edited and added to their sources. This makes it possible to better discern what each author wanted to convey about Jesus and the meaning of discipleship. Still, from a student's perspective, the composition of the gospels is likely far more complex than first imagined. Rather than being written by disciples of Jesus named Matthew, Mark, Luke, and John, each of the gospels was written anonymously. Rather than being eyewitness accounts, each of the gospels is a blend of oral and written traditions about Jesus along with creative additions by the gospel writers. Moreover, two of the gospels were based on an earlier one. Finally, all of the gospel writers shaped their stories of Jesus to address their own social and historical contexts decades after his crucifixion by the Romans.

All that said, students who encounter these ideas for the first time often still want to know which gospel is the most historically accurate. Or, after learning that these gospels were *not* written by eyewitnesses, they wonder how we can know whether the gospels accurately convey what Jesus did and said. As we saw in Chapter 2, these are questions about the historical Jesus. Such questions are difficult (if not impossible) to answer, and they are not central to our task here. The goal of this introduction is to understand and appreciate the differing gospel stories of Jesus in their own historical contexts. We have already seen how Mark's gospel presents Jesus as the suffering messiah. Now, we examine how Matthew reshaped the Gospel of Mark to address the historical situation a decade or more after the destruction of the Second Temple.

The Structure of the Gospel of Matthew

The first indication of Matthew's creative reshaping of Mark's gospel lies in the different way he structured his gospel compared to Mark. A comparison with one scene in the Gospel of Mark illustrates the point. The opening chapter of Mark's gospel says that Jesus "went into the synagogue and was teaching" (Mark 1:21). The response from the crowd is astonishment because "he taught them as one having authority and not as the scribes" (Mark 1:22). The Gospel of Mark shows *that* Jesus teaches but not *what* he teaches. The Gospel of Matthew uses this same scene from Mark, but with a major difference: Matthew's version of the scene comes in Matt 7:28–9, standing as a conclusion to three full chapters telling us what Jesus taught (Matthew 5–7). This extensive collection of teachings is the first of five sections of the gospel that contain sayings of Jesus. In between these collections of sayings, called discourse sections, one finds the story about Jesus, the narrative sections. The result is a gospel that alternates between teachings by Jesus and stories about Jesus. Each of the discourse sections is marked by a concluding formula, such as "when Jesus had finished saying these things" (Matt 7:28; 11:1; 13:53; 19:1; 26:1). This alternating structure (see the outline in "Basics on the Gospel of Matthew") contributes to the depiction of the Matthean Jesus as a teacher and guide for Christ-followers in the late first century CE.

Basics on the Gospel of Matthew

The following outline illustrates the Gospel of Matthew's five-part alternation of narrative and discourse. The narrative sections are often a loose collection of traditions about Jesus, while the discourse material collects sayings of similar types.

I	Introduction: Jesus's birth narrative	1–2	**Outline: Matthew's reshaping of the story of Jesus**
II	Five-part alternation of narrative and discourse	3–25	
	A. The beginning of Jesus's ministry	3–7	
	1. Narrative: baptism, temptation, and gathering of disciples	3–4	
	2. Discourse: Sermon on the Mount	5–7	
	B. Ministry in Galilee	8–10	
	1. Narrative: the healing ministry of Jesus	8–9	
	2. Discourse: instructions for the twelve disciples	10	
	C. Opposition to and conflict with Jesus	11–13	
	1. Narrative: stories of conflict	11–12	
	2. Discourse: parables of the kingdom	13	
	D. The power of Christ and life in the church	14–18	
	1. Narrative: nature, miracle traditions, passion predictions	14–17	
	2. Discourse: parables and instruction on life in the community	18	
	E. Journey and teaching in Jerusalem	19–25	
	1. Narrative: testing of Jesus	19–22	
	2. Discourse: "woes" and teaching on the coming judgment	23–5	
III	Passion narrative and resurrection accounts	26–8	

We have no certainty about where Matthew was written. However, there is good evidence for locating its origin in Antioch of Syria. Matthew is cited frequently in the letters of Ignatius, bishop of Antioch, in the second century CE. Another early Christian text that was used in Syria, the Didache, makes frequent use of the Gospel of Matthew. Finally, in Matt 4:24, the author adds to the material he gets from his Markan source, inserting the phrase that Jesus's fame "spread throughout all of Syria."

Location and author

Although the gospel was written anonymously, church tradition associated it with the disciple Matthew. It is unclear why the association would be with Matthew in particular. Perhaps someone with the name of Matthew was prominent in the early communities that read this gospel. The gospel's focus on Jesus in relation to the Torah suggests a Jewish author, as do the ambivalent references to gentiles (e.g., Matt 5:47; 6:7, 32; 10:5).

The Matthean Jesus and Jewish Tradition

In Chapter 1, I discussed the trauma of the Babylonian exile and how the end of the exile came when Persia conquered Babylon. However, the post-exilic period was not easy. It took an extended period of communal recovery and redefinition for the Jewish community to move forward. Two key events took place during that time: the rebuilding of the Jerusalem Temple and the establishment of the Torah as central to Jewish life.

Now, some five hundred years later, the destruction of the Second Temple brought a renewed crisis of identity and a new threat to communal survival. With one major symbol of Judaism gone, Jewish leaders studied the Torah with renewed vigor as a way of defining and sustaining the post-Temple Jewish community. The author of Matthew can be seen as one such leader. He was also a Christ-follower. This is the context to keep in mind as we explore this gospel's focus on Jesus and Jewish tradition, especially the Torah of Moses.

READING

Read Matthew 1–2.

EXERCISE

Notice the different explicit and implicit ways that the author connects the story of Jesus to traditions from the Hebrew scriptures. (Hint: for an example of an implicit connection, compare Matt 2:16 with Exod 1:15–16.)

The story of Jesus's birth as related in Matthew 1–2 (Special M material) opens with a genealogy that links Jesus to King David and Abraham, two key figures for Judaism in the first century CE (see Matt 1:1). Once this lineage for Jesus is established, the gospel moves to the story of his conception and birth. In Matthew's gospel, an angel appears to Joseph in a dream explaining why he should follow through on his impending marriage to Mary despite her surprising pregnancy. The angel predicts that "She will bear a son, and you are to name him Jesus, for he will save his people from their sins" (Matt 1:21). The focus on Jesus as teaching in the Gospel of Matthew suggests that a significant part of his saving activity includes advocating a life of righteousness through obeying the Torah. This is because Torah obedience is a way of avoiding sin.

Following this important statement, the narrator uses the first of 14 **fulfillment citations** (see also Matt 2:15, 17, 23; 4:14; 5:17; 8:17; 12:17, etc.). As we saw with the apostle Paul, Christ-followers often creatively reread the Jewish scriptures to interpret their experience of Jesus within the history and tradition of Judaism. This is certainly the case for the author of Matthew, who turned to the biblical prophets to show how Jesus "fulfilled" scripture. The first fulfillment citation offers an example of such a creative reading of an ancient prophetic text, Isaiah 7, to fit a new context. In its eighth-century context, the prophet Isaiah used the symbol of a newborn child to signal the imminent invasion of Assyria. But this symbol serves a new purpose as it is cited in the opening of the Gospel of Matthew: the phrase "God is with us" suggests a prophetic fulfillment connected to the birth of Jesus.

> All this came about in order to fulfill what had been said by the Lord through the prophet: "Look, the virgin shall conceive and bear a son, and they shall name him Emmanuel," which means, "God is with us." (Matt 1:22–3; compare LXX Isaiah 7:14)

Moreover, in the Gospel of Matthew, the fulfillment citation helps to frame the entire gospel with the idea of God's presence mediated through Jesus. The very last verse of the gospel offers the closing frame, where the resurrected Jesus pronounces "And remember, I am with you always, to the end of the age" (Matt 28:20). Literary features such as this framing device point to the creative thought behind the gospel's composition.

Gender and Matthew's Genealogy (Matt 1:1–17)

As is typical for biblical genealogies, the Matthean genealogy of Jesus traces his patrilineal line. Atypically, four women are mentioned in the midst of this line of fathers – Tamar, Rahab, Ruth, and the wife of Uriah (that is, Bathsheba). Scholars have puzzled over why these four women are listed. One possibility lies in the women's marginal status. All four of these biblical figures are portrayed as sexually suspect or as foreigners with whom God worked in unconventional ways (or both). They may be included in the genealogy to put Mary in this same line. Some readers of the gospel argue that the women's presence in the genealogy is a way of subverting patrilineal tradition. They also point to the genealogy's conclusion, which deviates from the patriarchal formula used throughout the genealogy: Joseph is not described as the man who "begot" Jesus. Instead, he is listed as "the husband of Mary, of whom Jesus was born" (Matt 1:16). The shift in wording may be a way of indicating that in the Matthean birth narrative that follows, Joseph is not the biological father of Jesus. Whatever the reason for including the four women plus Mary, the genealogy places Jesus in a line of honorable masculine ancestry that includes – through Joseph – both the founding father of Judaism and the founder of Judea's royal dynasty line.

More of the author's creativity is evident in how the story of Jesus's birth alludes to Moses, another central figure in the Jewish tradition. In the opening lines of Exodus, the Egyptian Pharaoh orders the slaughter of all sons born to Hebrew women (Exod 1:15–16). Similarly, in Matthew's birth story, King Herod (the same client king discussed in Chapter 2 of this textbook) orders the killing of all children younger than two years of age. Like the biblical Pharoah, Herod's aim is to eliminate a perceived threat to his power (Matt 2:16). While we have no historical evidence that Herod ordered a mass murder of young children, the brutality of the character of Herod in the gospel does reflect the nature of his reign. Moreover, Herod did have several of his *own* children executed during his rule. Additional literary allusions to Exodus include Joseph and his family fleeing by night to Egypt to save his family from Herod (Matt 2:13–14). There is even a shared motif of trickery: Herod realizes that the three eastern astrologers (Greek, *magoi*) have failed to report back to him as instructed, much like the Hebrew midwives ignore the instructions of the Pharaoh in Exodus (Matt 2:1–16). In these ways, the story of Jesus's birth in the gospel recalls the story of Moses, who was highly esteemed in the Jewish tradition as both prophet and lawgiver by the first century CE.

The Matthean birth story would resonate with the first-century CE audience of the gospel in other ways as well. In the aftermath of the destruction of Jerusalem and the Second Temple by Rome, the story of the infant Jesus's escape from a murderous ruler would signal resistance to Roman imperial power, including Rome's local representatives. On this last point, notice how closely the story links Jewish leaders to Herod's nefarious acts. Frightened by news of the birth of "the king of the Jews," the client king Herod asks the chief priest and scribes about the expected birthplace of the messiah. The story depicts the local Jewish leaders informing Herod without hesitation. They even quote a scriptural passage that reinforces the identity of the messiah as a "ruler" (Greek, *hegoumenos*; Matt 2:3–6). In other words, the gospel portrays the Jewish leadership as cooperating with Roman power and stoking the fears of Herod.

The Matthean Jesus, Righteousness, and Torah Obedience

READING

Read Matthew 5–7.

EXERCISE

How does the Matthean version of Jesus's blessings differ from the Lukan version (Matt 5:3–12; compare Luke 6:20–6)?

In Matthew 5–7, the Matthean Jesus delivers what is known as the **Sermon on the Mount**. Much of this material comes from the Q source, as a comparison with Luke 6:20–5 demonstrates. Matthew 5–7 also make up the first of the five discourse sections in the gospel. More like a series of teachings than a sermon, this first discourse develops central themes of the gospel. It builds on the connection of Jesus to the Torah of Moses, beginning with the setting of the discourse. The Matthean Jesus ascends to a mountain to teach about the law, much like the figure of Moses, who ascended Mount Sinai to receive the commandments from God (Exod 19:20; note the location of the sermon on a "level place" in Luke 6:17).

The discourse also builds on the idea of "righteousness" (Greek, *dikaiosune*). Words built from the Greek root *dike* (pronounced "deekay") have a range of meanings that include being just or fair or doing what God requires. For example, being "righteous" (*dikaios*), Joseph wants to avoid publicly humiliating Mary (Matt 1:19). The idea of righteousness is also present at the inauguration of the Matthean Jesus's ministry. When John the Baptist resists the idea of baptizing Jesus, Jesus responds, "Let it be for now; for it is fitting for us to fulfill all righteousness" (Matt 3:15). Then, in his first extended teaching in the gospel, the Matthean Jesus turns repeatedly to the concept of righteousness. He pronounces a blessing on those who "hunger and thirst for righteousness" (Matt 5:6) as well as on those who are "persecuted because of righteousness" (Matt 5:10). He warns his audience that ". . . unless your righteousness exceeds that of the scribes and Pharisees, you will never enter the kingdom of heaven" (5:20 NRSV). Later in the discourse, the Matthean Jesus urges his listeners not to worry about food or clothing but to "seek first for the kingdom of God and its righteousness" (Matt 6:33).

The repeated use of *dike* words shows that acting justly is a central concern for the author. In fact, some form of the *dike* root occurs more than twenty-five times in the gospel. What, then, does "righteousness" look like for the author? How would one know if one was being righteous? For a Jewish person living in the first century CE, the answer would be clear – being righteous required obeying God's law, which was the same as doing the will of God. This is one of the central ideas developed in Matthew 5–7. The Matthean Jesus first asserts that he has come to fulfill the law and the prophets (thus reinforcing the fulfillment citations). He insists that not one bit of the law will pass away before "all comes to be" (Matt 5:17–18). In this way, the fulfillment of the entire law (not its destruction) is linked to eschatological events. Then, toward the end of the first teaching section, Jesus observes:

> Not all who say to me, "Lord, Lord," will enter the kingdom of heaven, but the one who does the will of my Father in heaven. Many will say to me on that day, "Lord, Lord, did we not prophesy in your name, and cast out demons in your name, and do many deeds of power in your name?" Then I will declare to them, "I never recognized you, depart from me, workers of lawlessness." (7:21–3 modified from NRSV)

With this statement, the Matthean Jesus contrasts doers of the will of God with doers of *anomia* – a Greek word that literally means "no-law." In other words, for this author, doing powerful acts in the name of Jesus is not enough without practicing obedience to the Torah. One can see this idea expressed more positively in the following example. Note the subtle changes that the author of Matthew makes to his source, the Gospel of Mark:

Gospel of Mark (10:17–19)	Gospel of Matthew (19:16–18)
And as he was setting out on his journey, a man ran up and knelt before him, and asked him, "Good Teacher, what must I do to inherit eternal life?" And Jesus said to him, "Why do you call me good? No one is good but God alone. You know the commandments."	And behold, one came up to him, saying, "Teacher, what good thing must I do to have eternal life?" And he said to him, "Why do you ask me about 'the good'? One only is good. If you want to enter life, keep the commandments."

Here, the author purposely rewords the story from Mark so that the word "good" is repurposed to become a question of *doing* good. In response, the Matthean Jesus states that entering "life" requires keeping the commandments. Contemporary readers might understand this statement to refer to the well-known "Ten Commandments," especially because Jesus goes on to list some of them in this passage. Nevertheless, in the context of first-century CE Judaism, "keeping the commandments" would mean obeying the whole of the Torah. We know that the author shares this view from the claim that not the smallest bit of the law would pass away before "all comes to be." The Matthean Jesus further emphasizes keeping the whole of the Torah with the following warning: "whoever loosens one of the least of these commandments, and teaches others to do the same, will be called least in the kingdom of heaven; but whoever does them and teaches them will be called great in the kingdom of heaven" (5:19 modified from NRSV).

Taken together, these passages define being "righteous" as obeying the Torah and describe such obedience as an entry requirement for God's kingdom. Along with this focus on obedience come instructions for how to practice it. The Matthean Jesus offers several examples of "making a fence around the law." This idea is found in the opening lines of a book in the Jewish Mishnah, a collection of early rabbinic teachings. The "fence around the law" refers to the practice of adding requirements to a Torah commandment to help ensure obedience to the Torah. Consider the "fence" that is constructed in the first of a series of such teachings in Matthew 5:

> You have heard that it was said to those of ancient times, "You shall not murder"; and "whoever murders shall be liable to judgment." But I say to you that if you are angry with a brother or sister, you will be liable to judgment; and if you insult a brother or sister, you will be liable to the council; and if you say, "You fool," you will be liable to the hell of fire. (Matt 5:21–2 NRSV)

Note the underlying logic of this teaching. If one does not even get angry or insult another Christ-follower, one is certainly not going to kill him or her. In this way, one can be sure to keep the Torah commandment. This same pattern of instruction continues in Matt 5:27, 31, 33, 38, and 43. In each case, the Matthean Jesus extends the requirements of the commandment, thereby offering a way for Christ-followers to exceed the righteousness of the scribes and Pharisees (Matt 5:20) and to be "perfect" or "complete," as he calls on his followers to be (Matt 5:48).

To be sure, from the author's perspective, Torah obedience is not the only entry requirement. At the conclusion of the gospel, the Matthean Jesus instructs his disciples to make disciples of "all nations" (Greek, *ethne*) and to baptize them (Matt 28:19). However, the gospel also includes final instructions for the disciples to teach those baptized "to obey everything that I have commanded you" (28:19–20). One who has read the gospel carefully knows that the Matthean Jesus has commanded Torah obedience.

The Matthean Jesus, Wisdom, and Torah

The gospel writer connects Jesus with the Torah in yet another way. Before the Gospel of Matthew was written, early traditions about Jesus associated him with the figure of personified Wisdom found in Jewish wisdom literature. For example, a Q saying features

Jesus defending himself against his opponents by asserting, "Wisdom is justified by her deeds" (Matt 11:19; Luke 7:35). In the Gospel of Matthew, this association of Jesus with personified Wisdom is developed further. Compare these sayings spoken by Wisdom in the second-century BCE book of Sirach and by the Matthean Jesus:

Come to me, those who desire me, and be filled from my harvest. (Sirach 24:19) Put your neck under the yoke, and let your soul welcome instruction; it is close by to find. (Sirach 51:26)	Come to me, all those who are weary and burdened, and I will give you rest. Take my yoke upon you, and learn from me; for I am lenient and humble in heart, and you will find rest for your souls. For my yoke is easy to bear, and my burden is light. (Matt 11:28–30)

Reading these passages together, we can see that the Matthean Jesus is speaking Wisdom's words. While the citation is not an exact quotation from Sirach, an audience familiar with the Wisdom tradition would make the connection between Jesus and God's Wisdom. Another statement about Wisdom from the book of Sirach is especially significant for understanding the Matthean Jesus. Following a speech by personified Wisdom, Ben Sira (the author of Sirach) claims, "all these things are the book of the covenant of the Most High God, which is the law that Moses commanded us" (Sirach 24:23). In other words, this Second Temple writer understands God's Wisdom and God's Torah to be the same thing! The link between the Wisdom tradition and Torah continued into the first century CE, so that when the Matthean Jesus speaks in the words of personified Wisdom, he speaks also as a personified Torah.

Thus, the Gospel of Matthew links Jesus with the Torah in multiple ways – Jesus teaches about the Torah, advocates obedience to the Torah, and in a sense embodies both Wisdom and the Torah. The Matthean Jesus expresses this last association most clearly in Matt 18:20, when he claims, ". . . where two or three are gathered in my name, I am there among them." Compare these words to the following saying from the same book from the Mishnah mentioned above: "when the words of Torah pass between two who are studying, the Presence is with them" (*Avot* 3.3). In Jewish tradition, "the Presence" (Hebrew *shekinah*) refers to God's presence. Like this rabbinic teaching about Torah study, the Matthean Jesus teaches his followers that gathering "in his name" will be a means to experience his divine presence. Given all that we have already seen in the gospel, the author does not mean that Jesus *replaces* the Torah. Instead, he understands that being a follower of Jesus offers a way of obeying the Torah – that is, of doing "the will of the Father" (Matt 7:21).

Matthew's Apocalyptic Vision and the Kingdom of Heaven

Read Matthew 13, 18, 22, and 25.

READING

Focus on the different ways that Jesus describes the kingdom of heaven and who can gain entry to it.

EXERCISE

Another distinctive element of the Gospel of Matthew relates to Jesus's instructions about the coming kingdom of God, most often referred to as the "kingdom of heaven" in this gospel. All the synoptic gospels contain at least some "kingdom" parables, where Jesus uses a short saying or story to describe an aspect of the impending reign of God. Unique to Matthew, however, is a recurring theme of judgment connected to the kingdom, described in different ways as a sorting out of the "righteous" from the "lawless." For example, two parables that occur only in Matthew refer to separating weeds from wheat at harvest time (Matt 13:37–40) and sorting good fish from bad out of a full fishing net (Matt 13:47–8). As we saw with the apostle Paul, judgment language is a standard element of Jewish apocalypticism. While Paul warned his gentile audience of the "wrath" that was coming (1 Thess 1:10; Rom 1:18), the author of Matthew conveys the idea of God's judgment even more graphically. The Matthean Jesus speaks of the "lawless" burning in fiery furnaces and describes weeping and gnashing of teeth (13:41–3; 49–50). In sharp contrast, he declares that "the righteous will shine forth like the sun in the kingdom of their Father" (Matt 13:41–3). This reference to "shining" recalls the apocalyptic imagery in the book of Daniel. As we saw in chapter three, the book of Daniel uses similar language to promise that the "wise" and "those who lead others to righteousness" will shine like stars forever (Dan 12: 3).

The harsh language of punishment is not reserved only for those outside of the Jesus movement. Chapter 18 features a disturbing parable that tells of an angry master handing over his slave to be tortured because he had not shown mercy to a fellow slave. Matthew's Jesus concludes by threatening, "So will my heavenly father do to you, if you each do not forgive your brother from your hearts" (Matt 18:35). While the Matthean Jesus assures the gospel audience that the merciful will receive mercy (Matt 5:7), he also makes clear that the unforgiving will be harshly punished.

The *Ekklesia* in the Gospel of Matthew

The Gospel of Matthew is the only canonical gospel that uses the Greek word *ekklesia*. As I discussed in the Prologue of this book, this Greek term was used in a number of contexts to indicate an assembly of people. English translations typically translate it as "church." The word occurs first in the Matthean version of the scene between Jesus and his disciples

at Caesarea Philippi (Matt 16:13–30). The author has expanded this story from the Gospel of Mark (8:27–30) to feature Peter as the "rock" on which Jesus will build his *ekklesia* (Matt 16:17–19). In this way, the author gives special attention to Peter as the foundation of a newly formed group of Christ-followers. Two additional references to the *ekklesia* are found in Matt

18:15. In this case, the Matthean Jesus instructs his followers about how to intervene in the case of a "brother" who sins against another Christ-follower. The instructions offer a policy for handling disputes in the assembly that could eventually result in exclusion from the group. Such policies are another way of building group identity that is reinforced by social boundaries.

The depiction of God in the Gospel of Matthew complicates a popular Christian tendency to distinguish the "wrathful" God of the Old Testament from the "loving" God of the New Testament. This misinformed distinction does not match the diverse ways that the deity is portrayed across both parts of the Christian canon. On the one hand, in the Matthean parables and in some other places in the New Testament, we find portrayals of a harsh and punishing God. On the other hand, multiple texts in the Hebrew Bible describe a loving and compassionate God. In Exodus 34, for example, God offers a self-description that includes traits such as merciful, gracious, slow to anger, loving, faithful, and forgiving. These divine traits are also regularly cited in the Psalms (for example, Psalms 86, 103, 145). The main point here is that all such depictions of God were shaped by biblical authors for different purposes in times and places long distant from us. The task of critical biblical scholars is to consider the function that varying portrayals of the deity may have served in the social and historical contexts in which they were formed.

For instance, in considering the punishing God in Matthew, we should recognize that the theme of divine judgment is common to both the prophetic and the apocalyptic genres. Moreover, historically, both types of writing often took shape during times of collective trauma. That the author of Matthew draws heavily on prophetic *and* apocalyptic traditions may be the result of the collective trauma still reverberating through Jewish communities in the decade after the destruction of the Jerusalem Temple. The Jewish experience of Roman domination in the first century CE shared much with earlier times of trauma for Israel and Judah. While we may find the language of burning hellfire, gnashing of teeth, and eternal punishment problematic because it suggests a harsh and unforgiving God, this language may have encouraged people who knew the ability of Rome to punish with fire and destruction. Biblical apocalypticism anticipates a day of reckoning that will bring God's justice to bear on unjust regimes. From this perspective, the Gospel of Matthew's apocalyptic vision of a coming kingdom of God would instill hope. Those suffering under Roman-appointed authorities could imagine that God would intervene on their behalf.

Finally, the theme of the kingdom of God also relates to Roman claims about imperial rule. The Latin word *imperium* conveys the notion of absolute power. From Rome's perspective, the emperor had complete godlike authority over the whole earth. We see this idea in the words of a famous Roman poet named Ovid:

Jupiter controls the heights of heaven and the kingdom of the triformed universe;
But the earth is under Augustus's sway. Each is both sire and ruler. (*Metamorphoses* 15:858–60)

FIGURE 8.2
Roman coin indicating the ruling power of Augustus as he subdues the earth under his foot.

Images of the emperor on Roman coins also included exaggerated claims of earthly authority (Figure 8.2). Given these assertions of Roman power, two scenes toward the end of the Gospel of Matthew are notable for their implicit challenges to Roman claims of *imperium*. The first case involves details that the author of the Gospel of Matthew added to the crucifixion scene from the Gospel of Mark. Only the Gospel of Matthew describes the temple curtain being torn in two, the earth shaking, tombs opening, and bodies being resurrected (Matt 27:51–3). The gospel writer uses these signs to mark Jesus's death as a literally earthshaking and life-giving event. These details are intended to make clear that Rome's power to put Jesus to death is far superseded by God's power to bring the dead to life. In the second scene, this divine power is extended to the resurrected Jesus when he appears to his disciples and proclaims, "All authority in heaven and on earth has been given to me" (Matt 28:18). In the Roman imperial context, this claim to rule over the cosmos puts Jesus far above the Roman emperor. He is on a par with the gods. In these ways, the gospel ends with indications of a subversive resistance to claims of Roman imperial power.

The Matthean Polemic against the Pharisees

Read Matthew 23, 26–8.

READING

What claims are made against the Pharisees in the series of "woes" in Matthew 23? Note the depiction of the chief priests and scribes compared to Pilate. Who claims responsibility for the crucifixion of Jesus?

EXERCISE

Far more blatant than the places where the gospel writer may subtly resist Roman claims to power are the many outright critiques of Jewish authorities. These authorities are designated as the Pharisees, chief priests, and scribes. The gospel regularly depicts the chief priests and Pharisees as attempting to entrap Jesus (Matt 22:15–46) and plotting to put him to death (Matt 21:46; 26:3–5, 14–15; 27:1). Meanwhile, the Matthean Jesus engages in rhetorical attacks against the Jewish leaders. The most extensive of these occurs in chapter 23, where the author draws on Q material to include a series of "woes" against the scribes and the Pharisees. This chapter presents a caricatured image of the "hypocritical" scribes and Pharisees. The Matthean Jesus builds a picture of his opponents as men who concern themselves with outward appearances (Matt 23:27–8) and legal regulations (Matt 23:23, 25) but are actually greedy and self-indulgent (Matt 23:25). The Pharisees are accused of caring nothing about justice, mercy, or faith (Matt 23:23). Rather than affirming that the kingdom of heaven is accessible to the poor in spirit (Matt 5:3), these leaders – according to Matthew – "shut the kingdom of heaven in front of people and do not permit them to go in" (Matt 23:13). The series of woes ends in judgment and condemnation, not just for the scribes and Pharisees but for "all of this generation" (Matt 23:36).

Who Were the Pharisees?

The earliest references to the Pharisees suggest that they began as a political party during the Maccabean period (167–63 BCE). They aligned themselves with certain Jewish leaders and opposed others. According to the Jewish historian Josephus, they counseled the people to accept Herod as their leader during his reign. He portrays them as having "the complete confidence of the masses," in contrast to the Sadducees, who were supported by "the people of highest standing," that is, the aristocracy (Josephus, *Antiquities* 13.13.5 §401). The political influence of the Pharisees is last attested in the early stages of the Jewish revolt against Rome of 66–70 CE. They joined the "principal citizens" in opposing the Jewish revolution, speaking out against starting an unwinnable war against Rome.

While our sources are limited in describing the Pharisees, we do know about some aspects of their beliefs and practices. In contrast to the Sadducees, the Pharisees followed the "traditions of the ancestors," an oral tradition that, according to rabbinic tradition, was given to Moses at Sinai along with the written law. They believed in the resurrection of the dead (again in contrast to the Sadducees). Perhaps most significantly, they thought that the same purity regulations that were practiced by the priests should be extended to the common people, presumably so that the people could stand in the same relationship to God as did the priests. Further, the Pharisees encouraged ritual practices that would distinguish or "separate" the Jewish people from sources of ritual impurity, such as gentiles. This may also be why they were called "Pharisees," a word that means "one who is separated." In a sense, by extending purity regulations beyond the priesthood, the Pharisees engaged in a sort of "democratization" of religion. This had appeal among the Jewish community. Commenting on this appeal, Josephus writes, "[the Pharisees] are able greatly to persuade the body of the people; and whatever [the people] do in terms of divine worship, prayers, and sacrifices, they perform them according to [the Pharisees'] direction" (*Antiquities* 18.1.3). Josephus's observations come some two decades after the destruction of the Temple. By then, the Pharisees had secured their place as the dominant group among the Jews. It is precisely such popularity that would elicit strong polemical rhetoric from a competing group.

Most problematically, the gospel lays the blame for Jesus's crucifixion on the Jewish people themselves rather than on the Romans. Only in this gospel does the Roman governor, Pilate, absolve himself of Jesus's death. He washes his hands before the crowd, stating, "I am innocent of this man's blood; see to it yourselves." To this, all the people respond, "His blood be on us and our children!" (Matt 27:25). Because the gospel was written after the destruction of the Temple, a statement like this encourages the audience to interpret the traumatic events of 70 CE as divine punishment. That is, it suggests that the generation following those who put Jesus to death was punished with Roman violence. Recall that Mark's gospel features a similar theme but implies that God's judgment was restricted to the Jewish leaders, the "tenants" of the vineyard. In contrast, Matthew's gospel blames *all* the Jewish people for the death of Jesus and the destruction of Jerusalem.

From a twenty-first-century perspective, we might wonder how a gospel so concerned with associating Jesus with the Torah of Moses and the lineage of Abraham and David could condemn the Jewish people and their leaders so harshly. However, our own experiences may help us understand the sort of polemic we find in the Gospel of Matthew. Members of different political parties of one nation often use judgmental rhetoric against one another. Similarly, Christian groups who hold different positions on social issues may direct inflammatory language toward each other. When opposing groups share a common identity, such as Americans or Christians, they often define themselves even more sharply against those whose positions they oppose. In the ancient world as in the contemporary one, group cohesion is often formed and reinforced through polemical rhetoric against other groups. The Gospel of Matthew reflects a historical situation in which a group of Jewish Christ-followers defined itself differently than other Jewish groups in the period after the Temple's destruction. The gospel was written by a Jewish Christ-follower who disagreed with the Pharisees about how to be faithful, Torah-observant Jews. Its depiction of Jesus attacking the Pharisees as hypocritical may reflect this disagreement more than actual hypocrisy on the Pharisees' part. Such in-group tensions existed to some degree even before the conflict with Rome. They likely increased in the aftermath of the catastrophic end of the Jewish revolt.

On this point, postcolonial theory provides useful insights into the gospel. Among other dynamics of colonization, which I discuss more in the next chapter, this theory points to how foreign domination creates internal tensions within, and rivalries between, indigenous groups. Unable to confront the actual source of their oppression, these groups often turn against one another. In the Gospel of Matthew, we find only implicit and infrequent critiques of an all-encompassing Roman authority but frequent and explicit attacks against local Jewish authorities. We will never know how the Jesus movement might have developed in relation to other expressions of Judaism without the events of 70 CE and the pressures of living under Roman domination. Indeed, such pressures may well have contributed to the growing popularity of the movement. What we know for certain is that after the destruction of the Temple, surviving Jewish communities – both the followers of Jesus and those aligned with emerging rabbinic Judaism – contended between themselves over issues of identity and belief.

Contemporary Voices: Decolonizing the Story of the Canaanite Woman (Matt 15:21–8)

Musa Dube is a biblical scholar from Botswana who specializes in feminist postcolonial interpretation of the Bible (see Musa Dube, *Postcolonial Feminist Interpretation of the Bible* (St. Louis, MO: Chalice Press, 2000)). Her interpretation of the story of the Canaanite woman in Matt 15:21–8 (the Matthean version of the story of the Syrophoenician woman in Mark 7:24–30) shows how the gospel's rhetoric demonstrates an interest in gaining power through the colonization of foreign lands. The change from the description of the woman as Syrophoenician in Mark to the archaic label "Canaanite" already suggests the author's interest in characterizing the woman as part of a people who must be conquered. In the Hebrew scriptures, the Canaanites are presented as the foreign enemy of the people of Israel. Dube highlights how Jesus and his disciples travel to a different land and then treat the "foreign" woman with indifference and disrespect. Jesus seems to ignore her altogether, while the disciples urge Jesus to send the woman away because she is shouting at them (Matt 15:22–3). Even when the woman is reduced to begging, Jesus responds by likening her to a dog, again suggesting that she is not worthy of his attention (Matt 15:25–6). While the woman's daughter is eventually healed because of the woman's faith (in contrast, Mark focuses on what the woman says; Mark 7:29), Dube is not impressed with this "successful" outcome. In Dube's words,

That the Canaanite woman is portrayed as accepting the "dog" social category assigned to her and that her request is granted on these conditions, however, has frightening implications for a narrative that foreshadows the mission. The non-Christian followers, who must be sought and taught to obey everything, are not integrated as equals who have something to offer. Instead they are welcomed as "dogs" who have come to follow, beg, and depend on their masters. (Dube 2000, p. 151)

Dube shows how the Gospel of Matthew portrays Jesus and the disciples as "traveling divine heroes" whose superiority must be acknowledged. This portrayal is part of the missionary thrust of the narrative, which concludes with the Matthean Jesus commanding his disciples to make followers of all nations (Matt 28:19–20). Dube argues that the Canaanite woman symbolizes the foreign nations in advance of this command. In her reading, the Matthean missionary effort is portrayed as a project of a superior power over an inferior people rather than a project among equals.

Such observations are part of Dube's project of reading for decolonization. This involves the use of reading strategies that break down colonial assumptions about Western superiority and privilege. These assumptions are not only located in the biblical texts but are also found in centuries of interpretations of the Bible.

Matt 25:31–46

The focus text for this chapter is a parable that occurs only in the Gospel of Matthew. The parable illustrates God's judgment of human conduct based on doing acts of charity. This is a familiar theme in the Hebrew scriptures. Proverbs 14:31 and 19:17 assert that caring for the poor honors God and will be rewarded. Deuteronomy 15:7–10 instructs the Israelites to give willingly to the needy, with the assurance that God will bless their efforts. The call to feed and clothe the needy and give hospitality to the traveler also occurs in the prophets (Ezek 18:7, 16; Isa 58:7) and in Job (31:32). In short, the Matthean parable draws on a well-known scriptural theme of caring for those in need.

The placement of the passage indicates the importance of this theme for the author. The parable concludes the final section of Jesus's teaching before the passion narrative begins in chapter 26. The passage opens with familiar apocalyptic imagery – the Son of Man coming in glory with his angels (Mark 8:38). In Matthew's gospel, this image is used to introduce a vivid scene of divine judgment. Here, the Son of Man sits on his throne as "the nations" or "the gentiles" (Greek, *ethne*) come before him (Matt 25:31–2). This image of the Son of Man executing judgment from a heavenly throne is unique to Matthew's gospel. In Mark 14:62, the Son of Man is seated at the "right hand of the ruling power." In contrast, in Matthew's text, the Son of Man *himself* executes judgment from his own throne. Rather than an apocalyptic figure who ushers in the reign of God (compare Mark 8:38–9:1), the Matthean Son of Man assumes the role of a ruling authority and heavenly judge. The author may have been familiar with such a figure from Dan 7:13, which describes a "Son of Man" who is given "dominion and glory and kingship." Perhaps for this reason, the image of the Son of Man shifts from that of a shepherd separating sheep and goats (Matt 25:32–3) to that of a "king" (Matt 25:34). This image of the resurrected Jesus as king links with the earlier association between Jesus and kingship in the gospel (Matt 13:41; 20:21). The image also anticipates the conclusion of the gospel, where, as we have seen, the resurrected Jesus announces that he has been given "all authority on heaven and on earth" (Matt 28:18).

As the parable continues, the king invites those on his right to "inherit the kingdom" on the basis of their acts of mercy – providing food, drink, and clothing to those in need, caring for the sick, providing hospitality to strangers, and visiting the imprisoned (Matt 25:35–40). Such actions recall the gospel's earlier emphasis on righteousness and mercy (Matt 5:7). Meanwhile, the unmerciful are condemned to eternal punishment (Matt 18:8). Given what we have already seen in the gospel, we should not be surprised to find that those who showed mercy are referred to as "the righteous" (Matt 25:37). Significantly, the righteous are not even aware of when they cared for the king. The passage suggests that it is not enough to be motivated to serve someone of higher rank (perhaps hoping to gain from doing so). Instead, the reward comes to those who extend care regardless of concerns of rank or status, attending "to one of the least significant of these brothers of mine" (Matt 25:40). If the righteous – the "sheep" – are rewarded for their care of these members, we can anticipate the plight of the "goats." They are also unaware of their lack of care for the "Lord," but then, they had not even cared for one of the least significant (Matt 25:41–6).

While all of this might seem straightforward, there are ambiguities in the parable that have lent themselves to shifting interpretations. First, since the Greek word *ethne* can be translated as either "the nations" or "the gentiles," readers have offered different interpretations regarding who is included in the judgment scene. Similarly, the identity of "these least significant brothers" is vague. Does the passage refer to the needy in general? Or are the "needy" only those in the community of Christ-followers? Christian interpreters in the third century CE tended to interpret the parable as referring *only* to the Christian community. They understood the "least of these" to be Christians as well as the "nations" who provided for them. These ancient interpreters thought the parable was meant to motivate Christians to perform acts of mercy for other needy Christians.

By the eighteenth century, different cultural conditions elicited a different reading of the passage. At this time, Christian groups were becoming more involved in foreign missionary work as part of the Western colonization of Africa and India. In this context, "the nations" were interpreted as a reference to all non-Christians, while the "least of these" was interpreted as referring to Christians. Defining the groups in this way meant that all non-Christians would be judged based on their treatment of Christians. Such a reading could have offered comfort to missionaries who felt oppressed and persecuted by suggesting that those who mistreated them would ultimately be punished.

At the same time, movement into these so-called "foreign" lands led to a growing recognition of the existence of the very large number of non-Christians who remained non-Christian. An interpretation of the parable that allowed non-Christians to receive rewards based on their charity toward Christians made room for the salvation of non-Christians. To be sure, many people today, including Christians, would be troubled by the idea that the parable referred only to a final judgment of non-Christians, especially when that judgment was based only on the charitable treatment of Christians! But in the world of eighteenth-century missionaries, this interpretation of the parable introduced the possibility of heavenly salvation without conversion to Christianity.

In both the early church and up through the twentieth century, one can also find a more disturbing and persistent interpretation of the passage in which the "goats" are assumed to be the Jews that did not accept Christ. Such a reading is problematic on several counts. First, there is nothing in the passage to identify the goats as the Jewish people. Second, this interpretation overlooks the way the gospel is thoroughly connected to the Jewish history and practice of the first century CE. Third, the reading ignores the basic intent of the passage; the parable says nothing about doctrinal belief or confessions of faith as conditions for judgment but focuses only on acts of mercy, a thoroughly Jewish idea.

The twentieth century brought yet another interpretation of the tradition that is far broader in scope than most earlier readings. In this case, "the nations" are understood as *all* peoples coming under judgment, and "the least of these" as *anyone* that is in need, regardless of their religious convictions. This reading has been important for those who lift up God's concern for the poor as a central theological conviction. The interpretation emphasizes the undogmatic aspects of the passage and promotes the idea of a "practical" Christianity that is grounded in acts of love toward other human beings. It links with an earlier saying of the Matthean Jesus: "Not all who say to me 'Lord, Lord' will enter the kingdom of heaven, but the one who does the will of my father in heaven" (Matt 7:21 modified from NRSV).

Given these diverse interpretations, what can we say about the author's original intent? The various themes of the gospel provide some clues. The gospel has a strong missionary emphasis – the Matthean Jesus sends out his disciples "like sheep in the midst of wolves" (Matt 10:16). They are to expect persecution and betrayal (Matt 10:21–3), and those who welcome the disciples and provide hospitality will be rewarded (Matt 10:40). The Matthean Jesus's last instructions to the disciples reinforce this missionary emphasis: they are told to go and "make disciples of all nations" (*ethne*). Note that *ethne* is also used to refer to the group that is called before the throne in Matt 25:32. Moreover, the reference to the treatment of "the least of these *brothers* of mine" suggests a concern for those within the community rather than for needy persons in general. Perhaps the gospel writer is acknowledging that the traveling missionaries of the Jesus movement do not rank very highly in the broader Roman culture and may not be well received as they travel from town to town. In this sense, the passage would serve to encourage Christ-followers to show hospitality to the traveling missionaries.

These differing interpretations of Matt 25:31–46 indicate the textual nature of the presentations of Jesus that are found in the New Testament. Because readers bring their own experience to reading the text, they regularly interpret the teachings of Jesus in ways that fit their own setting. This is not necessarily a problem, as it simply reflects how humans make meaning by engaging with narratives. Nevertheless, this human practice of making meaning through reinterpretation does not mean that *any* interpretation is acceptable. We now have the benefit of assessing how this Matthean parable was used in different settings. Reflecting on the history of biblical interpretation necessarily calls for a robust ethical reflection that wrestles with and takes responsibility for interpretive choices. For example, interpretations of the Matthean parable that assert that Jesus condemned all Jewish people are a part of the tragic legacy of anti-Semitic interpretations of the New Testament. Moreover, what are the ethical implications of an interpretation of the parable that elevates the treatment of needy Christians as the only criterion for heavenly reward? Even if we understand the original missionary focus of the text, contemporary readers have a responsibility to consider whether this ancient focus is still meaningful in a twenty-first-century context. I would argue that the parable is now best understood as one that recognizes the value of all people and the necessity of caring for anyone in need regardless of their religious affiliation.

CHAPTER EIGHT REVIEW

1 Know the meaning and significance of the following terms:
- fulfillment citations
- Q
- Sermon on the Mount
- Special L
- Special M
- synoptic gospels
- synoptic problem
- two-source hypothesis

2 What sources did the author of Matthew's gospel use to write his story of Jesus?

3 How does the structure of the Gospel of Mark differ from the structure of the Gospel of Matthew?

4 What effect does this different structure have on the presentation of Jesus?

5 How and why does the Gospel of Matthew relate Jesus to the Torah?

6 How does the theme of God's judgment relate to the gospel's historical and cultural setting?

7 Compare the interpretation of the Canaanite woman by Musa Dube with the interpretation of the Syrophoenician Woman (Mark 7:24–30) by Mitzi Smith (see Chapter 7). How does the difference between the two versions of the story in Mark and Matthew and the difference in their interpretive approaches change their respective understandings of this Jesus tradition? How do their two different interpretations affect your own understanding of the story?

8 (Focus text: Matt 25:31–46) Discuss how the different interpretations of the parable relate to their cultural settings. How might you read the parable in ways that link directly to your own setting? Do you find the Matthean theme of divine judgment problematic or useful? Explain.

RESOURCES FOR FURTHER STUDY

Aland, Kurt. *Synopsis of the Four Gospels*. Philadelphia, PA: Fortress Press, 1985.

Allison, Jr., Dale C., ed. *Matthew: A Shorter Commentary*. London and New York: T&T Clark International, 2004.

Boxall, Ian. *Discovering Matthew: Content, Interpretation, Reception*. Grand Rapids, MI: Eerdmans, 2015.

Kampen, John. *Matthew within Sectarian Judaism*. New Haven, CT: Yale University Press, 2019.

For more on postcolonial interpretation of the Bible:

Dube, Musa. *Postcolonial Feminist Interpretation of the Bible*. St. Louis, MO: Chalice Press, 2000.

Sugirthrajah, R.S. *Voices from the Margin: Interpreting the Bible in the Third World*. Maryknoll, NY: Orbis Books, 2016. This updated edition of a classic collection of essays includes a section on postcolonial interpretation.

The Gospel of Luke: Legitimizing the Jesus Movement in the Midst of Empire

9

Chapter Outline

Chapter Overview	155
Reading the Clues in the Lukan Prologue	156
The Lukan Jesus in Continuity with Israel's Past	158
God's Plan of Salvation for Israel and the Gentiles	160
The Lukan Jesus and Imperial Imitation	160
The Role of the Holy Spirit in the Lukan Narrative	164
The Travel Narrative and Lukan Parables	165
Focus Text: Jesus's Sermon in Nazareth (Luke 4:14–30)	168
Chapter Nine Review	170
Resources for Further Study	170

Chapter Overview

This chapter focuses on the first of the two-volume work known as Luke–Acts. Because this work is often thought of as a history of the early Christian church, I begin with the question of genre and ancient history writing. The chapter then discusses several themes in the Lukan narrative. It explores the author's interest in legitimizing the Jesus movement, in part by showing its continuity with the history of the people of Israel. Making this connection also enables the author to make his central theological claim: that Jesus and his followers are instrumental to God's plan for the salvation of the Jews and gentiles. The chapter also explores the gospel's narrative focus on the role of the Spirit in the Jesus movement, as well as the gospel's ambivalent relationship with Roman imperial power. In the last part of the chapter, I turn to the author's addition of an extended travel narrative, especially the unique Lukan parables that are part of this addition. Studying these aspects of the gospel will prepare you to see how the author develops them further in the Acts of the Apostles, the topic of the next chapter.

The New Testament: A Contemporary Introduction, First Edition. Colleen M. Conway.
© 2023 John Wiley & Sons Ltd. Published 2023 by John Wiley & Sons Ltd.

Reading the Clues in the Lukan Prologue

READING

Read Luke 1:1–4 and compare these verses to Acts 1:1–2.

EXERCISE

Based on your reading, why do you think the author is writing the gospel? How does he portray his task? What does he imply about the sources that we know he used? Why do you think the author mentions "most excellent Theophilus" in both Luke and Acts?

If your name was Theophilus and you lived toward the end of the first century CE, you might be the esteemed patron of a major, two-volume account of the life of Jesus and the growth of the Jesus movement. Both the Gospel of Luke and the Acts of the Apostles begin with prologues in which the author writes directly to a certain "most excellent" Theophilus (see Luke 1:1–4; Acts 1:1–5). Because of this, and because of the many thematic links between these two works, we can see that the same author wrote a two-volume work made up of the Gospel of Luke and Acts. Scholars refer to these two volumes as **Luke–Acts**.

We do not know who wrote the Gospel of Luke, but the opening prologue offers some intriguing details about how he viewed his work. The prologue is similar to those used by ancient Greek history writers like Herodotus and Thucydides. These historians both began their works with prologues, as did history writers closer to the time of the author of Luke–Acts, like the Jewish historian Josephus. Perhaps the author imitated this literary convention with the hope that it would elevate the status of his two-volume work. That would fit with both prologues' addresses to "most excellent **Theophilus**," which create the impression that the author is writing on behalf of a wealthy patron. Theophilus may have been a wealthy convert to the Jesus movement who commissioned the author to write the two-volume work. It is also possible that the use of this name is a literary device. Because Theophilus means "friend of God" or "God-lover," the figure may be intended as a stand-in for believers in general. In either case, the effect of the address to Theophilus is the same: it situates the author and his work in a learned setting of relatively high social status. As we will see, the narrative of the gospel does the same thing with Jesus.

The prologue also tells us more about the author and how he conceived of his work. He observes that "many have tried to write orderly accounts," implying that earlier accounts of Jesus have not been entirely successful. Whom does the gospel writer mean with his reference to "many," and what written accounts does he know of? This tantalizing verse leaves us wondering about the number of sources known by the author. It would seem that, at least, he has in mind the two sources that we know he used: the Gospel of Mark and the sayings source known as Q. Were there also other accounts of the life of Jesus that have been long lost? The author's claim that he is working with accounts that have been "handed down" by eyewitnesses and servants of the word reminds us that he also drew on oral traditions.

Beyond highlighting the links between the volumes and the author's literary skill, the prologues raise the question of genre. Because the prologues imitate the style of ancient history writing and because there is a second volume that tells of the growth and spread of the Jesus movement after Jesus's lifetime, we could consider Luke–Acts as a sort of history writing. But what sort? How does this type of history writing compare to our ideas of how modern historians write?

Ancient history writing was different than contemporary understandings of history writing. Much like ancient orators, ancient Greek and Roman history writers were concerned with shaping model citizens for the city-state or empire. Their goal was to write a persuasive narrative of events to convey a sweeping historical idea. To that end, ancient historians constructed dialogues between historical figures and created speeches by prominent men based on what they thought these people must have said in a given situation. By communicating what they thought must have happened, ancient historians shaped their accounts to match their interpretation of past events. Of course, modern historians also do this to a certain extent. But contemporary historians base their construction of past events on archival research of historical records, which might, for example, include actual recordings of speeches. This is an important difference. If we call Luke–Acts history, we need to keep this type of ancient Greek and Roman history writing in mind. The author of Luke–Acts writes a history insofar as he writes what he thinks must have happened based on his understanding of the significance of Jesus and the earliest believers. Like other ancient history writers, he creates speeches for his characters that convey major themes of the narrative.

Basics on the Gospel of Luke

I	From Galilee to Jerusalem		**Outline: the geographical structure of the Gospel of Luke**
	A. Prologue	1:1–4	
	B. Jesus in Galilee		
	1. Birth narrative and preparation for ministry	1:5–4:13	
	2. Ministry in Galilee	4:14–9:50	
	C. Jesus's journey to Jerusalem	9:51–19:27	
	D. Jesus in Jerusalem	19:28–24:53	
	1. Entry to Jerusalem and teaching in the Temple	19:28–21:38	
	2. Passion, resurrection, and ascension in Jerusalem	22:1–24:53	

The author of Luke was traditionally identified as a physician and traveling companion of Paul. While many have posited that the author of Luke–Acts was a gentile Christ-follower, it is just as possible that he was a Hellenized Jew like Paul. The date and location of the writing of Luke–Acts is unknown. Since the author used the Gospel of Mark as a source for his gospel but does not seem to know of the Gospel of Matthew, the gospel was likely written sometime around 80–85 CE. Scholars offer mixed assessments of the probable **Author, date, and structure** date of Acts, though most put it in the late first century or early second century. The structure of Luke–Acts is geographically organized. The Gospel of Luke begins in Galilee before moving to an extended travel narrative (Luke 9:51–19:27). Most of the travel section is unique to the Gospel of Luke. The gospel concludes in Jerusalem, preparing the way for the second volume to begin in Jerusalem.

The Lukan Jesus in Continuity with Israel's Past

READING

Read Luke 1–2.

EXERCISE

Pay attention to the ways that the birth narrative evokes ideas from Israel's past and note its focus on the Temple and Jerusalem.

One major goal of the author is to show how Jesus and his movement are in continuity with the history of Israel. The author finds ways to connect the Lukan Jesus to this history. This connection begins immediately after the prologue, where the author shifts his writing style so that the narrative begins to "sound" like the Hebrew scriptures. The author uses a type of Greek that imitates the Septuagint, the Greek translation of the Hebrew scriptures. The author also imitates the content of the Septuagint. For example, Luke's birth story (unlike Matthew's) first introduces the righteous priest Zechariah and his wife Elizabeth, who both live blamelessly "according to the commandments and ordinances of the Lord" (Luke 1:6). The mention of Elizabeth's infertility recalls the common theme of "barrenness" in the ancestor stories of Genesis (Gen 16:1–2; 25:21; 29:31), as does Zechariah's assumption that the couple is too old to conceive a child (Luke 1:18; compare Gen 18:11–12). The author also has his characters speak in a scriptural way in the birth narrative. Mary's song of praise (1:46–55) sounds like Hannah's song from 1 Sam 2:1–10. Both Mary and Zechariah speak of the blessings and mercy of God on Israel and of God's promise to the ancestors (1:55, 72–5). In this way, the story of the Lukan Jesus's birth is scripturally situated in the context of God's ongoing relationship with Israel.

The author's focus on Jerusalem and the Temple early in the story of Jesus creates another important connection between Jesus and the history of Israel. Only this gospel relates scenes from Jesus's infancy and childhood that show him inside the Temple. The first of these scenes occurs when the family brings Jesus to the Temple to offer the required sacrifice for a first-born male (Luke 2:22–32). The second occurs when Jesus is 12 years old and the family travels to Jerusalem for Passover. As Jesus's parents travel home, they discover he has gone missing. He is found back in Jerusalem, sitting with teachers in the Temple and displaying his precocious learning abilities (2:41–51). These early connections between Jesus and the Temple foreshadow the importance that Jerusalem and the Temple will have later in the narrative.

The author creates another link between the Lukan Jesus and the traditions of ancient Israel by portraying Jesus in the role of the rejected prophet. This portrayal first occurs on the occasion of the Lukan Jesus's first public teaching. The scene, set in a synagogue, begins with the Lukan Jesus reading from a scroll of the prophet Isaiah. Following the reading, Jesus announces to those in the synagogue that "no prophet is accepted in his hometown" (Luke 4:24). His statement foreshadows the conclusion of the episode, when Jesus's listeners violently reject him (Luke 4:16–30). I will discuss this important scene in more detail as the focus text for this chapter. The theme of Jesus as a rejected prophet continues when the author of Luke uses a lament over Jerusalem from the Q source, describing Jerusalem as "the city that kills the prophets and stones those who are sent to it" (Luke 13:34). In the Gospel of Matthew, this Q saying occurs in the context of woes against the Pharisees and refers to a list of past prophets that have been killed (Matt 23:`34–7). In contrast, the Gospel of Luke places the saying after some Pharisees warn Jesus about Herod's plans to kill him (Luke 13:31). This difference illustrates the author's more favorable depiction of the Pharisees compared to Matthew's. It also suggests that when Jerusalem is described as a city that "kills the prophets," Jesus will be one of those prophets. The last chapter of the gospel underlines the point. In describing Jesus after his death, two of his followers say he was "a prophet strong in work and speech" who was handed over to be killed by their chief priests and rulers (Luke 24:19).

By showing Jesus's connection with the long-established traditions of Judaism and with the Jerusalem Temple (a well-known cultic center), the author may have intended to alleviate suspicions about the otherwise unfamiliar Jesus movement. The Romans were familiar with Judaism as an ancient tradition and generally did not perceive Jewish ritual practices as a threat to Roman culture. This was not the case with newly imported foreign cultic practices.

A bit of background will help here. By the first century CE, the Roman empire was engaged in a program of restoring Roman cultural values, including honoring the traditional Roman deities. Indeed, one of Caesar Augustus's major programs was to restore Roman temples and reinvigorate traditional Roman rites. This came at a time when many people were attracted to non-Roman deities such as Isis (a goddess figure originating in Egypt) or to the cult of Mithras (a Persian-inspired tradition). Both of these cults required personal initiation rites and promised benefits to individuals who devoted themselves to the deity. In this context, while Jewish identity was relatively "safe," gentile Christ-followers might have been especially subject to suspicion. Jesus might have been viewed as another new god from the East who disrupted the practice of traditional Roman rites. Baptism would be seen as the required rite of initiation promising devotees special benefits. Showing how the new Jesus movement was a continuation of the "old" tradition of Judaism addressed such potential misperceptions.

God's Plan of Salvation for Israel and the Gentiles

The author also uses the link between the Jesus movement and the traditions of Israel to develop the gospel's theme of salvation to Israel *and* to the gentiles. In chapter 1, when the devout Simeon sees the infant Jesus in the Jerusalem Temple, he praises God: "My eyes have seen your salvation which you prepared in the presence of all people, a light for revelation to the gentiles and glory for your people Israel" (Luke 2:30–2). The Lukan genealogy traces the lineage of Jesus back to Adam, a figure representing all of humanity – that is, Israel and the nations (Luke 3:38). The Lukan Jesus's first public teaching, in Luke 4:16–30, includes God's outreach to the gentiles (see the focus text discussion below).

Elements of Luke's narrative project a mission to the gentiles backward to the time of Jesus. For instance, only Luke includes a sending out of 70 "others" ahead of him on a missionary journey to all the villages to which he was planning to go (Luke 10:1–12). The sending of these 70 is then followed by "woes" to unrepentant villages in the Jewish territory of Galilee (Chorazin, Bethsaida, and Capernaum), which are negatively contrasted with the repentant gentile cities of Tyre and Sidon (Luke 10:13–16). The theme of gentile inclusion also occurs at the end of the gospel. On the one hand, the Lukan version of Mark's "little apocalypse" includes a reference to Jerusalem being "trampled on by the gentiles, until the times of the gentiles is fulfilled" (Luke 21:24). This prophecy of the end of the reign of gentiles is in keeping with the idea of the restoration of the 12 tribes of Israel that the Lukan Jesus foretells (Luke 22:28–30). On the other hand, the inclusion of the gentiles is part of this restoration process, as Jesus declares that the "repentance and forgiveness of sins must be preached to all nations" (Luke 24:47).

The Lukan Jesus and Imperial Imitation

In addition to connecting the story of Jesus with the past history of Israel and God's plan for salvation, the author of Luke–Acts also links Jesus with the politics and culture of the Roman empire. To help understand the author's depiction of Jesus in the context of the empire, biblical scholars have turned to postcolonial theory. As you may recall from earlier discussions, postcolonial theorists study the effects of colonization on subjugated peoples. One such effect is that colonized peoples often imitate elements of the oppressing group. They may mimic the oppressors' language, clothing, or other cultural patterns of behavior. They might also adopt the oppressing group's concepts of power and authority and adapt them to their own uses. On the one hand, such imitation reveals some degree of attraction to certain cultural elements of the oppressors. On the other hand, the subordinated group sometimes mimics the ruling culture in ways that undercut or resist its authority. Indeed, postcolonial theorists observe that such forms of mimicry come quite close to mockery. Postcolonial theories often find a deep ambivalence in the relationship between colonized and colonizer. The narrative of Luke–Acts offers evidence of this type of imitation and ambivalence with respect to Roman power.

First, the author takes care to place the birth and ministry of Jesus in the context of Roman ruling authority. For example, in the Lukan birth narrative, Joseph and Mary must travel to Bethlehem because of a decree of the emperor, Augustus, "that all the world should be registered." The narrative portrays this call for an empire-wide census occurring when Quirinius was governor of Syria (Luke 2:1–2). Neither of these claims is historically accurate – there is no record of such a decree from Augustus outside of this gospel, and Quirinius was not the governor of Syria at the time of Jesus's birth. Such discrepancies remind modern readers that the point of the gospel is not historical reporting in the twenty-first-century sense of the word. Rather, the author wants to tell the story of Jesus in the context of Roman ruling authority. The same tendency occurs when the author prefaces the inauguration of John's baptizing activity with a list of no fewer than five Roman rulers and two high priests (Luke 3:1–2). While this is not imperial imitation per se, situating the inauguration of the Jesus movement against a backdrop of Roman imperial power elevates the significance of the narrated events.

Second, in addition to associating the story of Jesus with Roman power, the author uses titles for Jesus that were commonly used for the Roman emperor. The first emperor, Caesar Augustus, claimed divine descent in several ways. He was the adopted son of Julius, whose family claimed that they were descendants of Aeneus, the mythic ancestor of Rome and the son of Venus. According to rumor (perhaps begun by his own propagandists), he claimed Apollo as his own father. When the Roman Senate deified Julius Cesar after his death, Augustus commemorated the occasion by minting coins that included the Latin phrases "son of god" (*divis filius*) and "divine Julius" (*divis Iulius*), coins which then circulated throughout the empire (see Figure 9.1). This is the imperial context in which Luke tells a story of an angel announcing to Mary that her son will be called "son of God" (Luke 1:35). Again, Luke's genealogy is relevant here. At the conclusion of the genealogy, Adam is called "son of God." This reference has puzzled interpreters, especially because the genealogy is that of Joseph, Jesus's adopted father. However, this too has a parallel with Augustus, who traced his divine genealogy through his adoptive father, Julius, in addition to claiming that he was the son of Apollo.

FIGURE 9.1

A coin minted by Caesar Augustus around 18–19 BCE. In 44 BCE, following Julius's assassination, a comet appeared in the sky which many Romans took as a sign of his deification. The coin depicts Augustus with a flaming comet on his head. The reverse side depicts the comet with the tail directed upwards and the Latin words "divine Julius."

The title "savior" is used to describe Jesus twice in the birth narrative: once in Zechariah's song (1:69) and once in the angel's announcement to the shepherds (2:11). Looking ahead to Acts, Peter and the apostles refer to Jesus as ruler and savior (Acts 5:31), and later, the Paul of Acts says that Jesus is a savior brought by God (Acts 13:23). What may be surprising is that this title was commonly used for the Roman emperor. Similarly, Zechariah's prediction that Jesus would direct "people toward the way of peace" (1:79) would have resonated with one of the fundamental claims of Rome – that the empire brought peace to a war-torn world, the so-called *Pax Romana* (see box "The Priene Calendar Inscription"). Given this context, the author may have meant to subvert the Roman emperor's claim of authority by designating Jesus as savior and peace-bringer. If the point of these titles is to make clear that it is Jesus, not the emperor, who is the savior and bringer of peace, this would be a form of imperial imitation that was used to resist imperial power.

The Priene Calendar Inscription

The following inscription, dating from 9 BCE, was found in ancient Priene, located in modern-day Turkey. It marks the institution of a new calendar "for good luck and salvation" based on the birthday of Augustus. Moreover, the emperor's birthday is said to mark "the beginning of the good tidings" or "gospel" (Greek, *euangelion*). The calendar inscription illustrates the rhetoric typically used to describe the emperor. When early Christ-followers made similar claims about Jesus, this sort of imperial rhetoric would be the most immediate frame of reference. Note also the idea of Augustus as a gift from Providence who is deeply invested in humankind.

It seemed good to the Greeks of Asia, in the opinion of the high priest Apollonius of Menophilus Azanitus: "Since Providence, which has ordered all things and is deeply interested in our life, has set in most perfect order by giving us Augustus, whom for the benefit of humankind she has filled with virtue, as if for us and for those after us she bestowed a savior, who brought an end to war and established peace . . . and since he, Caesar, by his appearance (excelled even our anticipations), surpassing all previous benefactors, and not even leaving to posterity any hope of surpassing what he has done, and since the birthday of the god Augustus was the beginning of the good tidings (Greek, *euangelion*) for the world that came by reason of him which Asia resolved in Smyrna. . ."

Although the birth narrative proclaims Jesus as savior and peace-bringer, the fact that Jesus is executed by local Roman authorities complicates such acclamations. Far from a display of ruling power, the crucifixion of Jesus would appear to many as the utterly shameful death of a convicted criminal. One way that the Lukan narrative deals with this problem is by stressing the innocence of Jesus. In the Lukan trial scene, Pilate explicitly states that he can find no reason to charge Jesus with a crime (Luke 23:4, 14, 22). Only Luke's account includes a separate trial before Herod, governor of Galilee (Luke 23:8–16), who also does not charge him with a crime (Luke 23:15). Even the criminal who hangs crucified next to Jesus recognizes Jesus's innocence (23:39–43). Most striking is the way the author adapts the Roman centurion's statement at the death of

Jesus. In the Markan version, the centurion at the cross declares, "Truly, this man was a son of God" (Mark 15:39). The author of Luke edits this source and has the centurion declare, "Truly, this man was innocent" (Luke 23:47). This claim of innocence was likely intended to reassure believers that Jesus was an honorable man, innocent of any charges against him, despite the fact that he was executed by Roman authorities. This is a major way that the author of Luke adapts the passion narrative to legitimize the Jesus movement in its Roman imperial context.

Finally, having established the innocence of Jesus by way of the passion narrative, the author returns to imperial imitation. Just as the birth narratives draw on imperial rhetoric to present Jesus as a powerful savior, the ascension scene at the end of the gospel (Luke 24:50–2), which is repeated at the beginning of Acts (Acts 1:6–11), connects Jesus to Roman imperial status. In the ascension scene, the Lukan Jesus gives final words of instruction to his disciples and is then "lifted up" into heaven. An ancient Greco-Roman audience would associate such a heavenly elevation with a familiar imperial scene: the deification of the emperor after his death (see Figure 9.2). As mentioned earlier, beginning with Julius Caesar, the Roman Senate began a tradition of honoring a deceased emperor with divine status. The deification of Caesar Augustus in 14 CE was celebrated across the empire and commemorated with coins, temple dedications, and the establishment of priesthoods and cult rituals. For a first-century CE audience, the ascension scenes in the gospel and Acts would be a way of making Jesus's divine status and

FIGURE 9.2
Base of an honorific column in Rome showing the deification of a second-century CE emperor and his wife.

authority explicit. Indeed, the Lukan Jesus's ascension (which occurs without the vote of the Roman Senate!) calls to mind the most powerful position in the known world: the Roman emperor.

A third way that the author imitates cultural values is by depicting Jesus and his followers with traits that would reflect well on them in Greek and Roman contexts. Much of this occurs in the extended narrative of Acts, but the depiction of Jesus in the gospel prepares the way. The Lukan Jesus is shown to be educated and pious, traits that would resonate with Roman cultural ideas of proper manly deportment. The story of a precocious young Jesus learning from the rabbis in the Temple demonstrates his keen mind (Luke 2:46–7). Moreover, only this gospel explicitly presents Jesus as literate, as he begins his public ministry by reading from a scroll in a synagogue (Luke 4:16). Another important quality for a Roman man was *pietas*. While this Latin word is often translated as piety, it means something closer to duty or loyalty to the gods, as well as loyalty to one's family and country. The first-century BCE poet Virgil regularly described Aeneas, the hero of his epic poem about the founding of Rome, as *"pius Aeneas"* – that is, as dutiful or "pious" Aeneas. Similarly, the Gospel of Luke illustrates the "piety" (loyalty, duty) of Jesus. His piety is grounded in his parents' pious reverence for the traditions of Israel (Luke 2:21–4). It is then displayed in the frequent depictions of Jesus at prayer.

The Role of the Holy Spirit in the Lukan Narrative

The importance of the Holy Spirit is signaled in the opening chapter of the gospel. The parallel stories of Elizabeth and Mary conceiving and giving birth to John and Jesus repeatedly reference the role of the Holy Spirit. Even before John's birth, an angelic announcement foretells that he will be filled with the Holy Spirit, and both Elizabeth and Mary are reported to be filled with the Spirit (1:35; 1:41). In Mary's case, the Holy Spirit is responsible for her conception. When an angel announces that Mary will conceive a child, she asks,

> "How can this be if I have not known a man?" And the angel answered, "The Holy Spirit will come upon you, and the power of the Most High will overshadow you; therefore the begotten one will be holy; he will be called Son of God. (Luke 1:35)

The characters Zechariah and Simeon are also Spirit-filled, causing them to prophesy about John (1:67–79) and Jesus (2:27–32), respectively.

The prominence of the Holy Spirit continues in the depiction of the Lukan Jesus. First, John contrasts his own water baptism with the coming baptism of Jesus with the "Holy Spirit and with fire" (Luke 3:16). While the Spirit descends on Jesus in all the gospels, only in Luke's gospel do we find repeated references to Jesus being filled with the Holy Spirit. For instance, Jesus is "full of the Holy Spirit" as he is led by the Spirit into the wilderness to be tempted (4:1–2). He then begins his Galilean ministry "with the power of the Spirit" (4:14, 18). Another distinctive reference to the Holy Spirit occurs at Luke 12:11–12. There, the author adds a statement to Mark warning about blaspheming against the Holy Spirit (see Mark 3:29). The Lukan Jesus looks ahead to times of trial for Christ-followers, assuring them that "the Holy Spirit will teach you in that hour what you must say." As we will see, this prediction will be realized in the Acts narrative. Finally, pointing ahead to the role of the Holy Spirit in Acts, only in Luke's gospel does the resurrected Jesus instruct the disciples to stay in Jerusalem to wait for the Holy Spirit (Luke 24:49).

The Travel Narrative and Lukan Parables

Read at least three of the parables listed below, all of which appear only in the Gospel of Luke.

READING

Pay attention to the context in which the Lukan Jesus tells the parables. What do you think these different parables are meant to do? What comes as a surprise as you read them?

EXERCISE

Luke 10:25–37; 12:16–21; 15:3–7; 15:8–10; 15:11–32; 16:1–8; 16:19–31.

As shown in the outline above (see box "Basics on the Gospel of Luke"), the author structures his two-volume work with Jerusalem at the center. At Luke 9:51, the author builds toward this central placement of Jerusalem with an announcement: "When the days drew near for [Jesus] to be taken up, he set his face to go to Jerusalem." This statement begins an extended section of the gospel known as the **Lukan travel narrative** that continues all the way until Luke 19:57. This section (Luke 9:51–19:57) contains many parables and sayings of Jesus that are unique to Luke's gospel. Interwoven in this mostly Special L material (that is, material found only in Luke) are repeated reminders of Jesus's journey to Jerusalem (Luke 9:53; 13:33; 17:11; 18:31).

Luke's gospel has more parables than the other canonical gospels, and most of them appear in this section. These Lukan parables often highlight the radical nature of the Lukan Jesus's teaching, even while this "radicalness" is often lost on modern readers. They also connect to the broader themes of the Luke–Acts narrative. For example, the parable of the "Good Samaritan" (Luke 10:25–37) depicts two priestly men ignoring and passing by a crime victim lying on the roadside before a Samaritan comes to his aid with extraordinary generosity. This story is so well known that one might now be called a Good Samaritan simply for doing a good deed. But this easy application of the designation misses the point that few Jews in the first century CE would expect a Samaritan to be "good" or treat someone coming from Jerusalem as "a neighbor." Indeed, there was a history of animosity between the Jews and Samaritans.

Another series of three parables in Luke 15 features a common theme of recovering the lost. The Lukan Jesus tells these parables when his opponents complain that he "welcomes and eats" with "sinners" (Luke 15:2). The first parable concerns a man's search for the one sheep out of 100 that goes missing. The second one features a woman's search for her one lost coin out of 10. The third parable is a more extended story of a father who rejoices at the return of his wayward son. The "punchline" of this parable comes when the father's older son complains about the extravagant celebration over the return of the once lost son. The father tells him, "Child, you are always with me and all that is mine is yours. But it was fitting for us to celebrate and rejoice because, your brother, he was dead and has come to life, was lost and has been found" (Luke 15:31–2). This conclusion indicates that the story is not simply about the repentant son who has returned, but also about reproving the disgruntled brother.

All three of these stories of God's joy and recovering the lost may be the author's way of accentuating his theme of God's universal plan of salvation. From the author's perspective, both Jews *and* gentiles are part of this plan, with the gentiles being the recovered lost coin, or sheep, or wayward brother. Like the dutiful son who complains to his father, the grumbling Pharisees and scribes are not excluded from God's reign but continue to share in the inheritance even if the gentiles have been "found."

Another type of Lukan parable raises questions about wealth and the accumulation of possessions. These parables are set in the context of the gospel's theme of God's concern for the poor. This theme appears first in Mary's song in the opening chapter of the gospel. As mentioned above, it imitates Hannah's song in describing a God who changes fortunes, exalting the lowly and bringing down the rich and powerful (Luke 1:46–56). Soon after, the Lukan Jesus suggests that he has been chosen to "announce good news to the poor and release to the prisoner" (Luke 4:18). Then, in the Lukan version of the beatitudes, Jesus announces "Blessed are the poor" rather than "Blessed are the poor in spirit" as in Matthew's version (Luke 6:20; compare Matt 5:3).

Several Lukan parables contribute to the focus on God's concern for the poor. For example, in Luke 12:13–21, the Lukan Jesus tells a story in the context of a brother's concern to get his share of the family inheritance. Jesus first issues a warning against greed because "life is not in one's abundance of possessions" (Luke 12:15). Then comes the parable, which is about a man who builds large barns, stores up his large amount of produce, and decides that he can now relax for a while. But God calls the rich man a fool for his seemingly reasonable retirement plan. God tells the man that he will soon die and then asks, "The things you have prepared, whose will they be?" (Luke 12:20). The question suggests that the problem is the accumulation of wealth for oneself. A similar idea is conveyed even more vividly in the parable of Lazarus and the Rich Man. In this case, a poor, homeless man named Lazarus is rewarded after death by being in the company of Abraham, while an unnamed rich man suffers in fiery Hades after he dies (Luke 16:19–31). The conclusion to the parable suggests that it is the rich man's lack of compassion for Lazarus that is under critique, a compassion that he should have learned from Moses and the prophets – that is, from the Jewish scriptures.

Although the gospel thematizes concern for outcasts and the poor, there are puzzling elements regarding this focus. First, we find mixed messages across the two volumes. For instance, in keeping with the warnings about wealth that we see in the parables, later in the gospel, another rich young man is told that in order to "inherit eternal life" he must sell all that he has and distribute the money to the poor (Luke 18:22). Another character, a rich tax collector named Zacchaeus, is granted salvation when he pledges to give *half* of his possessions to the poor and compensate those he has cheated (Luke 19:1–9). Similarly, Acts 4:32–7 describes the Jerusalem Christ-followers as a group with no private ownership of possessions. However, when they sell their private possessions, they do not do so to give the money to the poor. Rather, the proceeds from their private possessions are distributed among the Christ group on the basis of need. A couple who violates this process by holding some private money in reserve is struck down dead (Acts 5:1–11). After this scene, the theme of possessions disappears altogether from the rest of the book of Acts. In fact, the word for "poor" never even occurs in Acts. Rather, as I discuss further in Chapter 10, the author appeals to the status-conscious members of his audience by portraying the followers of Jesus as civilized men who are comfortable associating with men of high status. In sum, there is no consistent message about wealth and possessions that is woven all the way through the two books of Luke–Acts.

Contemporary Voices: Latin American and Intercultural Interpretation of Luke

The Gospel of Luke's message about God's liberation of the poor and oppressed has played a central role in **liberation theology**. Working among poor communities in Latin America, liberation theologians argue that God has a "preferential option for the poor." According to Gustavo Gutiérrez (a Peruvian priest, theologian, and one of the founders of liberation theology), God's preferential option for the poor means that God stands on the side of the poor. Gutiérrez argues that God calls the church to be engaged in actions with and on behalf of the poor, especially actions directed toward ending unjust social structures.

More recently, Esa Autero has studied the Lukan poverty texts with two Bolivian Pentecostal communities (see Esa Autero, *Reading the Bible across Contexts: Luke's Gospel, Socio-economic Marginality, and Latin American Biblical Hermeneutics* (Leiden and Boston: Brill, 2016)). Autero describes the members of Group One as economically marginalized and those of Group Two as economically privileged. Autero's work is a model of intercultural interpretation of the Bible, which examines how insights from "ordinary" people can inform the academic study of the Bible. The excerpts

below show how the two groups relate differently to Luke 14:12–14. In this brief passage, the Lukan Jesus is invited to dine at the home of a Pharisee. While there, Jesus suggests to his host that he should not invite guests to his home who are likely to reciprocate (such as friends, relatives, and rich neighbors). Rather, the man should invite "the poor, the crippled, the lame, and the blind" (Luke 14:13).

Group One:

MARIA:	Sometimes one is invited [to a party] but one does not go.
. . . .	
PASTOR:	For example I have an engineer [as a friend] who has a lot of money and I am of little means and he invites me to his party. I feel ashamed to go there.
PASTORA:	True . . . we exclude ourselves.
PASTOR:	I have a Korean friend who invited me to his birthday party . . . the brother has a lot of money . . . and he invited me to his birthday party . . . so what do I bring

to him [as a gift]? What do I bring? You know what I brought him? A turkey [everybody laughs with the pastor]. And he liked the turkey [everybody laughs] . . .

JUANA: One peso for the turkey.

PASTORA: But for example if we are invited to his birthday party what can I bring to him . . . a quarter of a chicken? [Everybody laughs] A quarter of a chicken that's all there is . . . that's all there is.

JUANA: He already has everything. (217–218)

Group Two:

CARINA: The crippled, the lame, the blind and in reality all the needy people and why? Because the reward is divine and comes from God.

TANIA: The needy are the poor in spirit, to those who are ignorant of the word, and who have a great need . . . to receive.

MARIA: It is spiritual; it could have been rich, crippled, lame, [and] blind. It talks about the spiritual poverty.

CARINA: In addition, it says when you make a meal or a dinner; it does not talk about other things other than food. If we associate that the word is food, it talks about food not about giving other things. It does not talk about giving a coat or house or other things except food. (223)

. . .

JOSÉ: I am going to have a banquet . . . and I am going to invite you because we are friends. All of you but as a great idea I am also going to invite the drug users, street urchins from the canals.

MARIA: I would not go to your banquet (everybody laughs). (225)

What do you notice from listening to these contemporary voices interact with this Lukan passage? How might insights from these Bolivian readers deepen an interpretation of the passage?

FOCUS
TEXT

Jesus's Sermon in Nazareth (Luke 4:14–30)

As I discussed earlier in the chapter, the author positions this synoptic story of the rejection of Jesus near Jesus's hometown so that it is his first public act of ministry in the gospel (compare Mark 6:1–6). Also, while the Markan version of Jesus's rejection in his hometown is quite brief, the author of Luke expands the story. These changes indicate the importance the author placed in the narrative of Luke 4:14–30. As we will see, the passage introduces several themes of the Gospel of Luke and also points ahead to the narrative of Acts.

In Luke's version of the story, Jesus returns to Galilee after the temptation in the wilderness. He is "filled with the power of the Spirit" and quickly gains recognition and praise as he teaches in the synagogues (Luke 4:14–15). It is not until he comes to his hometown that the content of his teaching is reported. The scene unfolds in two parts. In the first part, Luke 4:16–22, Jesus's words gain high praise from his hometown audience. In the second part, Luke 4:23–30, things turn in a radically different direction.

I noted above the significance of the depiction of Jesus reading from a scroll as a demonstration of his literacy (4:16). In addition to the fact *that* Jesus reads, however, *what* he reads is also significant:

The Spirit of the Lord is upon me, because he has anointed me to bring good news to the poor. He has sent me to proclaim release to the captives and recovery of sight to the blind, to let the oppressed go free, to proclaim the year of the Lord's favor. (4:18–19 NRSV; compare Isaiah 61:1)

This passage draws on the prophet Isaiah to bring together several major themes of the gospel: the identification of Jesus with the rejected prophets of Israel, the role of the Holy Spirit, and the Lukan Jesus's attention to the poor and oppressed. All these themes were introduced in the birth narrative, and this opening statement of Jesus reaffirms their importance to the gospel. The story builds tension as Jesus rolls the scroll back up, hands it to the synagogue attendant, and then sits down to comment on the scripture. The Lukan Jesus's announcement that the scripture has been fulfilled in their hearing brings words of praise from the synagogue members (Luke 4:21–2). Here is another indication that the author of Luke wishes to tell a story that differs from his source, the Gospel of Mark. In the Markan version, people question Jesus's origins in a way that criticizes his presumptuousness.

"From where is he getting these things? . . . Isn't this the carpenter, the son of Mary, and the brother of James and Joseph and Judah and Simon? And aren't his sisters here with us?" And they were offended by him. (Mark 6:2–3)

In the Gospel of Luke, this line of questioning is changed into words of praise: "And all were impressed with him and amazed at the gracious words that came from his mouth, saying, 'Isn't this Joseph's son?'" (Luke 4:22). In Luke's telling, they are proud of Jesus as a hometown boy.

At this point, the scene shifts in tone. The author juxtaposes two different proverbs. With the first one, "physician heal yourself," the Lukan Jesus anticipates the skepticism of the crowd and their demand for proof of his wonders. With the second proverb, he predicts their rejection of him: "No prophet is acceptable in his hometown" (Luke 4:23–4; compare Mark 6:4). In Mark, this saying is a fitting conclusion to the offense the crowd has already shown. In Luke's version, the people have only praised Jesus before this point. Given that the rejection will not occur until after the author's expansion of the scene, in this version, the proverbs anticipate what is to come.

The scene continues with the Lukan Jesus offering a series of examples about how God worked (or not) with ancient Israel in the time of earlier prophets – Elisha and Elijah. The evocation of these prophets is another example of linking Jesus with the prophetic tradition of Israel, but it does more than that. By the time the Lukan Jesus has finished talking about these early prophets, the synagogue members have become so enraged with his words that they try to throw Jesus off a cliff (Luke 4:28–9). What has caused this sudden change in mood? The examples that the Lukan Jesus provides are both cases when God helped non-Israelites rather than an Israelite in a time of need – the widow in Sidon and Naaman the Syrian. Both of these figures represent the theme already introduced in the birth narrative: that God's salvation includes gentiles. The reaction of the crowd anticipates the theme of the rejection of Jesus (and, later, the followers of Jesus) by some in the Jewish community.

Although I conclude this chapter here, it is not the conclusion of the narrative of Luke–Acts. The author's story of God's plan of salvation continues in his second volume, and so I turn to the discussion of the Book of Acts in the next chapter. Here, I will note one more distinctive aspect of the gospel as a way of bridging to the next chapter. In the Gospel of Mark, the term "apostle" appears only twice (Mark 3:14; 6:30), while the designation of Jesus's followers as "disciples" is far more common. In the Gospel of Luke, the author regularly uses the term "the apostles" (Luke 6:13; 9:10; 17:5: 22:14; 24:10). He also introduces a quotation from "the Wisdom of God" (with no known source) that begins, "I will send them prophets and apostles, some of whom they will kill and persecute . . ." (Luke 11:49). In this way, the author directly puts the apostles in the line of rejected prophets, some of whom will be killed. This is just one of many ways that the gospel narrative anticipates the Acts of the Apostles.

CHAPTER NINE REVIEW

1 Know the meaning and significance of the following terms discussed in this chapter:
 • Lukan travel narrative
 • Luke–Acts
 • Theophilus
2 What are the different ways that the author of Luke connects Jesus to the story of Israel in the Old Testament? List as many as you can.
3 What are three main themes developed in the Gospel of Luke? How do these themes relate to one another?
4 How and why does the author situate the Jesus movement in relationship to the Roman empire and Roman values?
5 How does the author of Luke–Acts emphasize the role of the Holy Spirit? What importance does the Spirit have in the Jesus movement according to this work?

6 What are some character traits that were valued by elite men in Roman culture? How and why does the Gospel of Luke emphasize ways that Jesus and his followers exemplify these characteristics?
7 (Focus text: Luke 4:14–30) How does the story of Jesus's sermon at Nazareth in Luke 4:14–30 illustrate central themes of Luke–Acts, such as links to the story of Israel and salvation to Israel and to the gentiles? Why do you think the author of Luke–Acts portrays Jesus as preaching "good news to the poor" at the beginning of his ministry? What do you think it meant in his context? How might contemporary readers from diverse socio-economic backgrounds understand Jesus's teaching in this passage in a twenty-first-century context?

RESOURCES FOR FURTHER STUDY

Green, Joel. *Methods for Luke*. Cambridge and New York: Cambridge University Press, 2010.

Parsons, Mikeal, C. *Luke: Storyteller, Interpreter, Evangelist*. Peabody, MA: Hendrickson, 2007.

Shillington, V. George. *An Introduction to the Study of Luke–Acts* (2nd edition). London: T&T Clark, 2015.

Tannehill, Robert C. *The Narrative Unity of Luke–Acts: A Literary Interpretation*. Foundations and Facets. Philadelphia: Fortress, 1986–1990. A dated but detailed discussion of the thematic links between the two volumes.

The Spread of "the Way" in the Roman Empire: The Acts of the Apostles

10

Chapter Outline

Chapter Overview	**171**
Salvation to Israel and to the Gentiles in Acts	**171**
The Role of the Spirit in Acts	**174**
The Acts of Jesus and the Acts of the Apostles	**175**
Looking Beyond the Leading Men of Luke–Acts	**177**
Paul and the Spread of "the Way" in the Roman Empire	**179**
Focus Text: Acts 8:26–40	**180**
Conclusion: Luke–Acts' Ambivalent Response to Empire	**183**
Chapter Ten Review	**183**
Resources for Further Study	**184**

Chapter Overview

This chapter continues the discussion of the two-volume work known as Luke–Acts that began in Chapter 9. The chapter traces the development of themes from the first volume into the second, focusing on the expansion of the Jesus movement (referred to as "**the Way**") to gentiles, the role of the Holy Spirit in that expansion, and how the apostles in Acts continue the work begun by the Lukan Jesus. It also considers the role of marginalized characters in the story, especially from the perspective of contemporary readers. It then turns to the Paul of Acts, exploring how the depiction of Paul contributes to the book's themes. The focus text for the chapter features the Ethiopian eunuch, another character on the margins.

Salvation to Israel and to the Gentiles in Acts

The author of Luke–Acts weaves several themes across his two volumes. The most prominent of these themes in Acts concerns how God's plan of salvation extends to both Israel and the gentiles. In the Gospel of Luke, the author uses speeches (or songs) voiced

The New Testament: A Contemporary Introduction, First Edition. Colleen M. Conway.
© 2023 John Wiley & Sons Ltd. Published 2023 by John Wiley & Sons Ltd.

by his characters to present this divine plan of salvation. The gospel then ends with Jesus instructing the disciples to preach to "all nations" (*ethne*). Although this instruction suggests a focus on the gentiles, the first eight chapters of Acts involve preaching in mostly Jewish territory.

It is not until Acts 10 that outreach to the gentiles receives its own dramatic turning point. This chapter depicts the Jewish Christ-follower Peter and the God-revering gentile Cornelius coming together because of divinely inspired visions (Acts 10:3–33). Cornelius is described as a Roman centurion of the Italian cohort who "revered God with his entire household," gave alms to "the people," and "prayed all the time" to God (Acts 10:2). Later, we learn that the whole of the Jewish people speak well of him (10:22). In short, the author makes very clear that this is a pious gentile, not to mention a high-status man with slaves and soldiers who work for him (Acts 10:7).

On the basis of their divinely inspired visions, Peter travels to Cornelius's home in Caesarea. Meanwhile, Cornelius prepares for Peter's arrival by gathering his friends and relatives to await his coming. When Peter arrives and hears the details of Cornelius's vision, he articulates his understanding that "God is not partial, but in every nation, anyone who reveres him and acts justly is pleasing to him" (Acts 10:34–5). Peter then preaches to the gentile audience gathered in the home of Cornelius in Caesarea, just as he earlier preached to the Jews in Jerusalem and with similar results: the Spirit falls upon all who hear the word (Acts 10:34–44; compare Acts 2:14–48). At this, the narrator reports that the "circumcised believers" with Peter were "astonished that the gift of the Holy Spirit had been poured out also on the gentiles" (Acts 10:44). When Peter returns to Jerusalem, he faces criticism by "the circumcised" (that is, the Jewish Christ-followers) for his association with gentiles. He retells the events that led him to Cornelius "step by step" so that the gospel audience hears about the episode a second time (Acts 11:1–18). This repetition shows how important the Cornelius episode is to the author. On hearing Peter's narration, his critics withdraw their objections about a mission to the gentiles and offer the final words of the scene: "Then even to the gentiles, God has given the repentance leading to life" (Acts 11:18; compare Luke 24:47).

The dramatic events of chapters 10–11 depict a divine intervention that convinces all the Christ-followers in Jerusalem to welcome gentiles into the movement. Nevertheless, for the rest of the narrative, gentile inclusion proceeds because of Jewish rejection. This theme too was anticipated in the Lukan birth narrative, where Simeon follows his prediction of God's salvation with the statement that Jesus is appointed "for the falling and rising of many in Israel" (Luke 2:34). In Luke–Acts, Simeon's prediction means that some Jews will come to believe in Jesus ("rise") and some will not ("fall"). The theme that some Jews rejected the idea of following Jesus is especially prominent in the portrayal of Paul's mission in Acts. Repeatedly, Paul's preaching to synagogue assemblies causes dissent among some synagogue members, which leads Paul to redirect his attention to the gentiles (see, for example, Acts 13:42–51; 14:1–7; 17:1–15; 19:8–9; 28:17–28).

Basics on the Acts of the Apostles

Acts: from Jerusalem to Rome		**Outline: the geographic structure of Acts**
Prologue: introduction to the second volume	1:1–5	
A. Apostolic mission in Jerusalem	1:6–7:60	
B. Spread of mission beyond Jerusalem	8:1–12:25	
1. Spread of the mission in Palestine and Paul's call	8:1–9:43	
2. Initial mission to the gentiles as far as Antioch	10:1–12:25	
C. Paul's journeys	13:1–28:31	
1. The mission from Antioch to Asia Minor and Greece	13:1–19:20	
2. The journey to Rome by way of Jerusalem	19:21–28:31	

The structure of Acts builds on the geographic orientation of the Gospel of Luke. The gospel's travel narrative showed Jesus moving toward Jerusalem, where the gospel ends. Accordingly, the book of Acts begins in Jerusalem and moves outward. A major literary feature of the book are the many speeches the author creates for its characters to communicate his major themes. These speeches by Peter, Stephen, and Paul make up nearly a third of the book.   **Structure**

Noting these literary motifs helps to remind us that the author of Luke–Acts is composing a narrative, not recording events exactly as they unfolded. For example, we know that Paul believed from the outset of his ministry that God sent him to the gentiles (review Gal 2, especially 7–10), while the author of Luke–Acts suggests that he went to the gentiles only after he was turned away in Jewish synagogues. As discussed in Chapter 9, the author of Luke–Acts presents a version of "history" that makes sense for him in light of his understanding of Jesus and of the emerging community of Christ-followers.

While this group included both Jews and gentile Christ-followers, not *all* Jews joined the Jesus movement. Indeed, some were unconvinced by the Christ-followers' insistence that Jesus was the long-awaited messiah. To account for this fact, the author of Luke–Acts tells a story that shares some similarities with Paul's argument in Romans 9–11. For Paul, the rejection of Jesus by some of Israel occurs in the context of God's larger plan for the salvation of Israel and the gentiles. The author of Luke–Acts also puts this rejection in the framework of the history of Israel. His characters insist that there have always been some who rejected God's prophets.

Accentuating Jewish rejection also has another function. At the same time as the author of Luke–Acts portrays some Jewish authorities as hostile to the Jesus movement, he often goes out of his way to depict the Roman authorities as reasonable men who have no interest in quibbles among the Jews. Such a portrayal aligns with the author's interests in legitimizing the Jesus movement in the context of the Roman empire.

His audience can be reassured that the movement is peaceful and law-abiding – that is, compatible with life in the Roman empire. Even so, there are subtleties in the narrative that reflect the ambivalence toward Rome discussed in the last chapter. Note, for instance, the depiction of the Roman governor Gallio in Acts 18. On the one hand, he illustrates the theme of Roman indifference to the Jesus movement (Acts 18:14–15). On the other hand, his indifference includes a certain brutality. This is illustrated by how Gallio ignores a mob's violent attack against Sosthenes, a synagogue leader seemingly well disposed toward Paul (Acts 18:17; see 1 Cor 1:1).

Despite the repeated accounts of the Jewish rejection of Paul's message, he continues to preach to the Jews. Indeed, even at the end of the narrative, when he has finally reached Rome and is kept under arrest, Paul calls together the local Jewish leaders in Rome. He once more makes the case that he has done nothing against "our people or the customs of our ancestors." Even more, he tells the Jews that "it is for the sake of the hope of Israel that I am bound with this chain" (Acts 28:20). As has been the case throughout Acts, some people in Paul's audience are convinced but others refuse to believe. In response, Paul quotes an extended passage from the prophet Isaiah that begins as follows:

> Go to this people and say,
> "You will indeed listen, but never understand,
> and you will look, but will never perceive." (Acts 28:26 NRSV)

Other New Testament writings use this passage from Isaiah to explain why Jesus spoke in parables (compare Mark 4:12; Matt 13:14–15) or why some did not believe in Jesus (John 12:40; see also the use of Isaiah in Rom 9:27; 10:20–1). In Acts, the Isaiah quotation becomes a final statement supporting the mission to the gentiles. The last words of Paul in the book are "Therefore, let it be known to you then that this salvation of God has been sent to the gentiles and they will listen" (Acts 28:28). The combination of the Isaiah quotation with Paul's final words encourages a contrast between those gentiles who listen and those Jews who listen but "never understand."

Does such an ending suggest that the author has written a tragic story of the history of Israel? After all, though the Gospel of Luke begins with the claim that Jesus will be a light for revelation to the gentiles and for glory to Israel (Luke 2:30–2), the final section of Acts calls attention to Jewish rejection of Paul's gospel in contrast to gentile acceptance. This raises the possibility that the author of Luke-Acts offers a tragic story about Israel. Perhaps. Alternatively, in the author's view, the end of his literary work does not signal the completion of God's plan of salvation. Note that Acts concludes with a report that Paul lived in Rome for two whole years, "welcoming all," a phrase that leaves open the possibility of an ongoing mission to Jews and gentiles. In fact, there is no final word on Israel. Nor, by the way, is there a final word on the fate of Paul and his mission. In the end, the author leaves the narrative of Luke–Acts open-ended.

The Role of the Spirit in Acts

The Holy Spirit appears in Luke–Acts as a primary instrument through which God's plan of salvation is carried forward. At the end of Luke, the risen Jesus promises that his disciples will be clothed with power from on high (Luke 24:49). The beginning of Acts returns to the character of the resurrected (but not yet ascended) Jesus, who instructs the apostles "through the Holy Spirit" (Acts 1:2). He tells the apostles to stay in Jerusalem, where they will soon be baptized by the Holy Spirit (Acts 1:5).

This promise is then fulfilled during the Jewish spring harvest festival known as Shavuot (Pentecost in Greek). As the Lukan Jesus promised, the twelve apostles are filled with the Holy Spirit, and the "power" that they receive is manifested in an ability to speak in other languages (Acts 2:1–9). As the narrative continues, they will reveal the power they have to heal, raise people from the dead, temporarily blind someone, and cast out spirits.

The author explains what has occurred through one of the character Peter's several speeches in Acts. This speech begins with a long quotation from the Hebrew prophet Joel. The opening lines predict the reception of God's spirit:

> "And it will be in the last days," says God
> "that I will pour out my Spirit on all flesh,
> and your sons will prophesy and your daughters,
> and your young men will see visions,
> and your old men will dream dreams.
> Even on my male slaves and female slaves,
> I will pour out my Spirit in those days, and they will prophesy."
> (Acts 2:17–18)

By beginning Peter's speech with this quotation, the author asserts that the Spirit that is now active in the Jesus movement was predicted long ago in Israel's past. This idea is reiterated by references to the Spirit's inspiration of past figures like the psalmist David (Acts 4:25) and the prophet Isaiah (Acts 28:25). At the same time, the author of Luke–Acts inserts the phrase "in the last days" before the quotation from Joel, thus adding an eschatological interpretation to the prophecy; the Holy Spirit's "pouring out" on Jesus's followers becomes a sign of the "last days."

As the Lukan Jesus predicted, the Holy Spirit inspires the apostles to speak with boldness before rulers and authorities (Acts 4:13; 4:31). Moreover, the apostles enable others to receive the Holy Spirit by baptism, laying on of hands (Acts 2:38; 8:17; 9:17), or speaking "the word" (Acts 10:44). The Holy Spirit is so prominent in Acts that it takes on the role of a character, speaking to other characters (8:29; 11:12; 13:2; 16:6) and even moving them from place to place (8:39; 13:4). In some cases, the Spirit forbids the apostles to preach in certain places (Acts 16:6–7).

The Acts of Jesus and the Acts of the Apostles

Another way that the author weaves themes across his two-volume work is by depicting the apostles in ways that resemble the portrayal of Jesus. In Acts 1:8, the resurrected Jesus responds to the apostles' question about the restoration of Israel by telling them that it is not their place to know "the times or seasons" set by God:

> But you will receive power when the Holy Spirit comes upon you; and you will be my witnesses in Jerusalem, in all Judea and Samaria, and to the end of the earth.

Later in Acts, Peter describes God's empowering of Jesus in much the same way: "God anointed Jesus of Nazareth with the Holy Spirit and with power" (Acts 10:38). Thus, just as Jesus then "went about doing good and healing all who were oppressed by the devil" (Acts 10:38), the apostles in Acts set about preaching, healing, and casting out unclean spirits. In several places, their miraculous power is described in the same summary fashion: "Now many signs and wonders were done among the people through the apostles" (Acts 5:12; see also 2:43; 4:30; 6:8; 8:6; 19:11). But the author also recounts specific examples of these signs and wonders in the cases of Peter and Paul. Both apostles heal a lame man (Acts 3:1–10; 14:8–10), and both raise people from the dead (Acts 10:26; 20:7–12). Indeed, Paul himself may be raised from the dead (14:19–20). The author portrays the extraordinary quality of these apostles by having others perceive Peter and Paul as god-like, even while the apostles themselves insist that they are mere mortals (10:26; 14:8–15).

The apostles are also depicted in ways that mark them as respectable members of society – indeed, as civilized men who exhibit the traits of other elite men in their culture. As we saw in the last chapter, the Lukan Jesus is portrayed as literate and pious. The author continues this trend in Acts with the portrayal of the apostles speaking as if they were educated men even though they were not. Indeed, the author makes this connection explicit in the Jerusalem leaders' reaction to the apostles:

> Seeing the bold speaking of Peter and John and realizing that they were uneducated and common men, they were amazed and recognized that they had been with Jesus. (Acts 4:13)

This description not only calls attention to the apostles' ability to speak confidently – which was highly regarded in the Greco-Roman culture – but links their oratorical skill to their association with Jesus. Similarly, the apostles share the trait of piety with Jesus. They are closely linked to the Jerusalem temple and are regularly depicted as engaged in prayer (Acts 1:14; 2:42; 4:31; 6:4; 7:59; 10:30; 11:5).

The narrative of Luke–Acts also implies that being a Christ-follower can help one achieve the sort of self-control that was associated with manly conduct in the ancient world. This is most evident in the way Paul speaks with Roman officials. In Acts 24:24–5, Paul speaks to Felix about "justice, self-control and the coming judgment." Similarly, before the client king Agrippa, Paul describes his earlier life compared to his life as a Christ-follower. He relates how, earlier, he persecuted "many of the saints" and was "furiously enraged at them, pursuing them to other cities" (Acts 26:11). In other words, the Paul of Acts offers a picture of himself as a man out of control – that is, an "unmanly" man from the perspective of Roman elite culture. At the end of Paul's speech, the Roman governor Festus suggests that Paul is very educated but that so much learning is making him insane (Acts 26:24). The first claim bolsters Paul's status as an elite man. Paul denies the second charge by claiming the contrary: he is not out of his mind but speaks with "truth and moderation" (*sophrosune*) (Acts 26:25). The exchange implies that while Paul used to be a man out of control, now that he is a Christ-follower, he speaks truthfully and with the self-control that was so highly esteemed in the culture.

In summary, Luke–Acts tells the story of the early Christ-followers in a way that suggests that being a part of this movement would help one attain a life of virtue and thus be seen as a manly and respectable member of society. Jesus and his followers are presented as self-controlled, educated, and pious – in short, as civilized men. This is not to say that those outside of the Jesus movement would be convinced by such claims. From an outsider perspective, joining a movement that was populated by low-status people and dedicated to following an executed man would not help one's masculine status. But that is precisely why the author would use Paul to portray Christ-followers as virtuous. Paul's claims would be a way of reassuring Christ-followers that they had much to gain from participating in "the Way," even if outside critics suggested otherwise.

At the same time, the author acknowledges that the apostles also resemble the Lukan Jesus in their violent deaths. In the Acts 1:8 passage quoted above, the Greek word that is translated as "witnesses" (*martyres*) can also mean martyrs. Indeed, the English word comes from the Greek. To illustrate this point, the author offers a dramatic account of the martyrdom of Stephen, a Greek-speaking Jew (a "Hellenist"; see Acts 6:1–6). In Luke 13:34, Jesus laments over Jerusalem, describing it as "killing the prophets and stoning the ones who are sent to it." In Acts, Stephen asks the Jewish council, "Which of the prophets did your ancestors not persecute?" (see also Luke 11:47–8). Stephen's listeners become so enraged and out of control that they drag him out of the city and stone him.

Stephen's death at the hands of a mob is told in a way that recalls the death of Jesus. Just as Jesus commends his spirit to God at his death, Stephen prays for "Lord Jesus" to receive his spirit before he dies (Luke 23:46; Acts 8:59). Just before Stephen dies, he cries out, "Lord, do not hold this sin against them" (Acts 7:60). In the Gospel of Luke, a verse that is present in some ancient manuscripts and lacking in others reads, "Father, forgive them because they do not know what they are doing" (Luke 23:34). Perhaps a scribe observed the similarities between the deaths of Stephen and the Lukan Jesus and added the verse to the Lukan passion narrative so that Stephen did not appear more forgiving than Jesus! Finally, a righteous member of the Jewish council named Joseph buries Jesus, and devout Jewish men bury and lament over Stephen (Luke 23:50; Acts 2).

Notably, the author does *not* narrate the death of his two central characters in Acts, Peter and Paul. To be sure, both apostles are arrested, and Paul is the victim of mob violence more than once. But rather than tell the story of their martyrdom, the author offers stories of divine rescue. Twice, Peter is miraculously freed from prison by an angel of the Lord (Acts 5:19; 12:6–11). Paul and Silas benefit from divine intervention in the form of an earthquake that both opens the doors to their prison and unfastens their chains (Acts 16:25–7). Such instances of divine deliverance were a popular feature in Greek romance novels that were being written around the same time as Acts. Whether or not the author was familiar with this genre, he shares its interest in telling an entertaining story involving dramatic rescues of his heroes.

Looking Beyond the Leading Men of Luke–Acts

Our study to this point suggests that Acts is very much a story of men in the Jesus movement: Peter, Stephen, Philip, Cornelius, and especially Paul consume much of the narrative space. In this section, I interrupt – or perhaps better, I disrupt – the focus of the leading men in Acts to attend to several characters on the margins. I am aided by contemporary womanist and feminist scholars who offer new questions and observations.

The story of Peter's divine rescue mentioned above includes the brief appearance of a character named Rhoda, who is described as a *paidiske* (often translated as "maid"; Acts 12:13 NRSV). When the rescued Peter knocks at Mary's outer gate, it is Rhoda who goes to answer. When she hears Peter's voice, Rhoda is so overjoyed that she runs to tell the others, leaving Peter standing outside the gate. Scholars have long read Rhoda's part in Peter's story as comedic – she is viewed as a foolish woman intended to add lightness to the miraculous escape story. However, Margaret Aymer urges readers of Acts to take the character of Rhoda seriously (see Aymer, "Outrageous, Audacious, Courageous, Willful: Reading the Enslaved Girl of Acts 12," in Resources for Further Study). Aymer's reading begins with the recognition that Rhoda is not actually a foolish "maid." The Greek word *paidiske* means a young female slave, and an ancient reader would have recognized the character of Rhoda as an enslaved child. Knowing this does not change how the author intended the figure to function in his narrative. Greek and Roman literature of the period commonly applied the figure of a running slave for comedic effect. In this sense, Aymer observes that Rhoda "is not intended to be read or seen as a person" but viewed simply as a stock character (271).

Nevertheless, Aymer rightly urges an interpretation that acknowledges the dark side of Rhoda's slave status. First, her presence in the story "locates human trafficking and child slavery within the earliest church" (268). The story depicts Rhoda as the enslaved girl of Mary, mother of John, a Christ-follower who is wealthy enough to live in a house with an outer gate. The slave girl's presence in Mary's household challenges the idealized picture of the Jesus movement that Luke's narrative offers. It also raises questions about who is included in the liberating vision of salvation that launches the Lukan Jesus's ministry (266).

As Aymer observes, Rhoda functions as Mary's body double in the story, facing potential threats in place of her free-bodied owner (279). In the context of the story, James has already been killed, and Peter is in prison. Therefore, a knock at the door could signal danger. One can imagine that the joy that Rhoda expresses upon hearing Peter's voice also includes relief because she hears a familiar voice – an associate of her owner and not a Roman official.

In any case, Rhoda's announcement to the household is met with skepticism and rebuke. When she announces to those inside that Peter is at the gate, they rebuke her with one word: *mainei*, meaning, "You are insane!" (see also Acts 26:24; 1 Cor 14:23; John 10:20). It is at this point, Aymer observes, that Rhoda acts in a womanish way, "outrageous, audacious, courageous . . . willful" (quoting Alice Walker's definition of "womanish" in *In Search of Our Mothers' Gardens*). Despite having been put sharply in her place, Rhoda persists. She insists on the truth of her position, even if it means acting in an insubordinate way (Aymer, 281). Those who dismissed her come to realize that she is telling the truth. However, at that point, she has dropped out of the narrative altogether.

Although Rhoda's part is brief, recent work by Christy Cobb shows how, in her role as a truth-teller, she joins two other enslaved girls in the narrative of Luke–Acts (see Cobb, *Slavery, Gender, Truth, and Power in Luke–Acts and Other Ancient Narratives*, in

Resources for Further Study). In the Gospel of Luke, a *paidiske* identifies Peter as one of Jesus's disciples in the courtyard of the high priest (Luke 22:56). As we have seen, in Acts 16, a *paidiske* identifies Paul and Silas as "slaves (Greek, *douloi*) of the Most High God" who preach "a way of salvation" (Acts 16:17). Each of the three slave girls speaks the truth about the men in the narrative, even when the men themselves deny or silence them. As Cobb puts it, each of these young slave girls speaks truth to power. Even while the author gives them the leanest of parts in his extended narrative, contemporary readers can see them as momentary disrupters in a narrative that elevates and idealizes male apostles.

The Paul of Acts versus the Paul of the Letters

The Paul of Acts is a character constructed by the author, not the same Paul who wrote the undisputed letters. In this sense, the Paul of Acts is one of the earliest legendary accounts of Paul. The author presents Paul as a heroic figure who worked closely with the Christ group in Jerusalem. In doing so, he deviates in significant ways from Paul's own account of his ministry and mission. For example, in Acts, Paul returns to Jerusalem after every major trip. He visits Jerusalem five times across the narrative, reflecting the author's interest in situating the Jesus movement in continuity with Judaism. Meanwhile, as we have seen, Paul deliberately distances himself from Jerusalem in his account in Galatians and reports only three visits.

Another major difference concerns the two reports of the leaders' meeting in Jerusalem. Recall that when Paul describes his meeting with the Jerusalem leaders, he reports that those present agreed that he should continue his mission to the gentiles. The only stipulation was that he take up a financial collection for the poor (Gal 2: 7–10). In contrast, the account of the Jerusalem meeting in Acts includes a decision that gentile Christ-followers should be required to follow Jewish dietary regulations (Acts 15:19–29). An even more striking difference in the two accounts, given Paul's own insistence that he was called to be an apostle to the gentiles, occurs when Peter claims that God chose *him* to bring the gospel to the gentiles (Acts 15:7). In keeping with this difference, the Paul of Acts begins his preaching in synagogues, only turning to the gentiles when he is rejected by synagogue members (Acts 18:5–7). In this sense, one aspect of Paul that the author of Luke–Acts understands well (better than later interpreters of Paul) is Paul's Jewish identity. The Paul of Acts keeps Jewish rituals (Acts 18:18; 21:20–6), identifies himself as a Pharisee (Acts 23:6), and insists that he has done nothing against "the law of the Jews or against the Temple" (Acts 25:8). Finally, the narrative of Luke–Acts implies that once the agreement was made, the tensions around gentile inclusion were resolved. Paul's report of his later confrontation in Antioch with Cephas (that is, Peter) suggests otherwise (Gal 2:1–14).

Paul and the Spread of "the Way" in the Roman Empire

In the last chapter, I showed how the author took care to place the early Jesus movement (referred to as "the Way" in his work) in the context of the Roman empire. This interest is also evident in the story of Paul in the second half of Acts. Geographically, Paul travels extensively across the empire by land and sea, building on the spread of the gospel described in the first eight chapters. The author uses the sea voyages to add a sense of adventure to the story. As in other ancient accounts of sea voyages, the author occasionally shifts to the first-person plural. These "we" passages are a further indication of the author's literary finesse and familiarity with accounts of sea voyages in other Greek literature.

Twice in the narrative, Paul dramatically reveals his Roman citizenship. First, in Acts 16:35–9, Paul's revelation comes with a demand for an apology and earns him a personal escort from prison by the Roman magistrates. The scene offers another example of the author's interest in restoring honor to the male heroes of his story. The same pattern occurs in Acts 22:22–9, although, this time, Paul reveals his citizenship as he is about to be flogged, thus challenging the order of the Roman commander. Additionally, in this episode, Paul's citizenship status appears to surpass that of the Roman commander. When the commander points out that his own citizenship cost him a lot of money, Paul claims that *he* is a citizen by birth (Acts 22:27–9).

Paul's status is further reinforced by his access to the commander, affording him enormous protection by the Roman army against a conspiracy to kill him (Acts 23:12–35). The Roman officials who meet with Paul find him innocent of any wrongdoing, echoing the assertions of Jesus's innocence in the gospel (Acts 18:14–15; 24:26–30; Luke 23:6–10). Eventually, Paul's Roman citizenship enables him to avoid a trial in Jerusalem by requesting an audience with the emperor (Acts 25:7–12). His request is granted and results in a journey to Rome, where the narrative concludes (though with no account of a trial).

FOCUS
TEXT

Acts 8:26–40

In the Gospel of Luke, the extended travel narrative inserted by the author accentuates Jesus's steady progression toward Jerusalem, where the gospel concludes. In Acts, the narrative begins in Jerusalem and progresses outward. The events that occur in Acts 1–8 correspond to the Lukan Jesus's declaration, "you will be my witnesses in Jerusalem and all of Judea and Samaria and as far as the end of the earth" (Acts 1:8). This geographical expansion from Jerusalem to all of Judea and Samaria is the result of the persecution and scattering of Christ-followers from their base in Jerusalem (Acts 8:1). The Christ-followers who are scattered fulfill Jesus's command as they go from "place to place to preach the word" (Acts 8:4).

Acts 8:26–40 relates a story about one of the apostles, Philip, whom an angel of the Lord tells to go to a desert road that travels south from Jerusalem toward Gaza. A long, descriptive sentence introduces the character that Philip encounters on the road:

> Behold! A man, an Ethiopian, a eunuch, an official of Candace, queen of the Ethiopians, who was in charge of all her treasure, who had come to Jerusalem to worship, and was returning and seated on his chariot, was reading from the prophet Isaiah. (Acts 8:27b–28)

Recalling the discussion from Chapter 1, here is a character whose multiple intersecting identities are a feature in the story, creating a complex and ambiguous picture. The character is introduced as a man, but also a castrated man, or eunuch. In the ancient world, the manly status of a eunuch was contested, and few ancient writers used the term "man" alongside the term "eunuch." While recognizing this gender ambiguity, in my reading of the passage, I follow the narrator's lead and refer to the eunuch with male pronouns.

The man's ethnic identity, Ethiopian, would put him in the category of an exotic foreigner for the author and his audience (See Figure 10.1). Greek and Roman literature characterized Ethiopia as a mythic place – not necessarily a specific nation as much as a far-away region to the south. In an early example of **African American biblical interpretation** (in brief, interpreting the Bible through the diverse experiences of African Americans), Clarice J. Martin studied the ethnographic significance of the Ethiopian

FIGURE 10.1

Rembrandt van Rijn – The Baptism of the Eunuch (1626). Rembrandt's seventeenth-century painting shows the apostle Philip as a white European man, while the features of the "exotic" Ethiopian man are in keeping with ancient stereotypes about the appearance of Ethiopians. Neither of Rembrandt's foregrounded figures are historically accurate. Note that the artist leaves out the water for the baptism in favor of a full display of the Ethiopian's clothing.

man in Acts. She showed how the thematizing of Ethiopian dark skin in Greek and Roman literature supports a reading of the Ethiopian man in Acts 8 as an exotic foreigner. Martin suggests that because the encounter between Philip and the Ethiopian comes soon after the spread of the Jesus movement from Samaria, the baptism of an Ethiopian eunuch represents the fulfillment of Jesus's prediction of the movement spreading from Jerusalem to all of Judea, then Samaria, and then to "the end of the earth" (Acts 1:8). (See Martin, "A Chamberlain's Journey," in Resources for Further Study.) The author of Luke–Acts later associates the "queen of the south" with the "end of the earth" (Luke 11:31), which strengthens Martin's interpretation.

In addition to his ethnic identity, the eunuch is also depicted as powerful, wealthy, and educated. He is a *dunastes* – that is, a figure with power who oversees the queen's finances. His status makes it possible for him to ride in a chariot with a driver and to issue commands. He is also in the possession of an expensive scripture scroll that he is able to read. Even so, while wealth gives him high status, the man is dependent on a woman with even higher status. Added to this is the fact that in the ancient world, eunuchs were often also slaves. Is the man enslaved or free? We also learn in this opening description that the eunuch is a God-worshipper. He has traveled to Jerusalem to worship, and Philip finds him reading from the Jewish scriptures. This, too, is an ambiguous detail because the legal codes in the Jewish scriptures forbid the inclusion of eunuchs in the "assembly of the Lord" (Deut 23:1; see also Lev 21:17–20). The passage that the eunuch reads is one of the servant songs from the book of Isaiah, in which an unidentified figure is unjustly humiliated and killed. The eunuch wonders about the identity of the figure, asking Philip, "About whom does the prophet say this? About himself or about another?" (Acts 8:34). While the passage closely corresponds to the author's theme of Jesus's unjust execution, it may also allude to the humiliated status of the eunuch.

In fact, for the rest of the episode, the author refers to the man only as "the eunuch" (Acts 8:34, 36, 38, 39). Given this focus, the author may have in mind another passage from Isaiah: an oracle in which God promises to give eunuchs who keep the sabbath "a monument and a name," and in particular "an everlasting name that will not be cut off" (Isa 56:3–5). Even so, ironically, this eunuch remains nameless. Moreover, immediately after Philip baptizes the eunuch, the "spirit of the Lord" seizes Philip and carries him away. In a more recent example of African American interpretation, Demetrius Williams notes that while the eunuch goes on his way rejoicing, he does not receive the Holy Spirit. Nor do Peter and John come to him to lay on hands, as they did after Philip baptized the Samaritans (Acts 8:14–17). Williams observes that while the Joel prophecy in Acts 2 implies that the Spirit will enable *anyone* to prophesy, in fact only certain Jewish and gentile men prophesy in the book of Acts. In this way, the figure of the Ethiopian eunuch reveals the limitations of the supposedly universalizing promise of salvation of the Joel quotation in Acts. (See Williams, "Upon all Flesh," in Resources for Further Study.)

Nevertheless, because the figure of the eunuch challenges conventional identity categories of sex, gender, and social class, the eunuch can be productively read through the lens of queer theory (see box "Queering Paul's Letters" in Chapter 5). I have already noted the ways the figure destabilizes fixed identity categories, a central concern of queer theory. As Sean Burke (see Burke, "Queering Early Christian Discourse," in Resources for Further Study) observes, "the ambiguities in the character of the eunuch function rhetorically to destabilize and denaturalize ancient constructions of identity" (148). But the queerness of the eunuch also extends to his action in the narrative. When the eunuch asks, "What is to stop me from being baptized?" he explicitly pushes the question of his queer identity to the fore. The question is met with silence, creating yet another moment of ambiguity. Undeterred by this silence, or perhaps encouraged by it, the eunuch assumes agency for his own baptism. He commands the chariot to stop and goes down into the water, where Philip baptizes him (though Philip does not speak again in the story). In this way, the Ethiopian eunuch acts with purpose in order to be counted among the "all flesh" of Acts 2:17, even while his inclusion is not unambiguously endorsed in the narrative. (For more on the Ethiopian eunuch, see Resources for Further Study.)

Conclusion: Luke–Acts' Ambivalent Response to Empire

This chapter has demonstrated the way the author of Luke–Acts builds a picture of the movement he calls "the Way" across two volumes. Scholars often point to how the author offers a rosy picture of a unified movement where all the apostles agree about God's mission and their role in preaching and helping to spread the word. This picture does not match the reality of what we know about the early centuries of a diverse movement, as reflected by both Paul's letters and the ongoing production of texts during these same centuries that reflect this diversity. Indeed, as mentioned earlier, we might best view the Paul of Acts as an early Paul of legend whose story is told in a way that supports the themes of the narrative.

Taken together, the two volumes demonstrate a deep ambivalence with respect to situating the Jesus movement in the Roman empire. The use of imperial titles for Jesus appears to be a subversive imitation of the power claims made by and about the Roman emperor. For example, identifying Jesus with the imperial titles Son of God and Savior are assertions of the surpassing power of Jesus. However, while the narrative subverts Roman claims of power, it also adopts the broader cultural values of Rome. It implies that becoming a Christ-follower can help one achieve a life of virtue and therefore a degree of manly status. This ambivalence is also reflected in a different way. While the Lukan Jesus preaches good news to the poor and oppressed, a close look at the margins of the narrative shows the broad acceptance of hierarchical social structures. Nevertheless, some marginal characters can be read as disrupting the social status quo.

CHAPTER TEN REVIEW

1 Know the meaning and significance of the following terms:
- African American Biblical Interpretation (see Appendix for more detail)
- "the Way" (as used in the Acts of the Apostles)

2 What themes does the author continue from Luke to Acts? Give examples of places in Acts where these themes occur.

3 Some scholars argue that the book of Acts is primarily an exchange between elite men. What evidence from

the narrative would support this claim? What evidence would challenge it?

4 In what way are the slave girls in Luke–Acts disrupters and truth-tellers?

5 How might the author's presentation of Paul fit his overall themes? What do you think he was trying to accomplish with his picture of Paul?

6 Scholars debate whether the author of Luke–Acts had access to a collection of Paul's letters. What do you think? Support your answer with evidence from Acts and the undisputed letters of Paul. (Hint: You might narrow your focus to Galatians 1–2, Romans 9–11 compared to Acts 8–9, 13–15.)

7 (Focus text: Acts 8:26–40) What does the Ethiopian eunuch represent in the broader narrative of Acts? Describe some different interpretations of this figure by contemporary readers. What interpretations do you find compelling and why?

RESOURCES FOR FURTHER STUDY

Grimshaw, James P., ed. *Luke–Acts*. Texts@Contexts Series. London and New York: T&T Clark, 2019.

Tannehill, Robert C. *The Narrative Unity of Luke–Acts: A Literary Interpretation*. Foundations and Facets. Philadelphia, PA: Fortress, 1986–1990. A dated but detailed discussion of the thematic links between the two volumes.

For more on women and slaves in Acts:

Aymer, Margaret. "Outrageous, Audacious, Courageous, Willful: Reading the Enslaved Girl of Acts 12." Pp. 265–289 in Gay L. Byron and Vanessa Lovelace (eds.), *Womanist Interpretations of the Bible: Expanding the Discourse*. Atlanta, GA: SBL Press, 2016.

Cobb, Christy. *Slavery, Gender, Truth, and Power in Luke–Acts and Other Ancient Narratives*. London and New York: Palgrave Macmillan, 2019.

For more on the Ethiopian eunuch:

Burke, Sean. "Queering Early Christian Discourse: The Ethiopian Eunuch." Pp. 175–189 in Theresa J. Hornsby and Ken Stone (eds.), *Bible Trouble: Queer Reading at the Boundaries of Biblical Scholarship*. Atlanta, GA: Society of Biblical Literature, 2011.

Martin, Clarice J. "A Chamberlain's Journey and the Challenge of Interpretation for Liberation," *Semeia* 47 (1989): 105–135.

Williams, Demetrius K. "Upon All Flesh: Acts 2, African Americans, and Intersectional Realities." Pp. 289–310 in Randall C. Bailey, Tat-Siong Benny Liew, and Fernando F. Segovia (eds.), *They Were All Together in One Place? Toward Minority Biblical Criticism*. Atlanta, GA: SBL, 2009. Other essays in this volume include Asian American, Cuban, and Latinx approaches to the Bible.

The Gospel of John and the Johannine Letters: Turning Inward as a Strategy for Life in the Empire

Chapter Outline

Chapter Overview	**185**
Who Is the Johannine Jesus?	**186**
The Johannine Prologue: Jesus as Pre-existent Logos Made Flesh	**186**
The Johannine Jesus as God's Divine Agent in the World	**189**
The "I Am" Sayings in the Gospel of John	**191**
Knowing and Believing in the Johannine Jesus	**192**
Opposition from the World	**194**
The Problem of "the Jews" in the Gospel of John	**196**
Focus Text: John 17	**200**
The Johannine Letters	**201**
Chapter Eleven Review	**203**
Resources for Further Study	**203**

Chapter Overview

With the Gospel of John, we enter a different narrative world than that of the synoptic gospels. In this world, there is little talk of the kingdom of God, no talk at all of miracles, but plenty of talk of "signs" and "glory." Whereas the Markan Jesus performs miracles (*dunameis*) to indicate that the kingdom of God is near, the Johannine Jesus's **signs** (*semeia*) point to his divine identity and "reveal his glory" (2:11). Indeed, far from urging secrecy about his identity like the Markan Jesus, the Johannine Jesus speaks in bold, self-descriptive "I am" statements. These distinctive features of the Gospel of John have intrigued readers for centuries. Scholars have long debated the origins and composition of the gospel and how it relates to the synoptic tradition. Already in the second century CE, Clement of Alexandria, a Christian philosopher and teacher, tried to explain why the Gospel of John differed from the others to such a degree. Clement argued that because its author knew that the other gospel writers had "set out the outward facts" about Jesus, the author of John composed a "spiritual gospel." While this suggestion likely helped the Gospel of John secure a place in the canon alongside the synoptic gospels, it also led to misconceptions. On the one hand, there is no shortage of spirituality in the synoptic gospels. On the other hand, some elements of the Gospel of John may be more "factual" than the synoptic traditions (within the limits of our ability to know "facts" from this time).

Rather than labeling John as more "spiritual," and rather than arguing that the gospel writer wants to show Jesus's divinity (another common claim about this gospel), I will focus on highlighting the distinctive elements of the Gospel of John, especially its unique depiction of Jesus. We will also examine how the language of the gospel is more inwardly focused than that of the synoptic gospels. It seems designed to draw boundaries and create a sense of belonging by focusing on the idea of alienation from "the world." Toward that end, the gospel paints an oppositional world of light and dark, above and below, things that are from God and not from God, and belief and unbelief. Such dualistic language is used to emphasize that the Johannine Jesus is *not* of the world. He is described as one sent by God into the world to gather "his own" and give them the power to become children of God. One especially troubling aspect of the gospel is its negative characterization of "the Jews." We will discuss possible reasons for this antagonistic language and the implications of its presence in the Christian canon.

Who Is the Johannine Jesus?

READING

Read John 1–5.

EXERCISE

As you read the opening chapters of John, keep track of the different claims that are made about the identity of Jesus, including the different titles that are attributed to him. Note also how the Johannine Jesus describes who he is, where he has come from, and for what purpose he has come. What overall impression do you have of the Johannine Jesus in these opening chapters compared to the synoptic versions of Jesus?

The Johannine Prologue: Jesus as Pre-existent Logos Made Flesh

The identity of the Johannine Jesus is the central question running through the Gospel of John. The opening lines already begin to address this question in striking fashion with a focus on Jesus's origins. Recall how the gospels of Matthew and Luke use genealogies to trace Jesus's family line back to Abraham (Matt 1:1) and Adam (Luke 3:38). The Gospel of John traces the origin of Jesus even earlier. It opens with a poetic prologue that takes the audience back to a time before the created world: "In the beginning was the *logos* and the *logos* was with God and the *logos* was God" (John 1:1). Typically, the Greek term *logos* is translated as "word," which readers understand as "word of God."

This is one possible meaning of *logos*, but this translation alone does not fully capture the Greek word's multifaceted meaning. In ancient Greek and Roman philosophy, *logos* often refers to the universal rational principle that gives order to the entire cosmos. In the Gospel of John, reference to the *logos* being involved in the creation of "all things" shares a similar cosmic scope. In the writings of Philo, a first-century CE Jewish philosopher, *logos* refers to God's wisdom, and this meaning is certainly part of *logos* in the Gospel of John. We have seen the association between Jesus and personified Wisdom in the Gospel of Matthew. In John, the author uses *logos* to associate Jesus with the figure of divine wisdom. Like personified Wisdom in Proverbs 8, this *logos* is active in creation *with* God, bringing life and light into being (1:3–4). Most striking is the gospel's assertion that this pre-existent divine *logos* became flesh in Jesus (1:14). This idea of a divine being becoming embodied as a human, seen in a number of religious traditions, is referred to as **incarnation**. The link between personified Wisdom in the Jewish scriptures and the incarnate *logos* in John (that is, the Johannine Jesus) continues in the prologue as well as later in the gospel, as the table shows.

Personified Wisdom in Jewish scriptures (translations are modified from the NRSV)	Jesus as Wisdom in the Gospel of John
Sirach 24:9	John 1:1
Before the ages, in the beginning, he created me, and for all the ages I shall not cease to be.	In the beginning was the *logos*, and the *logos* was with God and the *logos* was God. It was in the beginning with God.
Sirach 24:7–8	John 1:14
Among all these I searched for rest, and looked to see in whose territory I might pitch a tent. Then the Creator of all instructed me and my Creator chose the place for my tent. He said, "Pitch your tent in Jacob, make Israel your inheritance."	And the Word became flesh and pitched a tent among us and we beheld its glory . . .
Sirach 24:17–22	John 15:1–2
I am like a vine sprouting grace, my blossoms bear the glorious fruit of glory and riches. Come to me, you who desire me, and take your fill of my fruits, for memories of me are sweeter than honey, inheriting me is sweeter than the honeycomb. They who eat me will hunger for more, they who drink me will thirst for more. No one who obeys me will ever have to blush, no one who acts as I dictate will ever sin.	I am the true vine and my father is the gardener. All branches that do not bear fruit, he removes. All that bear fruit, he prunes so they bear more fruit.
	John 6:34–5
	"Sir," they said, "give us that bread always." Jesus answered them: I am the bread of life. No one who comes to me will ever hunger; no one who believes in me will ever thirst.

(Continued)

Personified Wisdom in Jewish scriptures (translations are modified from the NRSV)	Jesus as Wisdom in the Gospel of John
1 Enoch 42 (modified from Robert Henry Charles's 1913 translation) Wisdom found no place where she might dwell. Then a dwelling-place was assigned her in the heavens. Wisdom went forth to make her dwelling among the children of humans, and found no dwelling-place: Wisdom returned to her place and took her seat among the angels.	John 1:11 He came to what was his own, and his own people did not accept him. John 13:1 ... Jesus knew that his hour had come to depart from this world and go to the Father.

The last two verses of the prologue, 1:17–18, compare Moses and Jesus. You may recall that the Gospel of Matthew links Jesus to Moses and the law to emphasize the importance of Torah obedience. In the Gospel of John, it is more the case that Moses is put in contrast with Jesus. The gospel distinguishes between Moses as a mediator of the law and the Johannine Jesus who mediates "grace and truth." This already hints at tensions regarding the authoritative position of Jesus compared to Moses. The statement in 1:18 that "no one has seen God" except the only begotten God/son (ancient copies of the gospel differ at this point) heightens the tension. The claim contradicts the scriptural tradition of Moses speaking with God "face to face" as a friend (Exod 33:11). Such bold assertions about Jesus vis-à-vis Moses, as well as an early statement that not all of Jesus's "own" accepted him (John 1:11), foreshadow debates in the narrative about the identity of the Johannine Jesus.

Overall, the prologue functions as a sort of overture to the rest of the gospel. The themes of the light coming into the world, the rejection and acceptance of Jesus, and the focus on belief will all recur across the narrative. At the same time, the term *logos* never occurs again in reference to the Johannine Jesus. Once the *logos* becomes flesh, the Johannine Jesus himself – as well as the characters that he encounters – will do the work of defining who he is. The point of the author of John's claim about Jesus's divine origin is to assist the audience in interpreting statements by and about Jesus that occur in the rest of the gospel.

Basics on the Gospel of John

The gospel has two main sections. The first part focuses on the signs (the Johannine term for miracles) of Jesus and concerns his time in the world. A clear break is indicated at 13:1, where the narrator reports that Jesus knew that his hour had come to depart from the world and return to the Father. John 11 and 12 serve as a transition to the second section. These two chapters narrate the last of Jesus's signs (11:1–44) and foreshadow his death and glorification (11:45–12:8; 12:27–36). The second part of the gospel then focuses on Jesus's "hour," that is, his death and resurrection. Together, the two parts of the gospel trace the journey of the Johannine Jesus coming into the world and then departing to return to his origin with God.

I	Signs of the Johannine Jesus	1–12	**Outline: the**
	A. Prologue: the *logos* coming into the world	1:1–18	**sojourn of the *logos***
	B. Belief and unbelief in response to the signs	1:19–11:44	**in the world**
	C. Transition: the final sign and foreshadowing of the hour	11:45–12:50	
II	Jesus's departure from the world	13–20	
	A. Farewell meal with the disciples	13	
	B. Farewell discourse and prayer	14–17	
	C. The hour of glorification	18–20	
III	Epilogue: Jesus's last meeting with his disciples	21	

Date and authorship

The question of the authorship of the gospel attracts even more scholarly attention than that of the authorship of the synoptic gospels. This is due to the intriguing figure of the "beloved disciple" (13:23; 19:26; 20:2; 21:7, 20), whom some have supposed to be the author. Although this disciple is never named in the gospel, scholars have offered dozens of theories about his or her identity, from the resurrected Lazarus to Mary Magdalene. Such attempts are speculative at best. In terms of identifying the author, they are also misguided. There is no compelling evidence that the beloved disciple is intended to represent the author. Meanwhile, church tradition says that a disciple of Jesus called John, the son of Zebedee, wrote the gospel in his old age in Ephesus. Again, because the gospel was written anonymously, this remains tradition rather than fact.

There are indications that the Gospel of John went through several editorial revisions before it reached its current form. The clearest evidence of this is at John 20:30–1. These verses sound as if they are concluding the gospel. However, after this apparent conclusion, the Gospel of John continues with chapter 21, which appears to be an epilogue that was added to the gospel. The chapter resolves issues of Peter's status after his denial of Jesus (21:15–19) as well as rumors about the beloved disciple (21:20–3). Chapters 15–17, known as the **Farewell Discourse**, contain Jesus's parting words to his disciples and are another possible addition to an earlier version of the gospel. Note that although chapter 14 concludes with Jesus saying, "Rise, let us be on our way," Jesus then continues speaking for three more chapters. Some scholars argue that what modern readers perceive as breaks in the text, and thus indications of editorial activity, are actually literary features that are also found in ancient Greek drama. Regardless of disagreements about the gospel's composition, most scholars think the gospel in its present form is the latest of the canonical gospels, probably undergoing a final editing sometime between 95 and 125 CE, or perhaps even later in the second century (Figure 11.1).

The Johannine Jesus as God's Divine Agent in the World

Following the prologue, the story gets underway. As in the Gospel of Mark, there is no birth narrative. Jesus first enters the narrative mostly by way of others' descriptions of him. He appears to draw followers to him simply by walking around. Moreover, those who encounter the Johannine Jesus offer an impressive list of titles to describe him. Just in the first chapter, the Johannine Jesus is called the "lamb of God," "rabbi," "messiah," "one written about in the law and prophets," "son of Joseph from Nazareth," "Son of God," "king of Israel," and "Son of Man." Apart from "lamb of God," we have already seen most of these titles in the synoptic gospels. What is different in the Gospel of John is that these more traditional titles become far less prominent in the rest of the gospel as they are replaced by new designations for Jesus.

Much more frequently than the traditional titles, the gospel depicts the Johannine Jesus as "the one sent" by God or as one "from above" (for example, 3:34; 5:38; 6:29, 44, 57; 7:16, 28–9; 10:36; 11:42). He is also called "the one coming into the world" (1:9; 11:27). Likewise, both the Johannine Jesus and the narrator frequently refer to God as the one who sent him. In fact, this type of reference to God occurs more than two dozen times! (See, for example, 3:17; 4:34; 5:23–4; 5:37; 6:38–9; 7:16; 8:42; 9:34; 11:45; 12:49, and so on.) This language represents the Johannine Jesus as a divine agent of God who was sent into the world to follow God's commands. In fact, this is how the Johannine Jesus describes his presence in the world. He claims that he can do nothing on his own but seeks only to do the will of the one who sent him. His words are not his own; he speaks as he has been instructed (5:19, 30; 8:28; 14:10). As a divine agent, he has been given "works" to complete by the Father (5:36). His teaching is not his own but the teaching of the one who sent him (7:16). He does as the Father has commanded (14:31).

This also suggests that the Johannine Jesus functions in a subordinate role to the Father. Indeed, he says just this when he tells his disciples, "the Father is greater than I" (14:28). Paradoxically, however, because the Johannine Jesus is so intimately associated with God, he can also say "I am in the Father and the Father is in me" and "the Father and I are one" (10:30; 17:22). He claims that those who know him also know the Father (14:7), and those who honor him also honor the Father (5:22–3). This paradoxical relationship recalls the opening lines of the gospel, where the *logos* is said to be both God and *with* God (1:1).

If the Johannine Jesus is an agent sent from God, "one coming into the world," he is also one who anticipates departing from the world and returning to the Father (13:1; 14:28; 16:5). Because he is not of this world but "from above" (8:23), his death can be spoken of figuratively as a "lifting up" (3:14; 8:28; 12:32) or even a glorification (12:23, 27–8; 13:31; 17:1). Again, note how different this depiction of Jesus is from, for example, the Markan Jesus. In Mark 14:36, an anguished Jesus prays in a place called Gethsemane to "have the hour pass from him." In contrast, almost as if commenting on this Gethsemane tradition, the Johannine Jesus states, "Now my soul is troubled. And what should I say, 'Father, save me from this hour'? On the contrary, I have come for this hour" (12:27). This decisive statement shows how in the Gospel of John, the crucifixion is not depicted as a sacrificial death for others. Rather, it signals Jesus's departure from the world back to his divine origins. It is the ultimate sign of his glory, which reflects the glory of God (17:4–5).

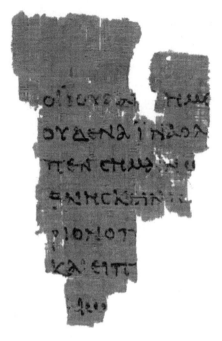

FIGURE 11.1

This famous papyrus fragment, Rylands Library P52, contains seven lines from John 18:31–3 on the front and lines from 18:37–8 on the back. The precise date of the fragment is unknown, but most scholars date it to the first half of the second century CE.

Contemporary Voices: Disability Studies and John 5:2–15

Over the past two decades, biblical scholars have begun analyzing the Bible through the perspective of disability studies. Two key components of disability studies are (1) questioning societal assumptions about what constitutes a so-called "normal" body and (2) challenging social structures that are built on such assumptions. In New Testament disability studies, a major focus has been on the healing stories in the gospels, especially those that appear to link sin with physical impairment. In John 5, for example, the Johannine Jesus heals a man who had suffered from a "weakness" for 38 years. Afterward, Jesus tells the man to "sin no more that nothing worse may happen to you" (5:14).

Reading the passage and its interpreters through the lens of disability studies, Helena Martin observes how readers have denigrated the man in John 5 with adjectives such as dull, unimpressive, crotchety, and lazy (see Helena L. Martin, "In Defense of the Disabled Man at the Bethesda Fountain (John 5:1–15)," in *Biblical Interpretation* 30.2 (2022)). In commenting on such interpretations, Martin observes,

Ableist prejudices are a widespread affliction, generated by a culture that privileges and assumes the normate body. Normate, coined by Rosemarie Garland-Thomson, refers to the socially constructed idea of a "normal" identity or body. Very few – if any – people actually occupy this space, yet societies tend to pressure people to conform to their constructed normates.

Martin's disability-informed study of John 5 offers a reading that uncouples the man's impairment from implications about his character. She notes how the man is described in ways that help to develop his character, rather than flatten him as the "paralytic" (a designation that never occurs in the story).

. . . [T]hree times [the author] refers to him as "the person" and once each "the one with an impairment," "the one who had been healed," and "the one who was made whole." With these words, the story directs our attention to, respectively: his personhood, his circumstances, and the fact of his having been healed by Jesus."

For more on disability studies, see Resources for Further Study.

The "I Am" Sayings in the Gospel of John

The gospel writer regularly presents Jesus talking with other characters, though these conversations often feature lengthy monologues from Jesus. This is another way that the Johannine Jesus differs from what we have seen in the synoptic gospels. Recall how the Markan Jesus commanded those he healed, as well as his own disciples, to say nothing to anyone about his identity. In sharp contrast, the Johannine Jesus speaks openly about his identity throughout the narrative. The gospel writer even calls attention to this point, as the Johannine Jesus tells the high priest, "I have said nothing in secret" (18:20, also 7:25).

This open speech involves the use of the Greek phrase *ego eimi* ("I am"). The Johannine Jesus uses this phrase across the narrative, both when he speaks with other characters and in longer discourses about himself. The phrase is used metaphorically. The Johannine Jesus describes himself as the bread of life (6:35, 48), the living bread that comes down from heaven (6:51), the light of the world (8:12), the gate for the sheep

　　　THE GOSPEL OF JOHN AND THE JOHANNINE LETTERS

(10:7), the good shepherd (10:11), the resurrection and life (11:25), the way, truth, and the life (14:16), and the true vine (15:1). Such self-descriptive statements are unique to the Gospel of John. They offer a rich array of images alongside the traditional titles applied to Jesus, like those in chapter 1. For this gospel writer, it seems that the identity of Jesus cannot be expressed fully with traditional titles like "messiah" or "king." He uses these metaphorical "I am" statements to symbolically evoke the life-giving significance of the Johannine Jesus.

In some instances, the "I am" phrase stands on its own. In English translations, these occasions are typically rendered "I am he" (John 8:24, 28, 58; 13:19; 18:6, 8). While grammatically correct, this translation dilutes the intended force of the phrase. In the Septuagint, especially in the oracles of Isaiah, this unmodified "I am" connotes divine, self-revelatory speech. For example, in the Greek Septuagint version of Isa 43:10, God declares that God's witnesses are to "know and believe and understand that I am" (*ego eimi*). This is perhaps an echo of Exod 3:14, when Moses asks God to reveal his name and God responds, "I am (*ego eimi*) the one who is" (see also Isa 43:25).

In the Gospel of John, Jesus's use of "I am" by itself carries a similar weight – it is revelatory language. This is most clear in the arrest scene. When the soldiers report that they are looking for Jesus of Nazareth, the Johannine Jesus replies, "I am." The author obviously intends to convey a more significant idea than Jesus simply identifying himself for arrest. We can tell this is the case for two reasons: first, because the phrase is repeated, and second, because the soldiers react by stepping back and falling to the ground (John 18:6)! This is not an action one would expect from those coming to arrest a man. It *is* a reaction that makes sense if the point is to show that these words are revelatory. The "I am" statement in the arrest scene is meant to reinforce the divine quality of Jesus for the gospel audience. To this end, note how Jesus's statement does not play a crucial role in the plot. In fact, after the dramatic reaction of the soldiers, the story proceeds as if they had not just fallen to the ground! The scene reminds us that, like the other three gospels, the Gospel of John has been shaped by its author to communicate a particular understanding of Jesus.

Knowing and Believing in the Johannine Jesus

READING

Read John 9 and 11.

EXERCISE

Pay attention to the questions and responses between the different characters or character groups in these two chapters.

The focus on who Jesus is and where he comes from in the Gospel of John serves another central theme in the gospel. Those who encounter the Johannine Jesus are called on to recognize who he is and to believe in him. This aspect of the narrative works at two levels – inside and outside of the story world. Inside the story world, the characters of the gospel are confronted with the question of knowing and believing in Jesus. Some form of the verb *pisteuo* (to believe or to trust) occurs 98 times in the Gospel of John. Compare this to the Gospel of Mark, where the verb occurs just 11 times (and Matthew and Luke, where it occurs even less). The Johannine Jesus asks the blind man whom he heals, "Do you believe?" (9:35–8). Martha, too, is asked whether she believes in Jesus as "the resurrection and the life" (11:25–6).

There are places where the words of the Johannine Jesus seem more directed toward the gospel audience *outside* the story world than to characters *in* the story. Notice, for example, how the conversation with Nicodemus blends into a more general speech about belief in the Son of God (3:11–21). Perhaps the Johannine Jesus is still speaking to Nicodemus at 3:15, but starting at 3:16, the third-person references to the Son and the Father suggest that these are now the narrator's words directed to the gospel audience. Another example of a blurring between the story world and the world of the gospel audience occurs in chapter 12, where Jesus has departed and gone into hiding (12:36). Soon after, Jesus "cries out" and then summarizes his teachings about belief in him and in "the Father" (12:44–50). Again, the summary seems to be intended for the gospel audience rather than characters in the gospel. This blurring of the story world and the world outside of the text suggests that in the author's view, those hearing the gospel face the same challenge as the characters in the narrative. Both groups are confronted with the question of belief in Jesus and both are called on to respond. Indeed, at the end of the gospel, the audience is told explicitly that these things were written so that "you all may believe that Jesus is the Christ, the Son of God" (20:30–1).

One major way that characters in the gospel come to believe is by seeing "signs" performed by Jesus. As mentioned earlier, the Johannine Jesus's signs (*semeia*) are intended to reveal his divine identity. In some cases, these signs become occasions for further conversation about who he is. The two primary examples are the story of the healing of the blind man (9:1–7) and the raising of Lazarus (11:38–44). In both accounts, the healing event is narrated in just a few verses. Both healing scenes are part of longer narratives that help the audience see a deeper meaning in Jesus's actions. The healing of the man born blind, for instance, becomes an occasion to contrast the "blindness" of the Pharisees with the sight of the formerly blind man. The Pharisees are unable to recognize the Johannine Jesus as one sent from God. In contrast, the once-blind man gradually sees who Jesus is. He moves from calling Jesus a man (9:11), to calling him a prophet (9:17), then asserts that Jesus is from God (9:33), and finally confesses his belief and worships Jesus (9:38–9). Similarly, the raising of Lazarus is preceded by a discussion between Jesus and Martha that prepares the reader to understand the event as an indication that Jesus is "the resurrection and the life" (11:25). The conversation also elicits Martha's full confession of faith before the sign even occurs (11:25–7).

These two examples illustrate a main theme in the gospel: that belief in the Johannine Jesus is the criterion for eternal life and salvation (3:16–18). This may seem unremarkable until we recall that not all the gospel writers make this point. For example, the Gospel of Matthew has a different emphasis. There, as we have seen, one enters the kingdom of heaven because one is Torah obedient, doing the will of God, and following Christ. But as the Gospel of John unfolds, characters are portrayed in terms of their recognition of and belief in Jesus as one sent by God. In fact, the gospel prologue prepared us for this theme. Already in the first chapter, the gospel contrasts the world "who did not know him" and his own "who did not accept him" with those who "received him" and "believed in his name" (1:10–12). The rest of this chapter will explore how the gospel develops the contrast between these groups in relation to the Johannine Jesus.

Opposition from the World

READING

Read John 14–17.

EXERCISE

Pay attention to the depiction of "the world" in these chapters in relation to Jesus and his disciples.

A pronouncement that comes early in the gospel is that the Johannine Jesus was sent by God to save the world (John 3:16–17). This conclusion is also reached by the Samaritans who declare that Jesus is "truly, the savior of the world!" (4:42). Despite these claims, the rest of the gospel suggests that "the world" is decidedly hostile toward the Johannine Jesus and his followers. This theme of hostility from the world is conveyed most strongly in the Farewell Discourse, the name that scholars give to the Johannine Jesus's parting words to his disciples in chapters 14–16. In this discourse, the Johannine Jesus acknowledges to his followers that the world hates him and therefore may hate them also (15:18). He explains how he will reveal himself to his followers but not to the world (14:22–3). Later, he acknowledges that his followers have affliction – or, more literally, "pressure" – in the world (16:33). Together, this language creates a sense of alienation on the one hand and group cohesion on the other. Note, for example, that the Johannine Jesus commands his disciples to "love one another" (13:34). This is quite different from Jesus's command in Matthew and Luke to love one's enemies (Matt 5:44; Luke 6:27). The Johannine command focuses on relations between Christ-followers, who do not belong to the world but rather have been "chosen out of the world" (15:19).

The Johannine Jesus also speaks of an ongoing struggle with "the ruler of this world." Earlier in the gospel, he claims that this ruler will be driven out (12:31). In the Farewell Discourse, Jesus tells his disciples that he will no longer be able to speak with them because the ruler of the world is coming (14:30). Nevertheless, the Johannine Jesus asserts also that this "ruler" has no control over him (14:30) and that the ruler has been condemned (16:11). Indeed, the Johannine Jesus proclaims that he has conquered the world (16:33). What should we make of these references to the "ruler of this world"? It is likely that the author had the figure of Satan in mind, although this designation explicitly appears only once in the gospel at 13:27. Nevertheless, it is also true that for the ancient audience, the Roman emperor was quite visibly "the ruler of this world." In either case, the audience is urged to believe that (appearances notwithstanding) the Johannine Jesus has gained a victory over the present earthly authority and therefore conquered the world. Maintaining such a belief would be both cathartic and challenging in a world in which the Romans exerted their power at will in the lands they occupied.

Some scholars interpret the gospel's polemical language regarding the world as an indication of **Johannine sectarianism**. This is a technical term that comes from the sociological study of religious groups. "Sect" describes a type of group that has withdrawn from the broader culture and defines itself in opposition to it. When applied to the Gospel of John, the term "sectarianism" involves a historical claim that there existed a distinct Johannine community that defined itself not only against those who did not believe in Jesus but also against other Christ-followers. As we will see below, the Johannine Letters may support the idea of Johannine sectarianism. However, not all agree that the gospel's polemical language provides evidence of sectarianism. There is no evidence outside of the Johannine literature for the existence of a separate "Johannine" community of Christ-followers that distinguished itself from other Christ-followers. It could be that the language of being "hated" by the world and not being "of the world" is a rhetorical strategy designed to *foster* a group identity rather than a reflection of an actual group (see box "Was there a Johannine Community?"). A Christ-follower encountering the Gospel of John might feel comforted by descriptions of mutual love between those who believe. Similarly, expressions of unity could create a sense of belonging. Finally, for those living under foreign rule, a narrative depicting a powerful divine figure who claimed to have conquered the world and its evil ruler would have a powerful appeal.

The Johannine Jesus promises another means of comfort in his parting words. He says that he will send another **Paraclete** after his departure (John 14:16). This Greek word (*parakletos*) literally means "one who is called beside to help" and is variously translated as comforter, advocate, intercessor, and counselor. The Johannine Jesus refers to the Paraclete as the "Holy Spirit" and the "Spirit of truth" who will be sent from the Father and can only come if Jesus departs (John 14:24; 15:26; 16:7).

According to the gospel writer, the figure of the Paraclete has many functions. It will guide and instruct the believers and remind them of Jesus's words (John 14:26; 16:12–14). This "spirit of truth" will speak and declare what is to come (16:13). It will also testify on behalf of Jesus (John 15:26; 16:8). These claims point to the role of the Paraclete in defending the gospel's claims about the identity of Jesus as God's divine representative who was sent into the world. Indeed, because the Gospel of John *itself* guides, instructs, and reminds later believers of Jesus's words, the implication is that the Paraclete has been active in the gospel's composition. Although Jesus promises that the Paraclete is to be with his followers forever (John 14:16), it also seems that the speaking, instructing, and guiding would necessarily be linked to individual leaders in the Jesus movement. In short, the range of functions attributed to the Paraclete mean that this figure is yet another unique and somewhat puzzling aspect of the Gospel of John.

The Problem of "the Jews" in the Gospel of John

READING

Read John 6, 8–9.

EXERCISE

Pay attention to the gospel's portrayal of "the Jews" in these chapters, especially the language used by the Johannine Jesus in his exchanges with this group. Here and in the discussion that follows, the quotation marks around "the Jews" is meant to signal the gospel's particular and problematic use of the designation *hoi Ioudaioi*.

In addition to a general opposition from the world, the Johannine Jesus encounters opposition from a group identified as "the Jews" (*hoi Ioudaioi*). We have already seen the negative portrayal of scribes, Pharisees, and chief priests in the synoptic traditions, but only in the Gospel of John do we find frequent use of the general phrase "the Jews" to refer to opponents of Jesus.

From the beginning of the gospel, this group persecutes Jesus (John 5:16), seeks to kill him (5:18; 7:1, 25), complains about him (6:41), claims that he is demon-possessed (8:48, 52), tries to stone him (10:31), and insists over Pilate's protests that Jesus must die (19:7). During the trial of Jesus, the narrative aligns "the Jews" with the Roman emperor. They hint to Pilate that releasing Jesus would be treasonous, and they openly claim that they have no king but Caesar (John 19:12, 15). In this gospel, "the Jews" cause fear in others. The parents of the formerly blind man will not speak to the authorities about Jesus because they are afraid that they will be expelled from the synagogue (John 9:22). This fear is reiterated later in the gospel when some Pharisees keep their belief in Jesus a secret, again because of the fear of expulsion (John 12:42).

The gospel's portrayal of "the Jews" as hostile opponents of Jesus is reinforced by the negative rhetoric directed at the Jews by the Johannine Jesus. The Jews are described as being from "below" and "of this world" (John 8:23). The Johannine Jesus wonders why he bothers speaking with them and finds much about them to condemn (8:25–6). Most troubling, the Johannine Jesus denies their claim that they are children of Abraham (a foundational truth for Jewish identity) and insists instead that their father is the devil, "a murderer from the beginning" and "the father of lies" (8:44). In his Farewell Discourse, the Johannine Jesus prepares his followers for expulsion from the synagogue and death at the hands of his opponents (John 16:2).

The Gospel of John also offers a paradoxical picture of Jesus in relation to Jewish ritual practices. On the one hand, the story of the Johannine Jesus unfolds in relation to the Jewish Sabbath and festivals (John 2:13; 5:1, 9–10; 7:2, 22–3; 14; 12:1). On the other hand, the rhetoric of the gospel frequently distances Jesus and his followers from

Jewish traditions in general. In speaking to "the Jews," the Johannine Jesus refers to "your law" (8:17; 10:34; 18:31) as if it is not also his law. Recall that the Matthean Jesus insisted that he came to *fulfill* the law. How different is this gospel's depiction of Jesus's attitude toward "the Jews" and "their" law! We see a similar distancing from the Jewish traditions in the gospel's references to "the festival of the Jews" or "the "Passover of the Jews" (2:13; 5:1; 6:4; 11:55). It is as though the gospel's author and audience no longer viewed these festivals as their own.

Understanding who the author of John meant by the term "the Jews" and why this group is portrayed so negatively has been one of the most important yet vexing problems of recent scholarship on the Gospel of John. The issue became particularly pressing in the aftermath of World War II, when the Nazi genocide perpetrated on European Jews became more widely acknowledged. Many Christians began to examine Christian complicity, not only in this horrific event, but also in contributing more generally to the long history of anti-Semitism. One part of this process has been reconsidering the portrayal of the Jews and Judaism in biblical texts like the Gospel of John.

A first step is to view the gospel in its late-first-century CE context (the setting of the gospel's composition) rather than as an accurate account of the time of Jesus. Here is a place where it is particularly important to maintain a distinction between the historical Jesus and the textual Jesus. Indeed, there is widespread agreement among biblical critics that the historical Jesus would not have distanced himself from the Jewish tradition in the way he is described as doing in this gospel. That said, even shifting the interpretive focus to the time of the gospel's composition can be problematic. Indeed, one prominent theory posits that the Gospel of John reflects a time when Jewish Christians were being driven out of their local synagogues because of their belief in Jesus. According to this theory, the Johannine Jesus's strong invectives against the Jews represent the Johannine community's reaction to being persecuted by local synagogue leaders (see box "Was there a Johannine Community?"). The problem with this interpretation is that the gospel is still perceived as an accurate account of Jewish misdeeds, if not in Jesus's time (Jews killing Jesus), then in the time of the gospel writer (Jews persecuting early Christians). From here, it is a short step to viewing the victimized church as superior to the persecuting synagogue (see Figure 11.2).

This dominant theory about the Gospel of John and the Jewish persecution of early Christians has serious limitations. A major problem is that the gospel reflects a one-sided view of this heated conflict in which Jesus's opponents are cast in the worst possible light. It is more likely that the animosity flowed both ways. Anyone who has ever had a bitter argument with a once-close friend should be wary of taking the depiction of "the Jews" in the Gospel of John at face value, whether in the time of Jesus or in the late first or early second century CE. Unfortunately, the historical details of this ancient argument are lost to us. The evidence from some second-century CE Christian writers suggests a concern about an ongoing attraction to Jewish synagogue life at a time when Christianity was emerging as a distinct practice. In other words, their worry seems to have been that Christ-followers were *returning* to the synagogue, rather than being *driven from* it. If this worry were present when the gospel was written, it would explain the gospel's strong emphasis on belief in Jesus. In this light, the gospel's depiction of Christ-confessors being rejected by the synagogue may have been a rhetorical

FIGURE 11.2
Medieval Christian image of the church preferred over the synagogue. The angel under Christ's arm on the left ushers in the church, while the angel under Christ's arm on the right violently drives out the synagogue, who is blindfolded and has lost her crown.

way of discouraging a return to the synagogue. Another possibility may be that in the author's local setting, the assembly of Christ-followers had already separated from the synagogue. If this is the case, the depiction of Jesus and "the Jews" in John's gospel may serve an explanatory role. It would explain (not necessarily accurately) how their current division came to be, projecting their own tensions back into the life of Jesus. It would not be the first time that we have seen traditional stories (in this case, the story of Jesus) retold to provide a meaningful foundation for a later community.

Was There a Johannine Community?

Beginning in the mid-twentieth century, scholarship on the Gospel and Letters of John has been dominated by the idea of a Johannine community and its relationship with the synagogue. In North America, the work of J. Louis Martyn has been enormously influential in the development of what we could call the "synagogue expulsion" theory (see Martyn, *History and Theology in the Fourth Gospel*, in Resources for Further Reading). Martyn famously described the Gospel of John as a "two-level drama." He meant that on the surface level, the gospel tells the story of Jesus, but on a second, deeper level, it tells the history of a distinct

group of Christ-followers living decades after the time of Jesus. A crucial part of this group's history, according to Martyn's two-level reading, was that the group was expelled from a synagogue community (John 9:22 and 12:42). A later stage of this history supposedly involved a split within the Christ-followers, based on a verse in 1 John that says, "they went out from us" (1 John 2:19).

Other scholars have challenged this type of "mirror reading" in which the interpreter assumes that one can accurately read a detailed community history through a narrative about Jesus. Scholars such as Adele Reinhartz have focused instead on the rhetorical strategies of the gospel. For instance, Reinhartz does not assume that the gospel's references to synagogue expulsion reflect historical events. Rather, she considers how the expulsion passages, along with the gospel's anti-Jewish language, might *shape* a group identity. In this reading, the language of the gospel works to discourage Christ-followers from participating in the Jewish synagogue community (the rhetoric of disaffiliation) and to promote ongoing relationships with a distinct group of Christ-followers (the rhetoric of affiliation; see Reinhartz, *Cast out of the Covenant: Jews and Anti-Judaism in the Gospel of John*, in Resources for Further Study).

Another line of scholarship suggests that none of the canonical gospels, John included, were written to address distinct audiences or groups of Christ-followers, such as a "Johannine community" or a "Matthean community" (see Baukham, *The Gospel for all Christians: Rethinking the Gospel Audiences*, in Resources for Further Study). The theory of a Johannine community will no doubt be an ongoing point of debate for Johannine scholarship.

Postcolonial criticism offers yet another way to understand the dynamics of the Gospel of John. As we saw in our study of the Gospel of Matthew, the destruction of Jerusalem by Rome opened the way for different Jewish movements to compete for power and the allegiance of the Jewish people. Our study of the Gospel of Mark suggested that the conflict of Jesus with the scribes and Pharisees from Jerusalem may reflect political as well as religious conflict between Christ-followers and collaborators with Rome. Both of these dynamics may be present in the Gospel of John. However, in this case, the gospel explicitly addresses the Judean leaders' *fear* of Rome and links that fear to their perception of Jesus:

> So the chief priests and the Pharisees gathered the council, and said, "What should we do? This man is doing many signs. If we allow him to go on like this, all will believe in him, and the Romans will come and destroy our place and our people." (John 11:47–8)

Here, the opponents of the Johannine Jesus view belief in him as a threat primarily to their safety and survival under Roman occupation rather than to their religious beliefs. They see Jesus as dangerous precisely because he might draw the unwelcome attention of Rome to their land. A postcolonial reading of Jesus's opponents in the narrative would be attuned to their concerns to ward off imperial violence. Indeed, although the chief priests and Pharisees are depicted as leaders of the Jews, they are in fact powerless before the empire. They can only hope to divert Roman attention from their nation by silencing Jesus and the crowds he attracts. In this sense, postcolonial theory can help readers see a potentially historically accurate element of the Gospel of John: its expression of the tension experienced by those of living under Roman occupation.

Note how the gospel writer uses irony in this scene to put a fundamental claim about the significance of the death of Jesus into words voiced by the chief priest:

> "You don't understand that it is more to your advantage to have one man die for the sake of the people than to have the whole nation destroyed." He did not say this on his own, but being high priest that year he prophesied that Jesus was about to die for the sake of the nation, and not for the nation only, but so that the scattered children of God might be gathered into one. (11:50–2 modified from the NRSV)

With this assertion, the gospel writer hints still more at the trauma of a colonized people. After all, the gospel was written after the whole Jewish nation *had* been destroyed by Rome. While the gospel writer does not acknowledge that brutal reality directly, this tragic irony should not be lost on us as contemporary readers.

FOCUS
TEXT

John 17

John 17 is a prayer that comes at the conclusion of the Farewell Discourse (John 14–16). There are a number of places in the gospel where the Johannine Jesus summarizes its message (3:31–6; 5:19–24; 12:44–50), but only here does such a summary come in the form of a prayer. This artfully crafted passage has three sections: the Johannine Jesus prays for himself in 17:1–5; he prays for his disciples in 17:6–19; and he prays for future believers in 17:20–4, before a concluding statement in 17:25–6.

In the opening section, the prayer points to the temporal dimension of the incarnation. At the time of his departure, the Johannine Jesus takes the audience back to the prologue, recalling the glory he had as the pre-existent *logos* in the presence of God (17:5) and acknowledging that the "hour" has now arrived (17:1). While this hour indicates his impending death, Jesus prays for glorification from the Father so that he may glorify God in turn. Jesus recalls the authority given to him by God over "all flesh" (17:2) but also the qualified nature of this authority. He claims that he may give eternal life only to those whom the Father has given him. Such language reminds the audience that Jesus does not act independently of God. It also explains why not everyone has believed in Jesus, an issue that we have seen trouble other New Testament writers, like Paul. Notably, the prayer includes a defining statement about eternal life: "This is eternal life; that they may know you, the only true God, and the one whom you sent, Jesus Christ" (17:3 modified from NRSV). This definition of eternal life, that is, knowing God and the one whom God sent, is another way of stating the central purpose of the gospel. Note that for the gospel writer, gaining eternal life is not something that happens when one dies. It does not mean, for example, "going to heaven." According to the Johannine Jesus, eternal life is a present reality available for those who recognize Jesus and God as presented in the gospel.

Scholars refer to this idea as **realized eschatology**. That is, the tradition of a future judgment and salvation available in the "last days" is transformed into an already realized state of affairs in the life of a believer. We see indications of this realized eschatology earlier in the gospel when the Johannine Jesus paradoxically proclaims, "the hour is coming and is now here" (4:23; 5:25; 16:32). Indeed, he regularly teaches about the present possibility of eternal life (5:24; 6:47, 54; 10:28; 11:25–6) and the present reality of judgment (3:19; 5:22–4), both of which are linked to knowing and believing in Jesus and God.

In the second part of the prayer, the Johannine Jesus petitions God on behalf of his disciples who will remain in the world once he is gone (17:6–19). The petition uses language that reinforces a sense of alienation from the world. For instance, Jesus refers to the disciples given to him by God as coming "from out of the world" (17:6). He specifically prays on their behalf and *not* on behalf of the world (17:9). Indeed, the Johannine Jesus claims that the world hates his disciples because, like him, they do not belong to the world (17:14, 16). For this reason, they need protection from the world and from the "evil one" (17:11–12, 15). The term "evil one" likely designates a supernatural evil power. However, as noted earlier, from the audience's perspective such a reference could also include the earthly authorities in whom this evil is manifest – the Roman emperor, as well as local governing authorities. Meanwhile, the Johannine Jesus also prays for an experience of unity and oneness among his followers, such as he experiences with God (17:11). In these ways, the petition on behalf of the disciples contributes to the inward turn of this gospel. It helps to construct a group identity that draws strength through its perception of victimization and alienation.

Finally, the prayer reaches forward to the future to address believers who were not immediate disciples of Jesus but "will believe because of their word" (17:20–4). This group may include the audience of the gospel, as well as other future believers. The hope for unity or "oneness" extends also to these future believers (17:23). The prayer's reference to future believers lacks the urgency or imminent apocalyptic expectations that we saw in the letters of Paul. Instead, the prayer projects a sense of ongoing existence of Christ-followers in the world (17:20). The Johannine Jesus asserts that by becoming "completely one," believers will show the world that he was sent by God and that believers are loved by God (17:22–3). The prayer concludes by returning to the gospel's beginning as the Johannine Jesus reiterates ideas from the gospel prologue. He highlights the eternal relationship between the Father and the Son, whom God loved "before the foundation of the world" (17:24; see 1:1). Though the world does not know God (17:25; see 1:10), Jesus's role is to make him known (17:26; see 1:18). In the prologue, those who believe in Jesus become God's children (1:12–13). In Jesus's closing words of the prayer, those to whom Jesus has made God known are infused with the love of God and the abiding presence of Jesus (17:26; see 1:12–13).

The Johannine Letters

Read 1, 2, and 3 John.

READING

What similarities do you see between the Johannine Letters and the Gospel of John?

EXERCISE

The texts of 1, 2, and 3 John, although quite different from one another, are commonly grouped together as the Johannine Letters. This is the case even though 1 John is not actually a letter and none of the texts indicates the name of its author. For a long time, readers assumed that the same person, John the Son of Zebedee, wrote both the gospel and the letters. We have already seen that most scholars no longer think this disciple wrote the gospel. And despite the overlap in words and phrases between the gospel and the Johannine Letters, grammatical differences in the Greek text point to different authors. It may be that the letters were written by the same person who revised the original gospel or simply by someone familiar with the gospel's language and traditions.

The longest of these three texts, 1 John, most closely reflects the ideas of the Gospel of John. In fact, the opening verse of 1 John recalls the opening verse of the gospel, with its reference to what was in "the beginning" (1 John 1:1; see John 1:1). Likewise, the opening section of the letter contains the dualistic language of the gospel. The world of 1 John is characterized by light versus dark, love versus hate, obedience versus disobedience, and children of God versus children of the devil (1 John 1:5–7; 2:9–10; 3:10). The Paraclete is also mentioned but is identified as Jesus Christ (1 John 2:1). The letter shares the same animosity toward "the world" as we saw in the gospel (1 John 2:15–17; 3:13; 4:4–5), and it reiterates the commandment that the letter's audience should believe in Jesus and love one another (1 John 3:23; 4:11). Such evidence points to some type of relationship between 1 John and the Gospel of John.

Many scholars have focused on 1 John 2:19 as a clue to understanding the occasion for the writing of this text. Here, the author refers to a group "who went out from us, but were not from us." This verse, in addition to the repeated references to those who "hate their brothers" (1 John 3:15; 4:20; see also 2:11), suggests that a break occurred in the author's community. There are several places in 1 John that work to bolster the group solidarity of the audience over against those who left. The author refers to the coming of an "antichrist" and the presence of "many antichrists" just before he writes about those who left the group (1 John 2:18). Later, the author defines the term as one who "denies the Father and the Son" (1 John 2:22). In a similar way, the author claims that "every spirit that confesses that Jesus Christ has come in the flesh is from God, and every spirit who does not confess Jesus is not from God" (1 John 4:2–3 NRSV). The authority of the writer is reinforced with statements such as "the one who knows God, listens to us. The one who is not from God, does not listen to us" (1 John 4:6).

We cannot be certain about the chronological relationship between 1 John and the Gospel of John. The dominant theory has been that 1 John was written *after* the Gospel of John, reflecting a later stage in the life of a particular group of Christ-followers. This theory suggests that the controversy in 1 John was no longer with the synagogue but was internal to the community and involved differing ideas about Christ. However, as mentioned above, it may be that some Christ-followers were returning to the synagogue and no longer confessing that Jesus is the messiah and Son of God. If this is the case, the controversy could have generated the type of animosity toward "the Jews" that is reflected in the gospel. The fact is that the author's references to those who left are vague, suggesting that they were not the main focus of his composition. Perhaps the most we can say is that 1 John is concerned with shaping and strengthening the identity of a group of Christ-followers, and the author does so in ways that coincide with the worldview and language of the Gospel of John.

The brief letters of 2 and 3 John draw on the same language but apply it to different situations. For example, 2 John, written from "the elder" to an "excellent lady," uses the same language of truth and love versus deceivers. The letter also refers to "the antichrist," a term which is used in a general sense for those who do not adhere to the author's claims about Jesus (2 John 1:4–7). (Note that while the figure of "the antichrist" looms large in some Christian imaginations, the references in 1 and 2 John are the only places the term occurs in the New Testament.) 2 John also specifically discourages the recipient from offering hospitality to those who do not come with the "teaching of Christ" (2 John 1:10–11). 3 John is even more specific. It refers to a conflict between the author and a certain Diotrephes, who does not recognize the author's authority (3 John 1:9). These texts, together with 1 John, reflect an ongoing tradition that flowed out of a "Johannine" way of conceiving of Jesus, God, and the believers' role in relation to the world.

CHAPTER ELEVEN REVIEW

1 Know the meaning and significance of the following terms:
- Farewell Discourse
- incarnation (especially for the Gospel of John)
- Johannine sectarianism
- Paraclete
- realized eschatology
- signs (as used in the Gospel of John)

2 In the Gospel of Matthew, one must obey the Torah commandments to enter the kingdom of heaven. What does one need to do according to the Gospel of John? How is this shown in the gospel?

3 What is the dominant theory about why the Gospel of John depicts Jews rejecting Jesus and Jesus as hostile to "the Jews"? What are the problems with this theory, and what might be an alternative understanding of the background of this theme in John?

4 How might postcolonial theory inform our view of tensions between Jews and Jewish Christ-followers at the time the gospel was written?

5 (Focus text: John 17) How does Jesus's prayer in John 17 represent a shift from the expectation in some other New Testament texts (e.g., Paul) of the coming of the last days? How do you understand the gospel's definition of "eternal life"? How might the gospel's idea of eternal life appeal to people living in the late first or second century CE?

6 What similarities are there between the Johannine Letters and the Gospel of John?

RESOURCES FOR FURTHER STUDY

Baukham, Richard, ed. *The Gospel for all Christians: Rethinking the Gospel Audiences*. Grand Rapids, MI: Eerdmans, 1998.

Brant, Jo-Ann. *John*. Grand Rapids: MI: Baker Academic, 2011.

Brown, Raymond Edward. *The Gospel According to John*. Vol. 29, 29A. The Anchor Bible. Garden City, NY: Doubleday, 1966 and 1970. A dated but detailed critical study of the gospel.

Conway, Colleen M. *Behold the Man: Jesus and Greco-Roman Masculinity*. Oxford: Oxford University Press, 2008.

Conway, Colleen M. *John and the Johannine Letters*. Nashville, TN: Abingdon Press, 2017.

Lieu, Judith. *I, II, III John: A Commentary*. Louisville, KY: Westminster John Knox Press, 2008.

Reinhartz, Adele. *Cast out of the Covenant: Jews and Anti-Judaism in the Gospel of John.* Lanham, MD: Lexington Books/ Fortress Academic, 2018.

For more on disability studies and the Bible:

Melcher, Sarah, Mikeal C. Parsons, and Amos Yong, eds. *The Bible and Disability: A Commentary.* Waco, TX: Baylor University Press, 2017.

Moss, Candida R., and Jeremy Schipper, eds. *Disability Studies and Biblical Literature.* New York: Palgrave Macmillan, 2011.

Following Christ in the Empire: Diverse Approaches in the New Testament

12

Chapter Outline

Chapter Overview   205

The Revelation to John: Visions of "Conquering" Roman Power   206

Focus Text: Revelation 17–18   213

Hebrews: Platonic Perspectives on Christ   214

1 Peter: Living as Aliens and Accommodating to the Empire   218

Conclusion: Three Different Relationships to the Roman Empire   221

Chapter Twelve Review   222

Resources for Further Study   222

Chapter Overview

As we come to the end of this Introduction to the New Testament, this chapter compares how three different writers connected belief in Jesus as the messiah to daily life in the broader culture of the Roman empire. The Revelation to John, Hebrews, and 1 Peter represent three different literary genres, as well as three different responses to the experience of living under imperial rule as a Christ-follower.

I first discuss the Revelation to John, a text that expresses a resistant and hostile stance toward the empire. Even with its coded language, it contains the most blatant attacks on Roman rule in the New Testament. I then turn to Hebrews, which appears less concerned with Rome than with the relations of the Christ-followers to the Jewish sacrificial cult. Still, the effects of imperial conquest (in this case, the lasting effects of Alexander's conquest) are evident in the appropriation of a Greek philosophical framework to talk about Jesus. Moreover, the emphasis in Hebrews on the alien status of believers suggests the author's unease with the current state of world affairs. The third book, 1 Peter, offers another form of accommodation to life in the empire. As in Hebrews, 1 Peter contains references to exile and alienation. But 1 Peter also offers guidance for Christ-followers who face difficult questions of accommodation versus resistance to Roman power.

The New Testament: A Contemporary Introduction, First Edition. Colleen M. Conway.
© 2023 John Wiley & Sons Ltd. Published 2023 by John Wiley & Sons Ltd.

The Revelation to John: Visions of "Conquering" Roman Power

READING

Read Revelation 1–5, 12–21.

EXERCISE

Note how the first three chapters are structured. Who is speaking and to whom? How does the structure change as the book continues? What images and events are featured in chapters 12–21?

In English, the title of the book I discuss in this section is typically translated "Revelation to John." The Greek word for "revelation" in the title is *apokalypsis*, which is sometimes left untranslated so that the book is called the "Apocalypse of John." Because "apocalypse" has come to mean a frightening, catastrophic event in popular usage (some years ago, for instance, the US media named a big snowstorm "snowpocalypse"), the title can be misleading. Recall that the Greek word *apokalypsis* simply means "uncovering" or, as it is translated here, "revelation." Nevertheless, the word **"apocalypse"** in the title is also useful because in biblical scholarship it designates a literary genre. There are many examples of this genre from the Second Temple period (see "Eschatology versus Apocalypticism," chapter two). One biblical example is Daniel 7–12, and many more examples of the genre from the Second Temple period are not in the Bible. Here, I focus on two questions: What is "apocalyptic" (in the sense of the literary genre) about the Apocalypse of John? And what is the point of this apocalyptic book?

The literary genre of apocalypse purports to reveal divine wisdom to its audience and occurs in two general forms: heavenly apocalypses, which feature tours of heaven by the seer, and historical apocalypses, which predict divine intervention against foreign rulers. Both of these literary types typically include the use of symbols; references to numbers, animals, or strange beasts; and an angelic mediator who interprets the meaning of these. The Book of Revelation draws on all these generic features. It opens with John's vision of a flaming-eyed, white-haired, bronzed-footed "one like the Son of Man" who recites messages to be written to seven communities in cities around Asia Minor (Map 12.1). As the book continues, the seer offers the audience visions of God's heavenly throne room, cosmic battle scenes, and eventually the gruesome destruction of a so-called "whore of Babylon." Such scenes make it an "apocalypse" in the literary sense.

As for the question of the book's purpose, it may not be what you expect. Many modern appropriations of the Revelation to John – whether in film, websites, novels,

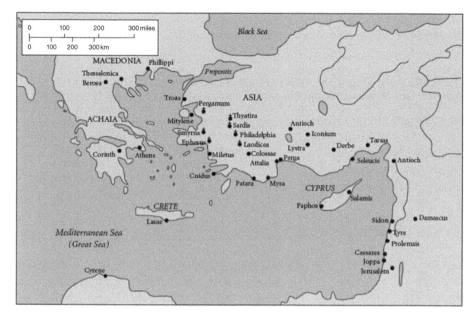

MAP 12.1

Cities of Revelation. Redrawn from Steven L. Harris, *Understanding the Bible* (6th edition). McGraw Hill, 2003, page 597.

or sermons – are designed to instill fear in the audience. The book certainly contains plenty of frightening images: torturing locusts with scales and scorpions' tails (Rev 9:1–10), seven-headed dragons ready to devour a newborn child (Rev 12:1–17), and a multiheaded, leopard-like beast rising from the sea (Rev 13:1–3), to name a few! But this popular use of the Book of Revelation to scare people is a long way from what the ancient writer had in mind for his audience. Consider the fact that the book offers repeated assurances of rewards to those in his audience who "conquer," provides dramatic visions of angelic worship (Revelation 4–5), and concludes with a promise that God will live among humans and wipe away their tears (Rev 21:3–4). Such images demonstrate that in its ancient context, the work was not intended to frighten its readers. Its purpose was to provide hope and comfort, encouraging Christ-followers living under Roman rule.

Because the Book of Revelation contains direct addresses to groups in the cities of Asia Minor, we can be more specific about the experience of Roman rule in this region. First, most scholars now agree that there is no evidence for an official Roman policy of persecution of Christians. Indeed, as we have seen throughout our discussion of the New Testament, there was little recognition of Christians as a group distinct from Jews for much of the first century CE. However, following the Jewish revolt in 70 CE, Jewish people living throughout the empire (including Jewish Christ-followers) may have been the target of ongoing local hostility. At a few points, there may also have been specific targeting of Christ-followers. As discussed in Chapter 7, according to the Roman historian Tacitus, Emperor Nero blamed the Christians in Rome for a catastrophic fire that destroyed large sections of the city. Rumors of this accusation may have led to poor treatment of Christ-followers in their local communities.

Tacitus's Account of Nero's Persecution of Christians in Rome

The following quote from the Roman historian Tacitus is important as an early non-Christian reference to the crucifixion of Jesus and the origin of the Christians. Tacitus's statement that "the crowd called them Christians" suggests the term was a negative designation, which is consistent with its rarity in the New Testament. As we have seen, "Christian" occurs only three times in the Bible (Acts 11:26; 26:28; 1 Peter 4:16), adding to the impression that it was originally a derogatory label that was eventually appropriated by Christ-followers.

But neither human help, nor imperial benevolence, nor all the modes of placating Heaven, could stifle scandal or dispel the belief that the fire had taken place by order. Therefore, to put an end to the rumor, Nero substituted as culprits, and punished with the utmost refinement of cruelty, a class of men, loathed for their vices, whom the crowd called Christians. Christus, the founder of the name, had undergone the death penalty in the reign of Tiberius, by sentence of the procurator Pontius Pilatus, and the pernicious superstition was checked for a moment, only to break out once more, not merely in Judea, the home of the disease, but in the capital itself, where all things horrible or shameful in the world collect and are celebrated. First, then, the confessed members of the sect were arrested; next, on their disclosures, vast numbers were convicted, not so much on the count of arson as for hatred of the human race. And derision accompanied their end; they were covered with wild beasts' skins and torn to death by dogs; or they were fastened on crosses, and, when daylight failed were burned to serve as lamps by night. Nero had offered his gardens for the spectacle, and gave an exhibition in his circus, mixing with the crowd in the habit of a charioteer, or mounted on his car. Hence, in spite of a guilt which had earned the most exemplary punishment, there arose a sentiment of pity, due to the impression that they were being sacrificed not for the welfare of the state but to the ferocity of a single man. (Tacitus, *Annals* 15.44, modified from the Loeb edition)

Basics on the Revelation to John

Outline: John's vision of wrath and renewal	I	Opening vision of the Son of Man and messages to the churches	1–3
	II	The visions	4:1–22:7
		A. Heavenly worship	4–5
		B. Preparation for God's judgment	6–11
		C. God's wrath unleashed against Rome/whore of Babylon	12–18
		D. Final judgment and defeat of Satan	19–20
		E. New creation and a new Jerusalem	20:1–22:7
	III	Concluding warnings and exhortations	22:8–21
Date and authorship		Traditionally, the "John" of Revelation was thought to be the author of both the Gospel and Letters of John, who was also thought to be the apostle John. Now, few	

would identify the disciple John of the gospels as the author of any of these texts. In fact, scholars no longer think the same author wrote all of these texts. While there is no reason to doubt that the author of Revelation was named John, this was a very common name. We should simply consider him to be a leader among the groups of Christ-followers who were living in the cities in Asia Minor that are addressed in Revelation 2–3. He reports that he experienced the visions on the island of Patmos, located off the coast of Turkey (Rev 1:9). The date of composition is uncertain. Many have linked the writing to the imperial reign of Nero, given Tacitus's account of Nero's persecution of Christians (see box "Tacitus's Account of Nero's Persecution of Christians in Rome"). This would mean an early date in the 60s CE. Others have argued it was written during the reign of Domitian in the mid-90s CE. Both suggestions are based on efforts to connect the suffering described in the book to an instance of state-sponsored persecution of Christians. However, because we lack evidence for widespread Roman persecution of Christians, there is little reason to date the book to a particular emperor. The most we can say is that the book was written sometime in the second half of the first century CE.

The Revelation to John expresses a sense of crisis in two main ways: through the messages written to seven communities in Asia Minor and through its detailed accounts of visions. We look first at the messages. Although written in coded language, they offer insight into the lived experience of Christ-followers in these cities, at least as the author perceived it. In the message to Pergamum, for instance, John refers to the community living where "Satan's throne" is (2:13). Pergamum was a provincial capital and home to the first emperor cult in Asia Minor, which was dedicated to Augustus. The city was also home to a monumental altar to Zeus built on a high acropolis. In both of these cultic settings, performing one's civic duty would have included offering sacrifices for the welfare of the city and empire. If the reference to "Satan's throne" refers to either of these places, it would signal the author's opposition to these civic expectations. In this same message, the author refers to a certain "faithful witness" named Antipas "who was killed among you, where Satan lives" (2:13). We do not know anything more about this figure except that the author's description implies that he was martyred for his confession of Christ.

Two other messages reveal tensions with local synagogues, again by way of references to Satan. According to the author, both Smyrna and Philadelphia have a "synagogue of Satan," and at least some of the synagogue's members are "those who say they are Jews and are not" (2:9; 3:9). We do not know the details behind such language, but it is important to notice what the author is contesting. The author seems to oppose Christ-followers who are not truly Jewish by his definition. This critique is yet another reminder that while the New Testament writings depict the diversity within Judaism in the first century CE, they do not reflect a conflict of two different religions, as in Judaism versus Christianity. At issue in the Book of Revelation is whether Christ-followers can coexist comfortably with other Jews within the synagogue. Calling these synagogues in Smyrna and Philadelphia "synagogues of Satan" indicates the author's view that this coexistence is no longer possible.

Together, the seven messages in Revelation 2–3 provide an example of the postcolonial concept of **hybridity**, where a subjected group adapts the cultural expressions of power of its oppressor. In this case, the seven proclamations that open the book imitate the form of royal and imperial edicts. Such edicts were commonly used by imperial rulers for issuing instructions to local communities. Royal edicts began with a formal introduction of the authority issuing the edict, then moved to a direct address to its recipients. This direct address was introduced with a recognizable formula, such as "The words of ...." In Revelation, this formula is the Greek phrase *tade legei*, "This is what he says ...."

The main body of an imperial edict would express decisions made and sanctions given. The concluding section would reinforce the need for obedience. The seven proclamations in Revelation contain all of these elements. They begin by identifying the issuing authority in ways that emphasize Jesus's ruling power as the exalted Son of God. In each case, the authoritative voice of Jesus follows the phrase *tade legei*, translated in the NRSV as "these are the words." The address to each community identifies the community's merits and shortcomings before concluding with promises of rewards or sanctions. Note that Jesus's authority is exerted on multiple fronts in these messages: against those in the community who are accused of false teaching (Rev 2:14; 20–3), against those in the synagogue who are deemed to be non-Jews (Rev 3:8–9), and against those in the community who are going astray (Rev 2:4–5, 14–15; 3:14–19). In sum, the opening chapters of Revelation imitate imperial authority by presenting Jesus as one with the status and authority to issue formal edicts with an expectation of obedience.

As is the case with many examples of cultural hybridity, this imitation comes with a twist. On the one hand, rewards are promised to those who "conquer," which is consistent with Roman rewards being bestowed on those who are victorious in battle (Rev 2:7, 11, 17, 26, 28; 3:5, 12, 21). On the other hand, what the author means by his use of "conquer" is sobering. Believers are victorious if they remain faithful to the point of death, perhaps like Antipas did (see, e.g., Rev 2:10–11). If they conquer in this way, they are assured that, like Jesus, they will be rewarded with ruling power. They will hold authority over the nations, ruling them with a rod of iron (Rev 2:26–8; see also 12:11). They will be clothed in white robes (Rev 3:5) and given a seat with the risen Christ on his throne (Rev 3:21). This is another indication of imperial imitation in this New Testament text. The ultimate reward envisioned by those who feel oppressed by Rome is to become the one who rules over others.

As if to affirm that such a reward is possible, the text next transports the audience to a scene of heavenly worship in the throne room of God (Revelation 4–5). The vision continues the project of imperial imitation, in this case mimicking scenes of Roman court ceremonials. For instance, the audience "watches" as the 24 elders show their submission to the one seated on the throne. They cast off their golden crowns before God, much like supplicants bowing before the Roman emperor. They sing acclamations to God and the Lamb, echoing similar acclamations directed toward the emperor (Rev 4:10–11). The entire vision reinforces the idea that "the Lord God, the Almighty" (Rev 4:8) is the real ruler of the universe and rightful recipient of "glory, honor and power" (Rev 4:10–11). Honors are also given to the central figure in the heavenly throne room, the Lion/Lamb with seven horns and seven eyes (symbolic indications of strength and wisdom). He, too, is worthy "to receive power and wealth and wisdom and might and honor and glory and blessing" because of his self-sacrifice for people from every tribe and nation (Rev 5:12 NRSV). Overall, the scene asserts the ultimate ruling authority of God and the Lamb over the illusory authority of the emperor. It does this by offering a visual parallel to a court ceremony for the emperor, but one that surpasses in splendor and spectacle anything that could be found in Rome.

Having established who actually rules heaven and earth, Revelation goes on to display a cosmic conflict that occurs as the wrath of God and the Lamb is unleashed upon the earth and its inhabitants (Rev 6:15–17). The text's audience, along with the seer, John, "sees" gruesome scenes of war, death, and destruction that manifest God's final judgment over the unrepentant inhabitants of the earth. These judgments are deemed "true and just," as well as acts of divine vengeance on behalf of those righteous ones who were killed for "the word of God" and for their witness (Rev 6:9–10; see also 15:3; 16:5–7; 19:2).

More coded allusions to the struggle with Roman imperial power occur in the description of the two beasts (Rev 13:1–18). The first beast rises from the ocean much like the sea monsters symbolizing oppressive empires in prophetic texts (see Isa 51:9–11; Ezek 29:3–5; 32:2–6; Jer 51:34). In appearance, it combines the features of the four beasts that represent different empires in Dan 7:2–7. By combining these various biblical monsters into one beast, the author of Revelation implies that this beast/empire represents the worst of them all – the culmination of evil in the world. The question, "Who is like the beast and who is able to fight against it?" (Rev 13:4) might be exactly the question that someone living under Roman domination might ask. The claim that the beast has authority over "every tribe, people, language and nation" (Rev 13:7) would feel practically true to those who were subjected to Rome's power. A further clue to associating the beast with the Roman empire is the claim that "all the inhabitants of the earth will worship it" (Rev 13:8). This is a reference to the emperor cult, which was instituted to encourage allegiance to Roman rule.

The description of another beast in Revelation 11 evokes the role of the elite class in the cities of Asia Minor. These affluent men controlled the political, religious, and economic affairs of their communities in close association with Rome. They held political offices, as well as priesthoods in prominent local cults. Such men worked on behalf of the "first beast" (Rome) and made others worship this same beast (through participation in the emperor cult, Rev 13:12). The description of the second beast also suggests that local leaders had the authority to kill those who did not "worship the first beast" (Rev 13:12). Alternatively, they could cut off the livelihood of resisters by denying them participation in the local economy (Rev 13:15–17). For Jews living in the empire, including Christ-followers, offering a sacrifice to the emperor posed serious problems because it was an offense to Jewish monotheism (see Figure 12.1). Yet, refusing to support the local emperor cult meant refusing to perform a basic civic duty. The Book of Revelation suggests that such refusal caused local tensions that could turn violent.

FIGURE 12.1

Fourth-century CE catacomb painting illustrating how early Christians viewed their own experience of the Roman empire through the lens of the biblical text. Though it depicts a scene from Dan 3:12–18 in which three men refuse to honor the image of the Babylonian king Nebuchadnezzar, the bust of the king looks like a Roman emperor, and the officer demanding their veneration of the king is in Roman military attire.

The rest of the Book of Revelation provides graphic descriptions of the coming defeat and punishment of Rome and Satan. The angel's call to worship "the one who made the heaven and the earth, the sea and the springs of water" (Rev 14:7 NRSV) is juxtaposed with a picture of the eternal torment of those who worship the beast (Rev 14:9–11). Throughout these violent scenes, the task of the faithful believer is to endure (Rev 13:10; 14:12). The violence against Rome and Satan is carried out by others, whether by the angels of God, who pour bowls of God's wrath on the earth and lock up Satan in a bottomless pit (Rev 16:1–21; 20:1–3), or by the warrior rider who strikes down enemies with the sword of his mouth (Rev 19:11–18). There is no question about who will win these contests between God and his opponents. Instead, the main point of these visions is to depict God's vengeance on and punishment of his defeated enemies. The final scenes complete the fantasy of a fallen Rome and the defeated evil power of Satan. A new holy city of Jerusalem comes down from heaven to a new earth. The city is to be home to God so that God will live among the people (Rev 21:1–4). This is the hope offered to those living under the oppression of the empire.

Revelation 17–18

FOCUS
TEXT

Although I will discuss two other New Testament texts below, the focus text for this chapter is from Revelation, so I include it here. Revelation 17–18 expresses the most explicit anti-Roman sentiment in the entire New Testament. Up to this point, the author of Revelation has led the audience to visualize the wrath of God being exacted on Satan, the beast, the earth, and most of its inhabitants. In these chapters, the focus shifts to the city of Rome itself, personified as "the **whore of Babylon**" (Figure 12.2). The image of the "whore" is introduced in chapter 17. She wears royal colors, is adorned in jewels and gold, holds a golden cup "full of abominations," and sits on a bright red, seven-headed beast (Rev 17:1–6). On her forehead is the name "Babylon the great, mother of whores and of earth's abominations." Soon, her identity is revealed. She is "the great city that rules over the kings of the earth" (Rev 17:18).

FIGURE 12.2

Revelation's figure of the "whore of Babylon" has captured the imaginations of artists for hundreds of years. This 1809 pen and watercolor was done by the artist and poet William Blake.

In the author's time, this "whore of Babylon" could only have symbolized Rome. The author draws on Israel's past trauma with Babylon to symbolize the source of the community's present trauma. The figure of the prostitute is also familiar from Israel's scriptures. Prophets like Hosea and Ezekiel used a similar image as a way to critique their own people's waywardness. Here, the "whore" is used in reference to the enemy city. The fact that the woman is "drunk with the blood of the saints and the blood of the witnesses to Jesus" suggests the author is aware of instances of suffering at the hands of the Romans, perhaps under Nero. Revelation 17 concludes with a disturbing image of the destruction of the personified city: she will be stripped, eaten, and burned with fire (Rev 17:16). The gruesome description of her fate indicates the intense level of hostility directed toward Rome. It is also another troubling example of an ancient writer using violence against a female body to convey the judgment of God.

Revelation 18 opens with an angelic announcement of the city's demise: "Fallen, fallen is Babylon the great!" Thus begins a scene of destruction that reflects deep anger against Rome and the exploitative practices that produced its great wealth. Much of the chapter is modeled on Ezekiel 27, which details the luxury and trading practices of the city of Tyre before predicting the day of its ruin. Likewise, Revelation 18 details the luxury of Rome and its eventual destruction. Its demise is considered to be a just punishment for its destruction of other nations: "render to her as she herself has rendered" (18:6).

As we saw in the discussion of Revelation 13, the leaders of the Roman empire grew rich off the lands Rome conquered, as did those who cooperated with imperial expansion (see Rev 18:3). Notice the detailed list of the cargo sold to Rome by the "merchants of the earth," which concludes with a reference to trading in "human lives" – that is, slaves (18:12–13). While the details of this chapter may seem exaggerated, it coincides with other accounts of how the Roman elite disenfranchised the lower classes. The poor were cut out of local governing assemblies and often denied citizenship. They were also subject to price gouging. The Roman writer Plutarch offers an account of bread riots in Asia Minor caused by the hoarding of grain and resulting price increases. Such conditions help explain the bitterness reflected in Revelation 18.

Finally, note that while the chapter refers to Rome's destruction as a past event, the concluding verses return to the future tense: "With sudden violence Babylon the great city will be thrown down" (18:21). In fact, throughout the Book of Revelation, past, present, and future are intertwined. This enables the reader both to fantasize about the utter demise of Rome and to acknowledge that Rome's destruction remains in the future.

Hebrews: Platonic Perspectives on Christ

READING

Read Hebrews 1:1–14; 4:14–10:39.

Pay attention to the imagery used for Jesus in these passages.

If the Revelation to John is the clearest biblical example of resistance to Rome, the biblical book of Hebrews seems the most removed from such concerns. At first glance, there is little to suggest that the author has anything in mind but Jesus's relation to Jewish tradition, in particular the Jewish sacrificial cult. Nevertheless, the text is a fascinating combination of cultural influences and thus another example of the type of hybrid text generated in an imperial context. In particular, the author combines neo-Platonic ideas with Jewish scriptural and cultic references in the service of his unique image of Jesus. Like other images of Jesus that we have seen in the New Testament, this one draws on cultural images of Roman imperial authority. But Hebrews also contains themes of alienation and marginalization, suggesting that this author recognized the difficulty of living under that authority. Indeed, even the interest in the Jewish sacrificial cult may be a result of the pressures of imperial occupation.

Although Hebrews first circulated with the collection of Pauline letters, it does not purport to be by Paul. Even the earliest church writers did not think Paul wrote it. The second-century CE writer Origen asserted that "only God knows" who wrote it. Nor is Hebrews actually a letter. Aside from the concluding benediction and greetings (Heb 13:20–5), the text reads more like a homily. The literary finesse of the book suggests that the author of Hebrews was well educated. Compared to much of the rest of the New Testament, Hebrews uses a complex and sophisticated writing style.

The central image of the text is a distinctive one: the author presents Jesus as a high priest offering an atoning sacrifice for "the sins of the people" (2:17). Although there are references in other New Testament writings to the sacrificial nature of the death of Jesus (see, for example, Paul's sacrificial language in 1 Cor 5:7 or Rom 3:25), only in Hebrews is Jesus presented as the priest who carries out the sacrifice. Specifically, Jesus is depicted as a high priest according to the order of Melchizedek (Heb 5:10; 6:20; 7:1–3). If you have never heard of Melchizedek, there is a good reason. The name occurs only twice in the Hebrew scriptures. It appears first in a brief account in Gen 14:18–20, where Melchizedek is described as both a king and a priest who blesses Abraham. The second reference is in Ps 110:4, where the Davidic king is called "a priest forever in the order of Melchizedek."

For the author of Hebrews, this double identity of king and priest was important. Recall that a major role of the Roman emperor was that of high priest, *pontifex maximus*. Just as the Roman emperor mediated with the gods on behalf of the people, the Jesus of Hebrews is a royal priest who intercedes for those who approach God (Heb 7:25). Here, we see the author's understanding of the superiority of Jesus to earthly high priests, whether the Jewish high priest or the Roman emperor in his priestly role. In fact, this is another reason why the figure of Melchizedek is significant to the author. The author calls attention to what is missing from the brief mention of Melchizedek in Genesis: "no father, no mother, no genealogy" (Heb 7:3; Gen 14:17–20), in other words, there is a timelessness to the figure. Indeed, for the author, this lack of origins explains the eternal nature of Melchizedek's priesthood; the author describes the figure as "neither having beginning of days nor having end of life, like the Son of God, he remains a priest forever" (Heb 7:3). According to the author of Hebrews, the priesthood of Jesus is likewise permanent and eternal (Heb 7:23–4).

Basics on the Letter to the Hebrews

While this book has "letter" in its title, the only letter-like elements come in the last chapter, which contains exhortations and greetings. Otherwise, the book is more like a sermon in form.

Outline: a literary sermon	I	The superiority of Christ	1:1–4:13
	II	Christ's high priesthood	4:14–10:18
	III	Encouraging faithful endurance	10:19–13:33

Date and authorship Much about Hebrews remains unclear to modern scholars; the author, date, and place of composition are all difficult to determine with any certainty. The author is unknown, and the proposed dates for the book range from the 60s to the 90s CE. This range reflects a debate on whether the text was written before or after the destruction of the Temple in 70 CE. There is no explicit recognition of the Temple's demise, but the book's focus on the heavenly sanctuary and high priesthood of Jesus could be a response to its destruction. Similarly, the admission that "we have no enduring city" (13:14) suggests an awareness of Jerusalem's destruction. Given this, it seems most likely that the text was written post-70 CE. As for location, most scholars now think the text was directed toward the Christ-followers in Rome. There is one reference to location in Heb 13:24 ("those from Italy greet you"), which may indicate greetings from fellow Italians now living outside of Italy sending greetings to the community in Rome. The earliest text that quotes Hebrews, 1 Clement, is a letter written by the Roman bishop Clement in the late first or early second century CE.

The description of the high priesthood of Jesus also points to the fundamentally Platonic worldview of the author of Hebrews. The Greek philosopher Plato (427–347 BCE) believed that the objects that made up the earthly material world were imperfect reflections of the true ideal (and immaterial) forms of these objects. For example, in Platonic thought, a physical chair is merely a copy of the eternal idea of a more real and perfect chair. This **Platonic theory of forms**, as well as other aspects of Plato's thought, continued to influence Christian writers until well into the fifth century CE. The early stages of this influence are evident in Hebrews, which uses the Platonic idea of forms to elevate Jesus above the Jerusalem Temple cult. For example, the author claims that Levitical priests offer sacrifices in a sanctuary that is a "copy and shadow" of the heavenly one (Heb 8:5). In contrast, Jesus as high priest has entered not an earthly sanctuary – which would be merely "a copy of the true one" – but rather what is truly real: "heaven itself" (Heb 9:24). Even the law, according to the author, is but "a shadow of coming good things, and not the form itself of these things" (Heb 10:1).

The critique of the Jerusalem sacrificial cult in Hebrews is not unique among Second Temple Jewish literature. The Qumran scrolls describe the Jerusalem priesthood as corrupt and their own group as the true temple. Such critiques are not independent of imperial occupation. Recall that in our study of the gospels, we saw how assertions of Jesus's superiority over Moses reflected a form of inter-group competition, a competition that was heightened, if not created, by the dynamics of foreign rule. The fact that Hebrews draws on a Greek philosophical idea (one that continued to be transmitted by the Romans) to speak of Jesus's relation to the Temple cult in a Roman-ruled empire further reflects the long-term effects of imperial forces.

Another more direct link between the Platonic perspective of Hebrews and associations with imperial authority occurs in Heb 1:3. At this point, Jesus is described as an exact representation of God's real being. Here, the author draws on a standard Greco-Roman political theory in which an ideal ruler is understood to embody reason and law, or, to use the Greek phrase, divine *logos*. To speak of the relationship between Jesus and God as one of "exact representation" highlights Jesus's own exact image of divine essence and authority. This is another example of how a New Testament author lifts up Jesus while also subtly critiquing similar claims made about the Roman emperor. The fact that Jesus is an *exact* representation of God stands in contrast to the "shadows" and "copies," such as the Roman emperor. According to the author, these shadowy copies do *not* convey the true essence of their forms, unlike Jesus in relation to God.

While we can now read Hebrews in light of its Roman imperial context, we must also recognize the book's damaging legacy as a founding text for supersessionist theology (or "replacement" theology) in the Christian church. Those who support the view that God rejected the Jewish people in favor of Christians turn especially to Hebrews 8. This chapter includes an extensive quotation from the book of Jeremiah, which suggests that God has abandoned his covenant with the people of Israel in favor of a new covenant. The author quotes from the Greek translation of Jeremiah, which differs from the Hebrew text in a significant way. Compare the last line of each translation of Jer 31:31–4 below:

> The days are surely coming, says the Lord, when I will make a new covenant with the house of Israel and the house of Judah. It will not be like the covenant that I made with their ancestors when I took them by the hand to bring them out of the land of Egypt
>
> – a covenant that they broke, though I was their husband, says the Lord. (NRSV, using the Hebrew wording)
> – a covenant that they broke, and so I had no concern for them. (Wording from the LXX, the Greek translation)

Whereas the Hebrew text emphasizes God's intimate relationship with the ancestors of Israel and Judah, the Greek translation points to God's lack of care for them. This difference in the Greek translation may have occurred from a misreading of the Hebrew word for husband by the Greek translators. In any event, the use of the Greek translation in the context of a book where Jesus is said to have obtained a superior ministry and mediated a better covenant that is enacted through better promises (Heb 8:6) contributed to the development of Christian supersessionism. It does not help that the author concludes the section with the claim that the old covenant is obsolete, worn out, and will soon disappear (Heb 8:13). Such claims are in striking contrast to Paul's insistence that God's gift and the election of Israel are irrevocable (Rom 11:29). While many Christian theologians now reject supersessionist theology, this just means it is even more pressing that they contend with the book of Hebrews and the history of its interpretation. Situating Hebrews in its first-century CE context does not fully alleviate the problems the book creates for Jewish–Christian relations, but it can at least complicate a simple and anachronistic Christian versus Jewish interpretation.

Finally, while most of Hebrews concerns the image of Jesus as high priest, there are also exhortations directed toward the audience. These sections reveal how the author views the community's position in the world. For example, in a list of faithful ancestors, the "great cloud of witnesses" (12:1), the author points to times when some lived as strangers and foreigners on the earth in search of a better homeland (11:13–14). The author contrasts the ancestral search for a homeland with the present one. Recalling the scene at Mount Sinai, he depicts it as a terrifying experience complete with a blazing fire, darkness, gloom, a windstorm, and a voice warning of death that the audience begs not to hear (12:18–20). In comparison, he offers a "better homeland" (11:16), which is not a place "that can be touched" but rather the heavenly Mount Zion/Jerusalem (12:22). Like Jesus, who was executed outside the gates of Jerusalem, believers are to go "outside the camp," for they have no lasting city but are looking for the city that is to come (Heb 13:14). In these ways, the author offers a subtle critique of past searches for a homeland and of present imperial rule. Neither in the past nor in the present has the people's lived experience been permanent or ideal. Rather, using a Platonic perspective on reality, the author suggests that the experience of earthly life in the empire only leaves them longing and searching for a better homeland.

1 Peter: Living as Aliens and Accommodating to the Empire

Read 1 Peter.

READING

What is the tone of this letter? What do you think is its main purpose?

EXERCISE

The third and final example of the variety of New Testament responses to life in the empire is 1 Peter. Like Hebrews, 1 Peter uses a rhetoric of alienation, opening with an address to "aliens in the diaspora" (1 Peter 1:1). **Diaspora** is a transliteration of the Greek word for "scattering," and in a Jewish context it refers to Jewish people living as foreigners in regions outside of Palestine. Like Revelation, 1 Peter is directed toward communities scattered across Asia Minor. The regions listed in the first verse – Pontus, Galatia, Cappadocia, Asia, and Bithynia – are all Roman provinces in Asia Minor. Intended to circulate in this region, 1 Peter is an example of a "diaspora letter." It resembles other Jewish diaspora letters, like Jer 29:4–23, and some Septuagint texts, such as Baruch (a letter associated with Jeremiah's scribe) and the epistle of Jeremiah. These diaspora letters often evoke themes of alienation and exhort those living in exile to conduct themselves in particular ways. 1 Peter fits this pattern, as it contains an exhortation to readers to live "in fear" during their time of alienation (1 Peter 1:17) and to conduct themselves honorably as "aliens and strangers" (1 Peter 2:11). Some scholars have argued that this language should be taken literally and that the letter addresses actual communities of exiles living in Asia Minor. However, given what we have already seen in texts like the Gospel of John and Hebrews, it is more likely that the language of exile and alienation is used metaphorically to describe the relationship between Christ-followers and the world. They are no longer at home in the world but instead live as aliens in a foreign land.

A major theme of 1 Peter helps explain this feeling of alienation. Throughout the text, the author points to the experience of suffering on the part of the believers (1:6; 3:14; 4:12–19). There is no specific mention of physical suffering. Instead, the author suggests that the communities were experiencing the sort of local mistreatment discussed above. For example, the author refers to their being accused of doing evil (2:12). He urges them not to be afraid or intimidated (3:14) even if they are being slandered (3:16) and insulted (4:14). Notably, the author also exhorts his audience not to be ashamed if they suffer "as a Christian" but to glorify God in this way (4:16). As we have seen, this is one of the rare occurrences of the term "Christian" in the New Testament. That the author associates the designation with the experience of suffering offers a further illustration of the sense of fear and alienation that his intended audience may have been experiencing.

Basics on 1 Peter

I	Opening salutation and thanksgiving	1:1–12	**Outline: an elder's letter to the churches of Asia Minor**
II	Letter body: the identity and proper conduct of the people of God – accommodation and persistence	1:13–5:11	
III	Concluding greetings and wishes	5:11–12	

The text purports to be from "Peter, an apostle of Jesus Christ," but few scholars think that Peter was the author. A Galilean fisherman would not likely be able to read or write, let alone write with the sophisticated Greek style of 1 Peter. Moreover, there is nothing **Date and authorship** about the content of 1 Peter that suggests it was written by one of Jesus's first disciples. Rather, 1 Peter is an example of a **pseudonymous** early Christian writing (in Greek, pseudonymous means "false name"). See Chapter 6 for a discussion of the ancient practice of writing under a false name. Most scholars think 1 Peter was written in Rome, probably sometime after 70 CE.

However, 1 Peter illustrates a different approach to the experience of alienation than we saw in Revelation. Whereas the Book of Revelation takes an openly hostile stance against Rome, 1 Peter urges its audience to adhere closely to the standards of Roman society. They are to live honorably (2:12) and submit to all human authorities, whether to the emperor or to governors appointed by him (2:12–14). Indeed, they are to honor everyone, including the emperor, as the author takes special care to note (2:17). In strong contrast to Revelation, this may be an example of a biblical text that advocates participating in the emperor cult. Although many scholars have suggested that the author means to say, "Do anything to honor the emperor *but* offering sacrifice," there are no such qualifications in the text. On the contrary, the author's overall stance – that his readers should not give cause for gentiles to despise them – would suggest conformity perhaps even to the sacrificial emperor cult, as Warren Carter has argued (see Carter, "Going all the Way? Honoring the Emperor and Sacrificing Wives and Slaves in First Peter 2.13–3.6," in Resources for Further Reading). The author may be promoting a *public* accommodation to the civic demands of life under imperial rule while *private* convictions to Christ are maintained. Note, for example, how the author urges believers to revere Christ "in their hearts" (1 Peter 3:15). They are to do so while being zealous to "do good." This "doing good" likely refers to a general sense of civic good conduct, since no mistreatment will come to them if they conduct themselves in this way (1 Peter 3:13). Again, this is quite a contrast to Revelation, which encourages its audience to resist such conduct even if it means their death!

Contemporary Voices: Asian Americans, Perpetual Foreigners, and 1 Peter

Asian Americans have a long and painful history of being stereotyped as perpetual foreigners in their own country. Even while they are caricatured as the "model minority," Asian Americans are often perceived as not fully legitimate civic participants, even as native-born citizens.

Janette Ok has examined the rhetoric of alienation in 1 Peter in light of this Asian American experience (see Janette H. Ok, "Always Ethnic, Never 'American': Reading 1 Peter through the Lens of the 'Perpetual Foreigner' Stereotype," in *T&T Clark Handbook of Asian American*

Biblical Hermeneutics (ed. Uriah Y. Kim and Seung Ai Yang; London: T&T Clark, 2019), 417–425). She suggests this rhetoric encourages the letter recipients to designate themselves as perpetual foreigners with a goal of building a strong sense of group identity. Yet, Ok suggests, this same language could be problematic for Asian American interpreters of 1 Peter. As she argues,

the image of the perpetual foreigner functions for Asian Americans as a stereotype negatively imposed upon them. This stereotype, coupled with the author's theological language of being "resident aliens and foreigners" (2:11), may further marginalize Asian Americans and encourage a position of civic and political withdrawal, while at the same time strengthening their sense of ethnic-religious group identity (425).

In the end, Ok suggests that more work is needed to understand the effects that the rhetoric of alienation in 1 Peter may have on the political engagement of Asian American Christians.

In addition to advocating "doing good," the author assumes that the community should embrace the same hierarchical relationships that shaped the social structure of the Greco-Roman world. He does this by using a **household code** similar to what we have seen in the Deutero-Pauline letters (Col 3:18–4:1; Eph 5:21–6:9). Recall that Paul himself urged people to remain in whatever social position they were in when they became believers, with the possible exception of slaves (1 Cor 7:17). In 1 Peter, the author draws on such standard codes of conduct to encourage cultural conformity among the community of believers. As with the Deutero-Pauline letters, there is no ambiguity in the instruction for slaves to submit to the authority of their masters. But especially troubling is the added instruction that slaves should submit "not only to those who are good and gentle but also to those who are perverse" (1 Peter 2:18). So, too, wives should be submissive to their husbands (1 Peter 3:1). Husbands are to honor their wives, the "weaker female vessels" (1 Peter 3:7). The younger should submit to the elders (1 Peter 5:5). None of these exhortations would seem unusual to the readers of 1 Peter.

In sum, the letter urges its readers – whom it identifies as aliens and strangers in the world – to conduct themselves in ways that conform to the expectations of their society. It may well be that this was a deliberate strategy of accommodation that the author employed to help Christ-followers avoid ongoing harassment by their neighbors and local authorities.

Conclusion: Three Different Relationships to the Roman Empire

This chapter has shown the diverse ways that certain authors outside the gospels and Pauline tradition responded to the challenge of living as a follower of Jesus during the late first century CE in the Greco-Roman world. The Revelation to John, Hebrews, and 1 Peter all suggest that life in the empire was difficult at best and a life of suffering at worst. However, each text presents a different approach to this reality. The apocalyptic text of Revelation takes a stance of hostile resistance toward Rome. It engages the audience in an extended fantasy in which they are invited to witness God's violent destruction of Rome. This vision of divine justice includes the ultimate promise of a restored Jerusalem where God will live among the people and wipe away their every tear.

In contrast, Hebrews seems largely detached from the Roman political and economic sphere. It more directly engages the Jewish sacrificial cult, presenting an image of Jesus as a superior high priest and king. Nevertheless, this image is also a subtle way of pointing to Christ as superior to the Roman emperor. Likewise, the author's Platonic perspective allows him to highlight the perfection of Jesus seated in the heavenly temple alongside God, creating an unspoken contrast to the imperfections of the present earthly rule of the Roman empire. Finally, 1 Peter urges accommodation to Roman authority and culture, even while it recognizes the alienated position of its audience. In stark contrast to Revelation, it looks toward a way of peaceful existence in the world, one that enables believers to fit into their cultural surroundings while maintaining their commitment to Christ.

CHAPTER TWELVE REVIEW

1   Know the meaning and significance of the following terms:
   * apocalypse
   * diaspora
   * hybridity (in relation to postcolonial theory)
   * Platonic theory of forms
   * pseudonymous
   * whore of Babylon

2   What elements does Revelation share with the genre of apocalypse? What was this writing intended to do for its ancient audience?

3   How do the Revelation to John, Hebrews, and 1 Peter reflect distress in the audiences that they address? How does this compare with evidence of the persecution of Christians in Roman sources?

4   What is the difference between the apparent positions of Revelation and 1 Peter on the issue of honoring and sacrificing to the Roman emperor? How does this reflect the different ways that Revelation and 1 Peter respond to alienation in their audiences?

5   How does Hebrews, with its Platonic perspective, subtly critique the Roman empire by emphasizing how Jesus is an "exact representation of God's true being"?

6   How would you summarize in three sentences the different ways in which Revelation, Hebrews, and 1 Peter relate to their Roman imperial context?

7   (Focus text: Revelation 17–18) What does the whore of Babylon represent in Revelation? What evidence from these chapters makes evident the meaning of this figure? How might the symbolic elements in these chapters be useful and problematic in a twenty-first-century context?

RESOURCES FOR FURTHER STUDY

Barr, David L., ed. *Reading the Book of Revelation: A Resource for Students*. Atlanta, GA: Society of Biblical Literature, 2003.

Beal, Timothy K. *Revelation: A Biography*. Princeton, NJ: Princeton University Press, 2018.

Beavis, Mary Ann. *Hebrews*. Collegeville, MN: Liturgical Press, 2015.

Blount, Brian K. *Can I Get a Witness? Reading Revelation through African American Culture*. Louisville, KY: Westminster John Knox Press, 2005.

Blount, Brian K. *Revelation: A Commentary*. Louisville, KY: Westminster John Knox Press, 2009.

Carey, Greg. *Apocalyptic Literature in the New Testament*. Nashville, TN: Abingdon Press, 2016.

Carter, Warren. "Going all the Way? Honoring the Emperor and Sacrificing Wives and Slaves in First Peter 2.13–3.6." Pp. 14–33 in A.J. Levine and Marianne Blickenstaff (eds.), *Feminist Companion to the Catholic Epistles and Hebrews*. London: T&T Clark, 2005.

Collins, Adela Yarbo. *Crisis and Catharsis: The Power of the Apocalypse*. Philadelphia, PA: Westminster Press, 1984.

Horrell, David G. *1 Peter*. New Testament Guides. London and New York: T&T Clark, 2008.

Kovacs, Judith, and Christopher Rowland. *Revelation*. Blackwell Bible Commentaries. Oxford: Blackwell, 2004.

Schüssler Fiorenza, Elisabeth. *1 Peter: Reading Against the Grain*. Sheffield, UK: Sheffield Phoenix Press, 2015.

EPILOGUE: THE FINAL FORMATION OF THE NEW TESTAMENT CANON

As we arrive at the end of this introduction to the New Testament, I am well aware that our work together has indeed only been an introduction. We have not studied all 27 books of the New Testament, nor have we studied all the texts that were popular among early Christ-followers. To cover all of the New Testament canon, we would need to include the pseudepigraphal letters of James, Jude, and 2 Peter. The book of James is a set of instructions resembling instructions in Jewish wisdom literature. Like the author of the Gospel of Matthew, the author of James urges Torah obedience (James 2:8–17). The short texts of Jude and 2 Peter (which uses Jude as a source) both warn against unnamed opponents or false prophets who have "snuck in" among the faithful (Jude 4; Peter 2:1).

Meanwhile, outside of the canon, a wide array of writings offer yet more insight into early Christ-followers. We know from the diverse writings collected at Nag Hammadi in Egypt and other sources that there were many kinds of Christ groups in the first and second centuries CE, some of which produced texts that were not included in the New Testament. These non-canonical writings include multiple gospels, other writings in the "Acts of" genre, and other apocalypses. Also included in this collection are a number of so-called "gnostic" writings. I mentioned one of the more well-known gnostic texts, the Gospel of Thomas, earlier in this book. This writing is a collection of supposedly secret sayings that Jesus offered to the disciples. Another example is the Apocryphon of John, in which Jesus answers questions posed by the apostle John. This fascinating collection of writings awaits the student who wants to move even more deeply into the study of early literature connected to the Jesus movement.

One result of this continuing development of tradition among Christ-followers was that Christianity underwent a process of consolidation during the early centuries of the common era. The first generations of Christ-followers seem to have valued oral traditions about Jesus handed down by trusted leaders over written documents, which could be falsified. For example, the early church writer Papias, writing sometime in the late first or early second century CE, claims that he would benefit more hearing "the words of the elders" (meaning "any of the Lord's disciples") than from "information from books" (as recorded by Eusebius, *Ecclesiastical History*, 3:39). Only rarely did the earliest Christian authors mention authoritative written works of the "Apostles" alongside Jewish books of "Prophets."

This situation changed as Christianity grew and began to define itself as a centralized religious movement that was separate from Judaism (see Map 13.1). How, when, and to what extent this so-called "Parting of the Ways" occurred has been an ongoing

The New Testament: A Contemporary Introduction, First Edition. Colleen M. Conway.
© 2023 John Wiley & Sons Ltd. Published 2023 by John Wiley & Sons Ltd.

scholarly conversation. Some recent researchers have cautioned against taking the anti-Jewish rhetoric of the second century CE onwards as reflective of actual social realities. Indeed, archaeological evidence from late antiquity demonstrates a fluid coexistence of Jews, Christians, and pagans. For instance, some ancient grave inscriptions draw on a mix of Jewish and Christian symbols in a way that suggests porous social boundaries between these groups.

The process of canonization – that is, the designation of particular texts as authoritative scripture – took place over several centuries. In general, writings by Christ-followers that were especially popular in the emerging church, whether they were used regularly in the liturgy or were presumed to be connected to one of the original apostles, came to be part of a "New Testament." Another factor affecting the canonization process was the existence of diverse and conflicting positions on matters of belief and doctrine. For instance, a second-century CE Christian bishop named Marcion designated a very narrow collection of books as authoritative: a shorter version of the Gospel of Luke and a collection of 10 Pauline letters. Marcion rejected all of the Hebrew scriptures outright, along with what he considered to be a different, tribal deity of the Jews in the Hebrew Bible. This position was rejected as heretical by other church writers. In contrast to Marcion, the early church writers valued the Jewish scriptures, even if these writings came to be designated as a separate "Old Testament."

In the third and fourth centuries, theologians produced varying lists of what books were included in the Old and New Testament. Generally, theologians working in the Western Mediterranean included a broader range of books, while theologians working in the East had more restrictive lists. For instance, it took a long time for the book of Revelation to be recognized as authoritative in the Eastern churches. Nevertheless, by the end of the third century CE, the leading authorities in Christianity agreed on virtually all the books to be included in the biblical canon.

A new level of consolidation came in the early fourth century, when Constantine, who ruled from 306 to 337 CE, became the first Christian emperor of the broader Roman empire. At this point, Christianity began the transition from being a movement *under* empire to becoming the religion *of* the empire. Divisions among Christians were viewed as threats to the unity of the imperial realm. For this reason, over the following century, a series of ecumenical councils were convened to resolve theological disputes. Most of these councils focused on debates about the nature of Christ, but several councils (such as those at Hippo in 393 and Carthage in 397 and 418) produced authoritative lists of which books were included in the New Testament. Meanwhile, some early Christian writings associated with dissident Christian groups, or works whose connection to an apostle had not been established, were excluded. Many scholars point to an Easter letter written by a church leader named Athanasius in 367 CE as an important indicator of the end of the canonization process. The letter lists all 27 books of the New Testament as we now have it, albeit in a different order.

Finally, throughout this textbook, I have offered examples of how the ancient biblical texts relate to their ancient settings and of how contemporary biblical interpretations relate to contemporary culture. Moreover, we have seen how both ancient and contemporary writers reinterpret older texts in light of new social and cultural contexts. For example, the gospel writers shaped their stories of Jesus in light of their own

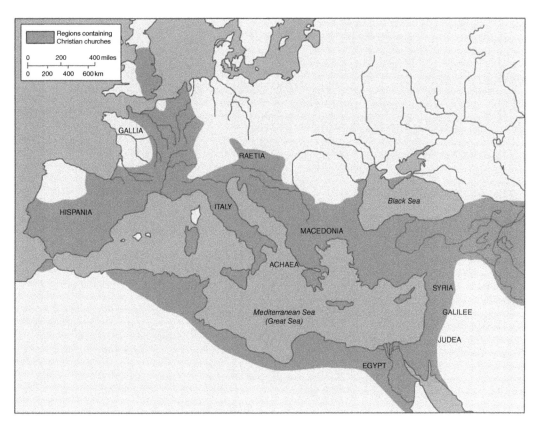

MAP 13.1
Spread of Christianity across the Mediterranean world by 300 CE. Redrawn from Bart Ehrman, *The New Testament: A Historical Introduction to the Early Christian Writings* (3rd edition). Oxford: Oxford University Press, 2004, p. 43.

circumstances while reinterpreting ancient scriptures to speak to their own understanding of God and Jesus. As I mentioned at the outset of this book, historical criticism helps us to understand these ancient concerns. It gives us eyes to see how the meanings of ancient texts shift as they are repurposed for different historical circumstances. Meanwhile, we have also seen how scholars who come to the text with the questions and concerns of the twenty-first century draw on a diverse set of critical perspectives for their interpretations. This range of contemporary approaches helps us to see the cultural and political influences that the Bible has, or could have, in our own time. While I have offered several interpretations from diverse perspectives in this textbook, what we have studied here has only scratched the surface of this scholarly work. New Testament scholarship, like any academic discipline, continues to develop in sync with emerging theoretical interests in the humanities. My hope is that you will continue to seek out a wide range of perspectives and approaches to aid in your understanding of the New Testament in its ancient and contemporary contexts.

GLOSSARY

African American biblical interpretation – forms of critical biblical study whose questions grow out of the experiences of people of African descent. Such study critiques racist interpretations of the Bible, highlights the presence of African characters in the Bible, and/or critically analyzes the diverse ways that scripture has been used in African American religion and culture. (See also **womanist interpretation**.)

allegorical interpretation – a method of interpretation that assumes multiple levels of meaning are present in a text, especially a deeper meaning that is evident beyond the literal meaning of the text. Paul's interpretation of Hagar and Sarah as "covenants" in Gal 4:21–31 is an example of allegorical interpretation.

apocalypse – a genre of writing commonly attested in the Hellenistic and later periods that describes a heavenly revelation to a human recipient, often a human recipient from Israel's distant past (for example, Enoch, Levi, etc.; see **pseudepigraphy**). The Book of Revelation in the New Testament is an example of this genre, although in this case, the author writes in his own name, John.

apocalyptic, **apocalypticism** – predicting or describing the end of the current, unjust age and the arrival of a new age through God's direct intervention in history. Similarly, **apocalypticism** refers to a worldview that emphasizes God's anticipated intervention that will bring the current, corrupt world order to an end. This end will involve the punishment of the unjust, rewards to those who have suffered, and the initiation of a new, just world order.

apocrypha – Protestant term for **deuterocanonical** books, in this case designating books that are not viewed in the Protestant tradition as fully **canonical**.

Babylonian exile – 586–538 BCE, a time when most of the elite who had been living in Judah (especially Jerusalem) were forced to live outside the land in Babylon (with many never having the chance to return).

canon and **canonical** – a "canon" is a collection of books that are recognized as divinely inspired scripture by a given religious community. Those books are recognized as "canonical."

client kings – Roman-appointed local leaders who ruled the provinces of Rome for the emperor (considered their "patron"), allowing some level of independence for the province and extended influence by Rome.

destruction of the Second Temple – 70 CE: occurred in the wake of a Jewish revolt against Rome and – along with the total destruction of Jerusalem in 135 CE after another revolt – represented the end of the local Jewish temple state and the recentering of much Jewish life in the communities outside the land (see **diaspora**).

deuterocanonical – books recognized as **canonical** by the Roman Catholic church, but not part of the Jewish Tanakh or Protestant **Old Testament**.

The New Testament: A Contemporary Introduction, First Edition. Colleen M. Conway.
© 2023 John Wiley & Sons Ltd. Published 2023 by John Wiley & Sons Ltd.

Deutero-Pauline letters designation for the disputed Pauline letters: 2 Thessalonians, Ephesians, Colossians, 1 and 2 Timothy, and Titus. See **disputed letters** of Paul.

diaspora – the "scattering" or dispersion of Jews throughout lands outside of Palestine, particularly during the **Babylonian exile** in the sixth century BCE and after the end of the **Jewish War** in 70 CE.

diatribe – an ancient form of philosophical discourse characterized by the use of an imaginary dialogue partner (an **interlocutor**) who poses questions and objections that are designed to enable one's argument to advance.

disputed letters – Pauline letters whose authorship is disputed on the basis of difference in tone, language, or theological positions, or because the letter presupposes a stage in the institutional organization of the Jesus movement that likely postdated Paul. These letters include 2 Thessalonians, Colossians, Ephesians, 1 and 2 Timothy, and Titus.

dynamic equivalence – a translation that aims to produce a meaning-for-meaning translation of a (biblical) text, diverging from a word-for-word translation as necessary to produce a more understandable equivalent meaning.

ekklesia – a common Greek word, meaning "assembly" or "gathering," that could be used for civic assemblies, Greco-Roman **voluntary associations**, and synagogue groups. It is often translated as "church," its later meaning.

eschatology – an aspect of theology that is concerned with the end of the world, the end of humanity, or the end of the current order of the world.

Farewell Discourse – chapters 14–17 of the Gospel of John in which the Johannine Jesus speaks to his disciples to prepare them for his departure from the world.

formal correspondence – a word-for-word translation of a (biblical) text.

fulfillment citations – the repeated claim that aspects of Jesus's life story "happened in order to fulfill" or actualize the words of the **Torah** and the prophets. These citations constitute a distinctive emphasis in the Gospel of Matthew.

hardship catalogues – also known as *peristasis* (Greek for circumstances) catalogues, lists of difficult conditions used rhetorically in Greek and Roman philosophical literature to showcase one's virtue in enduring harsh conditions. Paul uses such catalogues to demonstrate his steadfastness as an apostle.

Hebrew Bible – scriptures shared by Jews and Christians.

Hellenistic and Hellenization – related to Greek history, language, and culture after Alexander the Great in the fourth century BCE; the spread of Greek culture across the eastern Mediterranean after the military conquest of Alexander.

historical Jesus – the Jesus who is the person behind, but still separate from, the narratives about him in New Testament writings. Scholars have drawn conclusions about the historical Jesus by paying attention to the ways these texts contain overlapping and distinctive traditions about Jesus's life and teachings, and by applying a set of criteria to Jesus traditions in the New Testament.

household codes – in Colossians (3:18–4:1), Ephesians (5:21–6:9), Titus (2:1–10), and 1 Peter (2:18–3:7), specific codes of conduct for how members of households in the community (including husband, wife, children, and slaves) should behave toward one another. These instructions generally mirror common expectations of behavior in Greco-Roman households, which means a strict social hierarchy of patriarch over wife, children, and slaves (in more or less descending order).

hybridity – a concept drawn from postcolonial theory that designates the blending of self-determination with elements drawn from the culture of a past or current oppressor. Different from a mere blending of diverse cultural elements in identity, hybridity refers to the complex identity formed in the midst and wake of the experience of domination.

incarnation – within the study of the New Testament, the idea of God becoming human and fully embodied in the person of Jesus, signaled especially by the Johannine phrase "word made flesh" (John 1:14).

intercalation – sometimes called a "sandwich" structure; a narrative technique, regularly used in the Gospel of Mark, in which one story or episode is interrupted in the middle by another, complete episode, followed by the ending of the first one. The "inside" episode often offers an interpretation or complication of the story that enfolds it.

interlocutor – in the context of New Testament studies, an imaginary dialogue partner addressed in the second person, used for rhetorical purposes to advance an argument.

Jewish War – the war between the Jews of Palestine and the Romans that began in 66 CE with an armed revolt by the Jews, and ended with the destruction of the Second Temple and the sack of Jerusalem in 70 CE.

Johannine sectarianism – the idea, derived from the sociological study of religion, that the Gospel and Letters of John are products of a "sect," in this case a distinct group that perceived itself as the unique bearers of the truth about Jesus.

Koine Greek – "common" Greek that evolved from the classical Attic dialect. It was the dialect spoken in the eastern Mediterranean during the Hellenistic and Roman periods. The New Testament and **Septuagint** are written in Koine Greek.

liberation hermeneutic – an interpretive approach that emphasizes the importance of the perspectives of oppressed peoples as well as biblical themes of justice and emancipation from oppressive conditions.

Lukan travel narrative – the section of the Gospel of Luke from 9:51 to 19:27 comprised of material from **Q** and **Special L**, in which Jesus travels from Galilee to Jerusalem teaching along the way. The section is a major expansion of the brief travel narrative in the Gospel of Mark.

Luke–Acts – designation used by biblical scholars to refer to the two-volume work – the Gospel of Luke and the Acts of the Apostles – written by the same anonymous author.

LXX – an abbreviation for **Septuagint**.

Markan priority – the theory that the Gospel of Mark was the first-written of the synoptic gospels and was used as a source by the authors of Matthew and Luke.

messiah – a Hebrew word meaning "anointed one," which during the **Second Temple period** came to designate a hoped-for anointed king who would deliver Jews from domination and/or a hoped-for anointed priest to replace the priests in Jerusalem who were perceived by some to be corrupt. The term is applied to Jesus in the New Testament.

messianic secret – a recurring pattern in the Gospel of Mark in which Jesus urges secrecy about his miracles of healing or about his identity.

occasion – in the study of Paul's letters, a term used to designate the circumstances that led to each of these, pertaining both to the situations facing the various urban Christ groups to which he wrote and to his own personal situation.

Old Testament – Christian term for the scriptures originating in ancient Israel. It and the Jewish Tanakh contain nearly identical books, but with differing order.

Onesimus – name of the person, often assume to be enslaved, about whom Paul writes to Philemon. Paul uses the name, which means "useful" in Greek, for rhetorical purposes in his letter.

oral traditions – with respect to the New Testament, traditions about Jesus that circulated orally especially during the first and second centuries CE. These traditions formed the basis of the written gospels, though continued to develop and circulate after the gospels were written.

Palestine – a designation that the Romans came to use for a province including the land of Israel and much of Syria. The word "Palestinian" was used to characterize inhabitants of that province and continues to be used to refer to descendants of non-Jewish people who lived in the region prior to the establishment of the modern state of Israel.

parables – brief, open-ended, comparative stories using metaphor that invite the listener to make conclusions about the nature of the comparison being offered. Jesus is depicted as speaking in parables in the **synoptic gospels**, often comparing the kingdom of God to everyday people, things, and events.

Paraclete – the figure that Jesus describes in the **Farewell Discourse** of the Gospel of John, who Jesus promises he will send to comfort and guide his disciples after he departs. In 1 John 2:1, Jesus is described as a "paraclete" as well.

parousia – Greek work meaning "presence" that Paul and other writers use as a designation for the anticipated return of Jesus at the day of judgment, that is, his "second coming."

passion narrative – from *passus*, a Latin word for "suffering"; the story of Jesus's trial, suffering, and death in the canonical gospels. An independent passion narrative may have predated Mark's gospel.

passion predictions – the instances in the gospels in which Jesus, referring to himself as the "Son of Man," anticipates his own approaching suffering and death. Jesus does this three times in Mark, in keeping with Mark's preferred pattern of repeating important information in triplicate.

Pastoral Letters – 1 and 2 Timothy and Titus, designated as "pastoral" because they offer instructions for leaders of Christ groups. Also known as the Pastoral Epistles, they were likely written in the second century CE. See **disputed letters** of Paul.

Platonic theory of forms – Plato's theory that non-material abstract forms possess a higher form of reality than the material world of sense perception.

pronouncements – short, direct sayings in the form of sharp responses to tricky questions posed by one's rhetorical opponent. The gospels feature Jesus offering such retorts to his opponents.

pseudepigraphy – attribution of a later text to a more ancient author. Such pseudonymous attribution was particularly common in the Greco-Roman period, when Judaism came into contact with a Hellenistic culture that was more focused on establishing ancient authorship of authoritative texts.

Q – a hypothesized source (Q stands for *Quelle*, the German word for source). The term designates a set of sayings of Jesus found in Matthew and Luke, but not in Mark.

Scholars have supposed that this shared material comes from an independent written source that the authors of Matthew and Luke incorporated into their gospels in different ways.

realized eschatology – the notion in the Gospel of John that the judgment and salvation of the last days is an already present reality for the believer. This is particularly seen in Jesus's words to the Samaritan woman, "The hour is coming and is now here" (John 4:23), as well as in the "I am" statements that emphasize Jesus's incarnational presence.

salvation history – a Christian theological interpretation of the Bible as a continuous history (from Genesis to Revelation) of God's saving work with humanity.

Second Temple period – beginning in 515 BCE, when Persian authorization made possible the rebuilding of the Jerusalem temple. The period ends in the late first century CE after this same temple was destroyed by Rome in 70 CE.

Septuagint – an ancient set of translations of Jewish scriptural books into Greek.

Sermon on the Mount – Jesus's mountaintop speech in Matthew 5–7, in which Jesus is presented as a figure like Moses, interpreting the **Torah** and giving instructions to his followers.

signs – from the Greek *semeia*, a term used in the Gospel of John to refer to Jesus's miraculous deeds and reveal his identity. Some scholars hypothesize that the author of John used an early written "signs source" comprised of a collection of Jesus's signs. See John 2:1–11; 4:46–54; 5:1–9; 6:1–14, 16–21; 9:1–38; 11:1–44.

social memory – a common set of memories passed on to succeeding generations and celebrated in common rituals that help to define a group by its shared past (also known as "collective memory").

Special L – material that is found only in the Gospel of Luke.

Special M – material that is found only in the Gospel of Matthew.

supersessionism – the idea that Christianity and the Christian church have superseded and thus replaced Judaism and the people of Israel.

synoptic gospels – the gospels of Matthew, Mark, and Luke, which have a strong similarity in their story structures and content, as well as some instances of shared exact wording. "Synoptic" means to "see together."

synoptic problem – the question of how to understand the similarities and differences between the **synoptic gospels** of Matthew, Mark, and Luke. See **two-source hypothesis**.

textual criticism – the collection and analysis of different manuscript readings, e.g., different readings in Hebrew manuscripts and early translations of Hebrew manuscripts of books in the Hebrew Bible.

Theophilus – the figure addressed in the prologues of both the Gospel of Luke and the Acts of the Apostles, the name means "God-lover" and possibly refers to the gospel writer's patron.

the Way – unique designation used in the Acts of the Apostles for the Jesus movement, especially in the latter half of the narrative. Both the narrator and the character of Paul in Acts use the term.

Torah – the first five books of the Bible, namely Genesis, Exodus, Leviticus, Numbers, and Deuteronomy. Jews often distinguish between this "written Torah" and the "oral

Torah" given to Moses, transmitted through the sages, and embodied in the Mishnah and other authoritative Jewish writings.

two-source hypothesis – the theory that Matthew and Luke both drew directly from the Gospel of Mark and the sayings source **Q** to compose their accounts.

typological interpretation – a form of allegorical interpretation that reads figures in the Hebrew Bible/Old Testament as patterns, or "types," that prefigure elements (often Christ) in the New Testament or later Christian theology.

undisputed letters – refers to the general scholarly agreement that Romans, 1 and 2 Corinthians, Galatians, Philippians, 1 Thessalonians, and Philemon were letters written by Paul himself. This conclusion is based on the letters' shared vocabulary, themes, and rhetorical style, as well as their assumed composition dates around the 50s CE.

vice list – a list of standard vices often used rhetorically as in the service of a larger argument. Vice lists appear widely in the Hebrew Bible/Old Testament, in Greek and Roman literature, in Second Temple writings, and in the New Testament.

voluntary associations – a variety of social clubs, professional guilds, unions, and religious groups that developed in the Hellenistic age. These associations (of which synagogues and churches were two) were the center of Mediterranean social life through the Greco-Roman period. The members of the associations met, often in the name of a god, over leisurely meals in which eating, drinking, singing, discussion, and storytelling all took place. In their ancient Mediterranean context, synagogue groups and Christ-followers both within and outside of synagogue contexts can be viewed as types of voluntary associations.

whore of Babylon – female figure in the book of Revelation who personifies the corrupt city of Rome. Revelation 17–18 presents a vision of her violent destruction.

APPENDIX: A BRIEF OVERVIEW OF SOME INTERPRETIVE APPROACHES TO THE BIBLE

What follows does not represent *all* of the ways that biblical scholars have studied the New Testament and the Bible more generally. Instead, for easy reference, I briefly describe the approaches that I refer to or draw on in this textbook. At the end of this appendix, I list additional resources that offer more extensive overviews of the many ways that scholars have studied the Bible. While the descriptions below are intended to distinguish one approach from another, in many cases, these interpretive approaches overlap. Indeed, the nature of many contemporary academic interpretations of the New Testament is that they draw on more than one critical theory in their attempts to read the Bible for the contemporary world.

Contextual interpretation is a broad category to describe biblical interpretations that foreground the social location of the interpretive perspective (such as African American, Asian American, Latin American and so on). In fact, all interpretations of the Bible are contextual, that is, they are all undertaken from a specific social location. Contextual interpretations call attention to this fact by explicitly interpreting the Bible through the experience of living as a minority population or living in a non-Western nation. Contextual interpretations are often justice oriented. They address situations of oppression and inequality as these situations relate to the use and interpretation of the Bible.

Critical masculinity studies of the Bible emerged out of a focus on gender in feminist studies. Masculinity studies attends to the ideological concept of "masculinity" or "manliness." Prominent theories of masculinity have focused on the concept of hegemonic masculinity, a form of masculinity that legitimates the subordination of women as well as other forms of masculinity. New Testament masculinity studies includes the interpretation of texts that reinforce the hegemonic masculinity of the Roman empire, as well as interpretations that point to ways that some male figures in the New Testament challenge or subvert Roman hegemonic masculinity. With respect to the Bible, masculinity studies includes analysis of how biblical writings construct ideas about manliness and how these constructions relate to hierarchical systems of gender injustice.

Cultural criticism of the Bible involves analysis of how the Bible has been represented in the broader culture across different times and places. The analysis may include the long-term effects on the broader culture that result from these representations. Cultural criticism often focuses on the use of the Bible in the visual arts, film, television, and

The New Testament: A Contemporary Introduction, First Edition. Colleen M. Conway.
© 2023 John Wiley & Sons Ltd. Published 2023 by John Wiley & Sons Ltd.

other artifacts of popular culture such as advertising or comic books. Another term used for this sort of analysis is "reception history" of the Bible.

Decolonizing biblical interpretation involves efforts to deconstruct colonial frameworks that continue to influence biblical interpretations. Such efforts are especially prevalent among African scholars, whose decolonizing readings come from an African-centric perspective, drawing on African knowledge systems and African ancestral heritage.

Disability studies focuses on the different ways human beings are valued on the basis of their perceived physical or mental "abilities." These studies challenge "ableist" prejudices against differently abled people. For example, reading the New Testament through the lens of disability studies shows the problematic nature of healing stories in the gospels that associate sin with disability and faithfulness with healing and wholeness. Scholars working in the framework of disability studies also highlight ableist assumptions underlying some traditional interpretations or analyze passages in the Bible in which disabilities have a positive function.

Feminist criticism of the Bible dates back at least to Elizabeth Cady Stanton's Women's Bible published in 1895. Although Stanton did not call her project "feminist criticism," her interest in offering interpretations that resisted androcentric readings of the Bible was a precursor to what would emerge as an academic discipline in the 1970s. Feminist biblical criticism includes a range of reading practices aimed at addressing women's inequality, including analyzing biblical depictions of women (or lack of these depictions), the biblical use of feminine imagery in the Bible, and the effects of patriarchal interpretations of the Bible.

Gender criticism of the Bible describes a broad category of analysis characterized by consideration of how gender is typically (and often problematically) constructed as a relational and binary category. Its focus may be the construction of male characters in relation to female characters, but also gendered metaphors and images, and even the gendered nature of sacrificial animals.

Historical criticism encompasses much of the history of interpretation between the late seventeenth and the late twentieth century, at which point other interpretive approaches began to proliferate. The "historical" element includes searching for the meaning of the writing in its ancient context, as well as tracing the history of the composition of the writing itself. This latter aspect means asking questions about the author's sources for the work and analyzing how earlier sources were edited or adapted for a new literary composition (redaction criticism). Recent historically focused studies of the New Testament examine the relationship between oral and written transmission of biblical traditions, considering the role of shared social memories for transmission.

Intercultural criticism explores what insights into biblical texts emerge when one attends to diverse cultural experiences of the texts. In some cases, this includes an inter-religious reading, when a text from the New Testament is put in conversation with a scriptural text from another religious tradition.

Intersectionality in relation to biblical studies involves the analysis of how inter-secting categories of gender, race, class, and sexual orientation are evident in the Bible and biblical interpretation. Such an analysis includes consideration of one's mix of iden-tity categories and how that influences one's interpretation of the Bible.

Postcolonial criticism examines the effects of colonization on the Bible and bibli-cal interpretation. This often involves analyzing the role of the Bible in the colonizing efforts of Europe and the Americas. Early examples of postcolonial studies drew heavily on the concept of hybridity, which identified ways that colonized people imitate as well as resist the ideologies of the colonizing power. In New Testament studies, postcolonial studies includes analysis of the complex and often ambivalent relationship between the Jesus movement and the Roman empire.

Queer biblical interpretation involves reading biblical texts though the lens of queer theory. Queering biblical texts can mean producing readings that challenge the idea of sex and gender as fixed categories. Queer interpretations of the Bible also work to unmask the power dynamics of social constructions of sexuality and gender, especially how the idea of heterosexual as "normal" is used to police nonconforming expressions of sexuality.

Womanist biblical interpretation draws on the experience and perspective of Black women for analysis of biblical texts. It is also inherently intersectional as womanist scholars consider the oppressive social structures of racism, sexism, classism, and het-erosexism in their biblical analyses.

RESOURCES FOR FURTHER STUDY

Avalos, Hector. "Disability Studies and Biblical Studies: Retrospectives and Prospects." *Interpretation* 73 (2019): 343–354. DOI:10.1177/0020964319857604.

Bailey, Randall C., Tat-siong Benny Liew, and Fernando F. Segovia, eds. *They Were All Together in One Place? Toward Minority Biblical Criticism.* Semeia Studies. Atlanta: Society of Biblical Literature, 2009.

Dunning, Benjamin H. ed. *The Oxford Handbook of New Testament, Gender and Sexuality.* New York: Oxford University Press, 2019.

Elder, Nicolas A., "New Testament Media Criticism." *Currents in Biblical Research* 15 (2017): 315–337.

Junior, Nyasha. *An Introduction to Womanist Biblical Interpretation.* Louisville, KY: Westminster John Knox Press, 2015.

McKenzie, Steven L. and John Kaltner, eds. *New Meanings for Ancient Texts: Recent Approaches to Biblical Criticisms and Their Applications.* Louisville, KY: Westminster John Knox Press, 2013.

Sugirtharajah, R.S. ed. *The Oxford Handbook of Postcolonial Biblical Criticism*. London and New York: Oxford University Press. This book is forthcoming as a print volume, but individual articles are available online as they are published. DOI:10.1093/oxfordhb/9780190888459.001.0001

Yee, Gale A. "Thinking Intersectionally: Gender, Race, Class, and the Etceteras of Our Discipline," *Journal of Biblical Literature* 139 (2020): 7–26. This article offers a helpful description of the principles of intersectional analysis of the Bible, although the analysis is from a text in the Hebrew Bible rather than the New Testament.

INDEX

The letter b after a page reference indicates that the topic appears in a textbox. Page numbers in *italics* refer to illustrations.

abbreviations for biblical books 8
Abraham 65–9, 71–2, 76, 94, 186, 196
Acts of Paul and Thecla,   108–9, *110*
African American interpretation 181–2, 227
anti–Jewish language *see* "Jews" in the Gospel of John
apocalypse, genre of 37, 206–207, 227
apocalyptic and/or apocalypticism in the New Testament 52–4, 57, 65, 70–2, 74, 87, 102, 117, 143–146
and the historical Jesus 36–7
apocrypha 4, 21, 108, 227
Asian American interpretation 220–1b
Augustus *32,* 41*, 49*, 87, 145, *146*, 159, 160–3, *161, 256*

Babylonian empire 18–9, 138, 227
Ben Sira, book of 22, 143

canon or canonical 4, 6, 17–18, 223–224
chapter numbering 8b
circumcision for gentiles in Paul's letters 61, 63, 65–7, 72–3
as presented in Josephus 63–4b
citation of biblical passages 7–8
client king 30, 139, 227
Colossians, "Paul's" letter to 101–4
Corinth 47, 80–81, *81*
Corinthians, Paul's first letter to 83–9
Corinthians, Paul's second letter to 90–5
critical masculinity studies 3, 233
cultural criticism 233–4

Daniel, book of 37b, 57, 115, 117, 144, 206
deification of the Roman emperor *161, 163,* 163
Deutero-Pauline letters 99–108, 228
disability studies 191b, 234
diaspora 219

disputed letters of Paul 46, 228
dynamic equivalence translation 11

ekklesia 13–14, 144–5b
Ephesians, "Paul's" letter to 101–4
eschatology 35–6, 37b, 228
realized 200, 231
exile in Babylon 18–19, 138, 227

farewell discourse 189, 194, 196, 200–1, 228
feminist criticism or theory 3, 49b, 66, 67b, 122b, 177–9, 234
formal correspondence translation 11
fulfillment citations 138–9, 141, 228

Galatians, Paul's letter to 62–67
gender criticism 234; *see also* manliness and masculinity in early Christianity examples of,   74b, 93–4, 139b
gender and translation 11–12

The New Testament: A Contemporary Introduction, First Edition. Colleen M. Conway.
© 2023 John Wiley & Sons Ltd. Published 2023 by John Wiley & Sons Ltd.

heavenly apocalypse *see* apocalypse, genre of
Hebrew Bible 4, 6, 228
Hebrews, book of 214–18
Hellenistic or Hellenization 19–20, 30–3, 228
Herod 30–33, 114, 139–40
historical apocalypse *see* apocalypse, genre of
historical criticism 2–3, 225, 234
historical Jesus 14, 33–8
household codes 104–5, 111, 228
hybridity 210, 229, 235

Infancy Gospel of Thomas 41b, *42*
intercultural interpretation or criticism 167–8b, 235
intercalation 127, 127b, 229
intersectional interpretation 3, 23, 104–5, 235

Jewish War 114–15
"Jews" in the Gospel of John 196–200
Johannine community 198–9b
Johannine letters 201–3
John, Gospel of 185–201

King James Version 10

Latin American interpretation 167–8b
logos 186–8, 190, 200, 217

Luke, Gospel of 156–70
LXX *see* Septuagint

Maccabees and/or Maccabean 20, 29, 64, 147b
manliness and masculinity in early Christianity 74b, 93–5
Mark, Gospel of 111–31
Matthew, Gospel of 133–51
messiah 19, 22, 34, 84, 125, 229
messianic secret 120, 125b, 125–6, 229
monotheism 211

Nero, emperor 117, 207–9, 208b, 214

oral tradition(s) 29, 39–41, 117b, 156–7, 230
order of biblical books 5–7

parables 24, 37, 40, 121, 131, 144, 165–7
Paraclete 195, 202
passion narrative 117b, 126–8, 230
passion predictions 124, 230
Paul within Judaism 265–6b, 276
Pentateuch 3
Peter, first letter from 218–21
Pharisees 119, 146–9, 147–8b, 159, 193, 199–200
Philemon, Paul's letter to 57–9
Philippi 25, 47–8, *49*, 54

Philippians, Paul's letter to 55–7
postcolonial theory or criticism 3, 148, 149b, 160, 199–200, 210, 235
Priene inscription 162b
pseudepigraphy and pseudonymous texts 98–9, 223, 230

Q 135, 135b, 140, 159, 230–1
Queer theory 86b, 182–3, 235

redaction criticism 234
rereading and reinterpretation of scripture 18, 66, 75–6, 126, 138–9, 152, 224–5
Revelation, book of 206–14
Romans, Paul's letter to 69–77

Second Temple building and destruction of 19, 114–5, *115*, 121, 131, 136, 138, 140, 227
critique of 126, 216–7
expansion under Herod 30–3, *31–2*
focus in Luke–Acts 158–159
literature (in apocrypha or deutero-canonical), 21–2
period 19, 231
Septuagint (LXX) 19–20, 66, *72–3*, 158, 192, 219, 231

Sermon on the Mount 40,
140–2, 231
Sirach *see* Ben
Sira, book of
slavery and the New
Testament 24, 58–9,
104–5, 178–9
social memory 38–9, 231
Son of Man 125,
150, 190, 206
supersessionism 4,
67–8b, 218, 231
synoptic gospels
134, 231
synoptic problem
134–6, *135*, 231

Tanakh/TaNaK 4
Temple, Jerusalem 18
textual criticism 10–11b

Theophilus 23, 156, 231
Thessalonians, Paul's first
letter to 50–1b, 51–4
Thessalonians, "Paul's"
second let-
ter to 99–100
Thessalonica 47–8, *49*, 51
Timothy
Paul's co-worker 50–1b
"Paul's" first and
second letters
to 98, 105–8
Titus, General *115*, 115
Titus, "Paul's" letter
to 107b, 108
Torah, definition of 4
translations 9–13
two-source hypothesis (or
two–source theory)
125, 125, 136, 232

verse numbering 8b
voluntary association
87, 100, 232

whore of Babylon 206,
213, 213–14
Wisdom
and Jesus in the New
Testament 22,
143–3, 187–8
literature 22, 142–3, 223
Wisdom of Solomon,
book of 22
womanist interpretation
(of the Bible)
122b, 178, 235
women and female figures
in the Bible 25–7, 40,
90b, 107–8, 130–1,
139b, 178–9, 213–4